Blood Sacrifice
The Thaumaturgy Companion™

By Dean Shomshak and Ari Marmell

Vampire® created by Mark Rein•Hagen

CREDITS

Written by: Dean Shomshak and Ari Marmell.

Vampire and the World of Darkness created by Mark Rein•Hagen

Storyteller Game System Design: Mark Rein•Hagen

Developed by: Justin Achilli

Editor: Michelle Lyons

Art Director: Richard Thomas

Layout & Typesetting: Becky Jollensten

Interior Art: Mike Danza and Drew Tucker

Front Cover Art: David Leri

Front & Back Cover Design: Becky Jollensten

OVERHEARD

"They're covering my mullet."
— Chad Brown

"They fill the cherry pies with magma."
— Mike Chaney

"Go home, Ken."
— Ken Cliffe

"I thought that was an orc."
— Rich Thomas

"Hey, shut up. We're listening to banjo music."
— Dean Burnham

"There's a fairy in your booth."
— Laura Foutz

DEAN'S SPECIAL THANKS

My special thanks go to the Encyclopedia Britannica, the greatest game supplement ever published, and to all the folklorists whose research supplied inspiration for **Blood Sacrifice**.

ARI'S SPECIAL THANKS

To Dean, for having the patience to be a guiding hand on top of everything else he had to deal with, and to George, for not throttling me.

735 PARK NORTH BLVD.
SUITE 128
CLARKSTON, GA 30021
USA

WHITE WOLF
GAME STUDIO

Contents

I cannot just heave everything I know into the abyss. But I know it is coming. And when it comes, when I have made my sacrificial offerings to the gods of understanding, then the ruptures will cease. Healing waters will cover the land, giving birth to new life. burying forever the ancient, rusting machines of my past understandings And on those waters I will set sail to places I now only imagine. There I will be blessed with new visions and new magic. I will feel once again like a creative contributor to this mysterious world. But for now, I wait An act of faith.

-- Margaret Wheatly. A Simpler Way

Formerly, when religion was strong and science
weak, men mistook magic for medicine; now, when
science is strong and religion weak, men mistake
medicine for magic.

-- Thomas Szasz

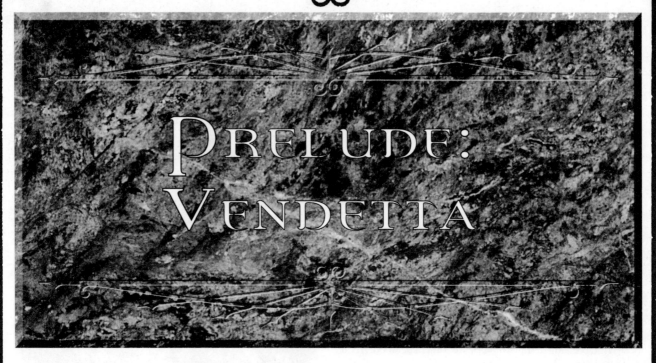

PRELUDE: VENDETTA

The itchy sensation of something crawling across the back of her hand — something unseen; something small; something with far, far too many legs — first greeted her return to consciousness. She felt only cold, an oblivion that could have lasted an eternity — and then, this.

Hold on! *Uno momento, por favor!* She couldn't be waking up. Her kind didn't fall unconscious. Torpor, yes. The sleep of day, absolutely. This, though, didn't feel like the end of her daylight slumber, and she sure as hell couldn't have been out long enough to have lain in torpor. Could she?

She seemed unable to move her arms or legs. She wasn't bound, so far as she could tell. Instead, her entire body suffered from some inexplicable languor, her limbs refusing to respond to her commands. Eyes still squeezed shut — more to decieve anyone who might be watching and reveling in her strange and helpless state into thinking her still asleep than because she feared what she might see — Carlota stretched forth her other senses. Sounds, scents, even currents in the air, all these and more painted a detailed portrait of the room around her. Her heightened senses were a gift taught her by one of the Tremere who'd run with her pack in the nights before every last one of the blasted Warlocks had been, well, blasted.

The spider (she knew, now, that it was a spider, as her skin had become sensitive enough to count legs) scuttled down the outer edge of her hand, tickled its way across her palm and disappeared onto the cold stone floor. The cloying, sickeningly-sweet scent of mold clung to the walls like a coat of paint. The room was not terribly large, or so she judged by the feel of the sluggish air currents that rustled past her face. It was probably somewhere between three and five meters on a side. It…

Madre de Dios! She wasn't alone. Rather, she might be alone now, but someone had been there recently enough. The feeble popping sound of a wick and the ever-so-faint touch of warmth suggested a candle burning somewhere across the chamber.

Where the fuck was she? How the hell had she gotten here? Carlota tried to relax, and remembered….

***

They'd gone to kill that fucking Tremere, some Camarilla stooge who actually thought he could set up shop in the jungles of Peru, just plunk his ass down in Sabbat territory. *Imbécil!* Leaving Antonio, her pack priest, to guard the perimeter, she and the rest of the Muerte Repentina pack burst through the door of the magus' ramshackle hut — the Warlock's wards proved simple enough for Carlota to shatter — and things started to go wrong almost instantly.

The Tremere didn't look like much. A young (or at least young-looking) black man with features that screamed urban America, clad in jeans, T-shirt and mud-caked Air Jordans, he could have been one of thousands of post-adolescent inner-city thugs. The Warlock, though, was undoubtedly morethan immediately met the eye. Arcane sigils and diagrams covered the inside of the shanty. In all her years, Carlota had never seen the likes of such Thaumaturgical rites and runes. He was definitely more powerful than he looked — and the fucker knew they were coming.

It was Javier; it had to be. No wonder the little *bastardo* hadn't come back. He'd gotten himself caught, probably killed, and he'd ratted the rest of them out in the process. Fuck! Well, served her right for using a ghoul in the first place, the others would no doubt tell her; she should have done more than broken his wrist the last time he'd fucked up.

Bernardo was the first of the Muerte Repentina to fall. The Pander's skin abruptly reddened, his eyes bubbling. He screamed once, before the boiling blood in his veins burst through his eyes and mouth to drench the open doorway and the trees nearest the Warlock's hovel, filling the air with crimson steam and a singed, metallic tang.

Isabella died next. She leapt at the Tremere, letting loose an ear-splitting primal shriek from her throat even as her hideous claws burst from her fingertips. Carlota had seen the

Gangrel — newly recruited after so many of that bestial clan had finally seen the Camarilla for the load of *mierda* that it was — in frenzy before. She had no doubt at all that the Tremere was about to become little more than quivering chunks of meat scattered across the creaking floorboards.

A sudden gesture and a whispered word from the Warlock set Isabella's clothes and hair aflame. When last Carlota saw her, the Gangrel was gripped in the depths of the red fear, racing into the jungle and screaming as slabs of roasted flesh sloughed off her smoldering body.

Either Antonio still waited outside, despite the fact that things were clearly going to hell in a hand basket, or something unpleasant had befallen him as well. That left Carlota alone against a magician who, in a matter of moments, had put down two of the fiercest Cainites she'd ever run with.

That was just fine by her. A grin splitting her face like a scar, the Lasombra raised both arms before her, her *kisengue* — a human shinbone wrapped in black rags — clasped in her left hand. For the first time, the Tremere's expression changed; he looked ever so slightly puzzled.

When Carlota called on Santisima Muerte, when the air shimmered and an obscenely large crossbow suddenly occupied her left fist, puzzlement shifted abruptly to panic. The wooden bolt sprang forth from the weapon like a striking adder almost before the startled magus recognized what he'd just seen was a variation on the Path of Conjuring.

It was a perfect shot, one that should have ended the conflict instantly. Instead, Carlota watched — chagrined, but not especially surprised — as the projectile disintegrated mere inches from impact.

Truly alarmed for the first time, the Tremere stabbed two fingers toward his foe. Carlota choked as a torrent of vitae poured forth from her gaping jaw, flowing through the air like a crimson river until it struck — and was absorbed by — the magus' outstretched hand. The Hunger gnawed at Carlota's belly, at her mind, like a caged animal; she ruthlessly crushed the rising frenzy, well aware that losing her capacity for rational thought in the face of a hostile blood magician was tantamount to suicide.

He recognized it too, watching as the Lasombra curled inward, nearly toppling over with the sudden weakness and the strain of resisting frenzy. A faint smile crossed the lips of the Tremere, revealing just a hint of extended fang. "Stupid Sabbat *chica*," he hissed, putting a deliberately mocking edge on the Spanish. "You're a dabbler in the arts. You should have known better than to mess with a true magus."

He was cocky now, his guard dropping. He knew — as she did — that she didn't have the blood to spare on further magics.

Carlota, however, was no mere thaumaturge — and a *wangateur*, protected in the faith of Palo Mayombe and favored of the Enkisi, had more tools at her disposal than some hidebound Hermetic blood wizard could possibly comprehend. Hidden from the Tremere's sight as she doubled over, the Lasombra's fingers snaked forth from the leather satchel she wore at her side, trailing shredded tobacco leaves and a glossy white powder in their wake. Magic surged through her as she drew on the power intrinsic to the plants and minerals of the world around her, supplementing her depleted stores of vitae with outside forces.

The Tremere hardly had the time to scream as he, like Carlota's feral companion moments before, erupted in a blazing pillar of fire. Carlota staggered through the open doorway and watched from outside as first the Tremere, and then the entire hut, burned to so much flickering ash.

She remembered a shifting of the air behind her, as though someone approached; she began to turn, expecting Antonio, and then….

Then — nothing.

***

Nothing. The battle with the Warlock was the last memory she could dredge up. Obviously *something* happened to her in that jungle clearing. She just needed to figure out what it…

"I know you are awake, Señorita Carlota."

The Lasombra's eyes popped open. She knew that voice!

"Javier!" Carlota tried to leap to her feet, to lunge toward her errant ghoul, but she found that her limbs still refused to obey her. "I'll kill you, you little *puta*!" she shrieked at him, snarling impotently. The sound of her grinding fangs reverberated throughout the room.

"I doubt this," he told her gently.

Now that her eyes were open, Carlota discovered there was little enough to see. The single candle she'd sensed was the room's only source of illumination. She could make out the barest outline of Javier's form, a patch of moving darkness that reflected the feeble glimmers of light. Javier — a skinny, rodent-like man with a heavy moustache and a notable overbite — stood across the room, beside the only door. Something lay in a sarcophagus or trough before him, though Carlota could not, from her angle, see what it might be. A second figure stood behind him, immersed so deeply in the shadows that the Lasombra could barely detect its presence at all. She realized too, ever so gradually, that she lay not on the floor, as she'd first believed, but instead on some sort of cot or platform several feet above the ground.

"You're dead," she barked furiously, her lips curled. "Nobody betrays— "

"Oh, please, Señorita. This, I have heard before. Have you not told me little else for almost a year now? 'Nobody betrays the Sabbat!' 'Nobody stands against the Sabbat!' 'Be grateful the Sabbat saw fit to allow you to serve, rather than eating you like the *comida* you are.' I have a new master now, Señorita, and you no longer frighten me."

Carlota felt herself gasp in astonishment — a habit she despised as a holdover from her weak, mortal life — as Javier stepped forward into the light, his left hand held before him, fingers together and palm upward as though offering her some token of his esteem. That hand hadn't worked in months, ever since Carlota snapped the wrist and refused to allow him to have it set. It should have been a permanent deformity — but here it was, good as new.

She noticed only then Javier's abnormal pallor, realized only then that no trace of a heartbeat reverberated through the chamber, and she understood.

"*Sí*," Javier said simply, reading her expression as easily as a street sign. "They were going to kill me at first. They hate us

— you — with a passion I have never seen. But they saw that I was not a willing servant, and decided that my knowledge of the Sabbat could work to their advantage. They permitted the Tremere to claim a haven in their territory, Señorita, because they knew — because I told them — it would draw your attention. And I — I was more than happy to stand beside them against…" His spittle left a watery crimson streak down the side of her face, a mark of shame that she could not even raise a hand to wipe off. "Against you."

"You will help us as well." The voice was rough, somehow abrasive. The figure behind Javier stepped forward then, and Carlota would have been amused were her situation not so precarious. The stranger wore a simple robe of untreated wool; feathered bracelets dangled from his wrists and ankles, and an obsidian-bladed knife hung at his waist. Hair the black of moonless midnight was swept back from his face and neck with a silver clasp. He stood before her, barefoot, a figure out of Central America's ancient past.

"Who the hell are you supposed to be?" she asked contemptuously.

"I am Javier's sire," he told her roughly, his accent strangely archaic. "And I am your new master. You will serve us well, in the time you have remaining in this world."

Carlota wanted to laugh — would have laughed — except that Javier, as if on cue, raised a second obsidian blade high, and thrust it down into whatever lay in the trough before him. A line of agony ripped through Carlota's gut. Incapable of any movement beyond speech, she couldn't even double over as she had in the Tremere's hovel. Instead she simply clenched her teeth, nearly cracking them in her determination to bite back the scream that welled up insider her.

How had he done that? Had Javier somehow created a baleful doll, or some other sympathetic effigy? It didn't seem likely; her own knowledge of *voudoun* was far too limited to allow such a thing, and Javier couldn't possibly have surpassed her in only two nights as a Cainite. His master might have created it, but…

"Look down, Señorita," the former ghoul taunted. Carlota tried, despite herself — and found that she couldn't do even that. *Nothing* moved, except her mouth and her eyes.

"What have you *done* to me?" Anger rose like a tide, sweeping away the creeping tendrils of fear that slunk through the back of Carlota's mind. How *dare* they treat her this way?

Javier and his sire silently turned the stone trough about, so that Carlota could finally see inside it….

She could only stare, eyes wide and weeping bloody tears of absolute despair, at her own headless body where it lay across the room, animate and twitching spasmodically.

It was no cot on which she lay, no platform. It was merely a shelf, a simple shelf, barely large enough to hold — her head. A head that, against all sense, against all logic, was still undead, still animate, still capable of feeling every cut, every torment that a hate-filled former ghoul could inflict upon her body with his razor-sharp blade. *Oh Dios, this can't be happening, this can't be real, let it end, please….*

It was not the end, despite desperate prayers to a God she hadn't spoken to since her Embrace. It was merely the beginning.

INTRODUCTION: IN VITAE VERITAS

To hear the vampire-wizards of Clan Tremere tell it, they all but invented Thaumaturgy. A few vampires practiced crude blood-sorceries before them, but this was not what you would call a real Discipline. When the clan's founders transformed themselves from mortal wizards into the undead, they rendered all other blood magic obsolete.

That's utter bosh. Few among the Kindred would deny the power and versatility of Clan Tremere's magic, but several other schools of Thaumaturgy flourish as well. Some of these sorcerous traditions date back to the dawn of history. Their practitioners still wield formidable power. **Blood Sacrifice** explores these alternate styles of Thaumaturgy: their origins, histories and occult practices, as well as many new paths and rituals.

WHAT'S IN THIS BOOK

Blood Sacrifice describes four styles of Thaumaturgy in detail. Chapter One describes Akhu, the blood sorcery that the Followers of Set preserve from ancient Egypt. Chapter Two provides information about Dur-An-Ki, the blood magic of Middle Eastern vampires, including — but not limited to — the Assamite clan. Chapter Three introduces Sadhana, the strange magical art of India's vampires. Chapter Four expands upon Wanga, the voodoo-inspired Thaumaturgy practiced in the Caribbean and South America.

The Appendix provides several new rituals for Necromancy and Koldunic Sorcery. It then describes Nahuallotl, the blood sorcery of a secretive Native American lineage

struggling back from the brink of extinction. The appendix concludes by discussing spontaneous talismans — magic items that seem to arise without anyone deliberately creating them and put the lie to anyone who thinks they understand the supernatural World of Darkness.

Each chapter includes three new paths and several rituals for that particular style of Thaumaturgy. Just as importantly, each chapter explains the concepts underlying the Thaumaturgical style, and describes the tools and procedures used in its rituals. Along the way, the chapter provides history and how the magic style fares in the modern nights.

FOR GOD'S SAKE, WHY?

Why write another book about Thaumaturgy? Haven't we done enough damage already? Let's face it, Thaumaturgy has a reputation as a way for powergamers to *get away with anything*. Once you look at Thaumaturgy in detail, though, it becomes rather less of a bargain. Thaumaturgy is perhaps the most difficult of all Disciplines to learn… but the reasons make great hooks for stories!

THE STUDENT'S QUEST

How do you *learn* Thaumaturgy? You cannot take night classes in blood magic at the local college. If you come from a vampire lineage that systematically teaches blood magic to its members, such as the Tremere or the Assamite sorcerers, your sire can teach you or arrange for a tutor. Vampires from other lineages must find a teacher on their own, and blood magicians do not advertise in the Yellow Pages.

What does the teacher demand in return for lessons? Instruction takes time — and every new blood magician becomes a potential rival for the teacher. At the very least, a thaumaturge might demand payment in cash, boons or immediate services. Surely, a sincere disciple would not mind hunting for her master and performing domestic chores for the duration of her apprenticeship? Oh, and perhaps fetching a few oddments, such as the skull of Cardinal Richelieu and a sample of the prince's vitae? As a hedge against betrayal, a teacher may also insist that the student accept a blood bond or some other supernatural compulsion.

Sooner or later, a student moves beyond her first teacher's resources. Suppose you want to learn the Pavis of Foul Presence and your teacher-mentor does not know it: You have to find someone else who does. Your mentor might not like you consulting other thaumaturges and perhaps passing on her trade secrets. The other thaumaturge might not like you passing on *his* path, ritual or other fruits of his mystical labors to your regular teacher. Studying under more than one master demands either great discretion or great diplomacy.

A thaumaturge can also seek the rare and hidden texts that reveal secrets of blood magic. Perhaps you can find the tomb of an ancient blood-sorcerer and raid his stash of grimoires… and hope that he really is still in torpor and did not leave too many occult guardians. Perhaps a blood-cult carved the instructions for a potent spell on the walls of its hidden temple. Once in a while, a book of blood magic even appears at elite auctions of art and antiquities, such as Sotheby's of London, provoking whirlwinds of intrigue among Cainite sorcerers.

A character can even try to research her own paths and rituals based on the legends and theories of her occult tradition. The Tremere excel beyond all other clans at the creation of new Thaumaturgy, but other blood magicians may innovate as well. Research takes years or even decades of experimentation. Magical experiments are frustrating when they fail… and can be dangerous when they *almost* fail, as illustrated by the famous story of The Sorcerer's Apprentice.

Both research and ritual often call for special ingredients that may present further challenges. Mere financial costs are typically the least of a thaumaturge's problems, though if a ritual consumes a flawless diamond every time you cast it, you might have to work on your cash flow. Ingredients may be intrinsically rare, such as wood from a 1000-year-old tree; dangerous or illegal to collect, such as a human child's heart; or come with mystical conditions, such as St. John's Wort gathered at the dark of the moon. Even the closest substitutions reduce a ritual's effectiveness.

The social barriers between lineages of vampires and schools of Thaumaturgy magnify other difficulties. The Tremere seldom teach their Hermetic style of Thaumaturgy to vampires outside their clan. Some Tremere hunt such outsiders, to preserve their secrets and supremacy.

The Thaumaturgical styles in **Blood Sacrifice** lack such close associations with a single lineage, but clan, ethnic and religious barriers remain. The proud Assamites, for instance, often view other vampires as unworthy of their magic. The Native American vampires who practice

REASONS TO RESEARCH

Like the vampires of the World of Darkness, the styles of magic in **Blood Sacrifice** are based on a blend of folklore and fantasy — the legends and fiction of the source cultures, as well as their actual occult beliefs. This reinforces the illusion that the World of Darkness could be a hidden side to our real world.

More importantly, this gives you more game material than we could ever publish. Libraries and bookstores hold treasuries of lore — everything from collections of folktales to scholarly anthropological studies — that can inspire more Paths, rituals, characters and stories.

Remember, though, that blood magic never precisely imitates the forms of mortal occult or religious beliefs. Don't feel too bound by "realism" (a dodgy concept for a game about vampires). Filter the myths and legends through the vampiric condition and the rules for Thaumaturgy to make something new that works within your game.

Nahuallotl tend to mistrust vampires who do not share their mortal ancestry. Students of Wanga generally must devote themselves to one of the Afro-Caribbean religions. Sadhana masters reputedly teach their art only to fellow undead brahmins. The Followers of Set care less for ancestry than members of many clans, but many will insist that would-be students of their sorcery also devote themselves to the Dark God. An "outsider" may have to pass grueling tests of loyalty and devotion from a prospective mentor… or else perpetrate an exceedingly dangerous fraud.

We urge players and Storytellers to view these restrictions as opportunities. The search for magic tuition, lore and ingredients can justify all sorts of stories. Does swashbuckling adventure — "Indiana Jones By Night" — appeal to you? Search for that lost temple or tomb. Do you prefer creepy, Lovecraftian horror full of hideous secrets and Slimy Unspeakables? What luck, a reclusive vampire savant in a decaying backwoods village is said to know the ritual you seek… and what an *odd* statuette he keeps on his mantelpiece. If you enjoy razor-edged intrigue, the challenge of opposed mentors should provide plenty of opportunities. Players can certainly take their fill of personal horror as their characters learn just how far they will go for the sake of magical power.

THE CHALLENGE FROM BEYOND

The styles of Thaumaturgy described in **Blood Sorcery** come from regions outside the "developed world" that most players and characters know. As Western vampires meet their counterparts in (and from) other lands, they encounter unfamiliar blood magic as well. Even in the Western world, the Tremere now face a minor (but growing) challenge to their long-assumed monopoly on Thaumaturgy. For centuries in the Camarilla, a vampire who sought sorcerous aid had to pay whatever price the local Tremere charged, and smile. The Tremere *antitribu* had the Sabbat over a barrel in much the same way.

Upheavals in both sects and among independent clans have broken that monopoly. The destruction of the Tremere *antitribu* forces the Sabbat to shop for alternative magical resources. The civil war among the Assamites has launched a diaspora of their blood magicians who petition both the Sabbat and Camarilla for protection. The Followers of Set vend their ancient occult prowess for their own obscure reasons. Foreign princes court the blood-brahmins just as mortal corporations recruit computer programmers from India.

In both fear and fascination, the Tremere seek to master the secret arts of these other thaumaturges. Long restricted to Europe and its colonies, Clan Tremere now seeks to expand its base. Globalization is the new buzzword around the chantries. Everyone else is doing it, and the ever-competitive Tremere vow not to be left behind.

In Africa and India, the Middle East and Central America, Tremere savants ponder obscure clues within ancient myths and excavate long-lost temples and tombs. Students kneel before undead sages, begging to learn their mystic lore, and cunning elders weave vicious schemes to capture those same sages and extract secrets through torture.

Other Tremere expand their clan beyond its European roots more directly, by Embracing childer from among these foreign populations, from Mexican *curanderos* to Indian holy men. Such childer bring an insider's view of their culture's magical traditions. The Tremere hope they can adapt native spells and conjurations just as the clan's founders adapted the Hermetic magic of medieval Europe. Thus will Clan Tremere assemble and synthesize all the magic in the world — or so they hope.

Some among the Tremere doubt this world-spanning program. The foreign Thaumaturgy may be too, well, *foreign*. To learn another culture's magic, Tremere students find they must learn and accept that culture's beliefs. Then, however… are they still Tremere? Can the clan's elders trust them? In seeking to encompass all blood sorcery within itself, will Clan Tremere shatter itself beyond hope of reunion?

Blood Sacrifice

Many impediments to learning non-Western Thaumaturgy boil down to religion. The Tremere clan culture is not very religious. Since ancient times, the West has denigrated and demonized magic. The Romans, so promiscuously tolerant of foreign religions, frequently launched waves of suppression against astrologers, fortune-tellers and all sorts of magicians. The Jewish Law likewise condemned all sorcery except the mystical Kabbalah. Christianity inherited a suspicion of magic from both sources. St. Augustine of Hippo declared that an appeal to *any* supernatural power other than God Almighty forged an implicit pact with Satan.

When European scholars rediscovered Greek and Roman learning in the later Middle Ages, they recovered the ancients' astrology, mysticism and magic — chiefly the *Corpus Hermeticum* — along with Greco-Roman law, medicine, math and rhetoric. Scholars pursued this occult lore at their peril. Pioneering Hermetics adopted a variety of dodges to forestall the inquisitor. Some wrapped their spells in prayer, and proclaimed that all magic worked by the sufferance of God. Others denied the mystical aspect of their spells, describing them as "natural magic" that exploited subtle forces of the planets, the elements and the human spirit. The founders of Clan Tremere came from this culture. Both as mortals and vampires, they saw their magic as a practical craft with no religious implications.

Not every culture separates and opposes magic and religion. Egyptian priests, Hindu brahmins and *voudoun houngans* combine the roles of priest and magician. Some anthropologists say that, "A priest has a congregation; a magician has a clientele." Many occult practitioners have both.

A practical, diligent Tremere must make a significant conceptual leap to learn the forms of sorcery described in **Blood Sacrifice**. Each magical tradition intertwines with a religious tradition. A student who says, "Never mind the sermon, just teach me how to cast the spell" does not learn much. A *bokkor* or brahmin believes his magic works *because* of his connection to the divine. He could no more divorce his magic from his faith than he could divorce the right side of his body from his left.

Some Tremere do make that leap. They learn to believe in the divine power behind the blood sorcery. Not all of them return to their clan to explain what they have learned.

Game Mechanics

All these divergent styles of Thaumaturgy consist of paths and rituals, just like the Hermetic Thaumaturgy of the Tremere, and *mostly* obey the same rules. All Thaumaturgy derives from the supernatural power within vampiric vitae. Schools of blood magic hold different beliefs about how to evoke and shape that intrinsic magic, however, and those beliefs explain their variations in magical style and content.

Tremere paths generally do not require any material ingredient to operate. The vampire might whisper a few magic words to herself or trace a brief gesture to aid her concentration. Some of the non-Hermetic paths, however, involve a small amulet or other material component to trigger or direct the magic.

Hermetic Thaumaturgy uses a Willpower roll for all path powers. This reflects the systematic and homogeneous nature of the Tremere's magic. Other forms of Thaumaturgy may use a different roll for each path, generally an Attribute + Ability roll.

Every ritual calls for an Intelligence + Occult roll, but the cultural milieus that underlie styles of Thaumaturgy make different assumptions about what Occult *means*. A Hermetic magus, a Santería *wangateur* and a Hindu *sadhu* possess very different bodies of esoteric knowledge and ritual practice — but the Storyteller System files them all under the blanket label of "Occult." Players may want to note these differences on the character's record sheet by adding a word to "Occult";

thus, "Occult, Egyptian" or "Occult, Wanga." Characters who have Occult 4 or higher can treat this as a specialty.

LEARNING TIMES

Just because a thaumaturge finds a teacher or grimoire does not mean she gains new Thaumaturgic powers instantly. Under reasonable conditions — no major distractions or interruptions, but normal nightly hunting and social duties — learning a new ritual takes this length of time:

Ritual Level	Estimated Learning Time
One	One week
Two	One month
Three	One season (three months)
Four	Two seasons
Five	One year
Six+	Storyteller's discretion

Under *optimal* conditions — when the thaumaturge can devote every waking moment to study — a character can cut these times in half. Major disruptions (such as attacks from rival sects) increase learning times.

CREATING NEW RITUALS

Before a character has a chance to invent a new ritual, the player and Storyteller must agree upon exactly what the ritual does. This includes defining the ritual's level. If a proposed ritual is beyond a character's ability, the player or Storyteller can suggest ways to reduce its power. The ritual might have a weaker effect, or difficult conditions (such as Willpower expenditure or exotic ingredients) may attend its use.

To create a ritual from scratch, a character needs an Occult Trait of 5 and a Thaumaturgy Trait one level higher than that of the ritual she hopes to create. First the character must research the ritual by whatever means her tradition defines as a source of occult wisdom. A mystical *sadhu* might read Hindu scriptures and meditate on their hidden meanings; in contrast, a wangateur would talk to other priests and the spirits of his faith. Then the player makes an extended action roll of Intelligence + Occult (difficulty 5 + the ritual's level, to a maximum of 10). To successfully create the ritual, the player must accumulate three times the ritual's level in successes. Rolling a botch means the character has to start over, assuming that nothing more heinous than a mess in the lab takes place.

Each increment of research and development takes time. The ritual's level sets the duration of each increment — the same length of time given in the table above for a character learning the finished ritual. Each time the player makes the R & D roll, the character must expend two blood points per level of the ritual.

Thus, if a character sought to invent a new second-level ritual, she would have to spend one month researching the ritual. The player would make Intelligence + Occult rolls at difficulty 7, accumulating six successes. She would need to spend four blood points per roll, and each roll would represent another month of effort.

CREATING NEW PATHS

Creating a new path is one of the most challenging feats a blood magician can attempt. A character needs a minimum Occult Trait of 5 and Thaumaturgy Trait of 5, as well as a laboratory that might also see use as a haven during the intense research.

First, of course, the player and Storyteller must agree upon the powers within the path. The player does not have to devise all the powers at once. In fact, it's a good idea to leave a slot or two vacant, in case you think of something better or more suitable at a later time.

To devise each level of the new path, the thaumaturge's player must accumulate five successes on an extended Intelligence + Occult roll (difficulty 5 + the level she researches). Each roll represents a full year of research and experimentation. The character also expends five blood points per level of the power. For most characters and most path levels, this means external reserves of blood. Rolling a botch means the character loses all accumulated successes and must begin work on that level of the path from the beginning — or something more terrible, at the Storyteller's discretion. A character must develop the powers in order — no skipping levels. The character's player must also spend the necessary experience points actually to *learn* the path. The first power level in the path costs seven experience points; subsequent levels cost four times the current level.

BLOOD MAGIC
ERRATA

The Level Five power for the Setite Sorcery path The Snake Inside was inadvertently omitted from **Blood Magic: Secrets of Thaumaturgy**. Here it is, and I'm a big dummy.

••••• TEMPERANCE

The final power of the Snake Inside puzzles Setites who do not fully understand their clan's seductive ways. What's the point of *preventing* addictions? Forcing an addict to abstain, however, can shatter many habits and force a complete lifestyle (or unlifestyle) change — not just an easily visible addiction.

Temperance renders a victim unable to take pleasure from satisfying an addiction. The physical or psychological craving still exists, but the substance or behavior that once gave such pleasure now provokes pain and disgust.

System: While the character is near the target, the player rolls Manipulation + Seduction (difficulty of the target's Willpower) and spends a blood point. The number of successes determines the duration of the Temperance effect.

1 success	1 scene
2 successes	1 night
3 successes	1 week
4 successes	1 month
5 successes	1 year

The victim suffers one health level of bashing damage from the nausea and pain of satisfying her addiction. Storytellers may impose other problems, too, based on the nature of the victim's addiction. For instance, an alcoholic forced to go cold turkey might need a successful Willpower roll to avoid vomiting when he drinks. Storytellers may also wish to impose withdrawal symptoms on those whose addictions would likely produce such a result for "coming off the junk."

The sorcerer's player must select one and only one craving for Temperance to affect. The character may use the power more than once, however, to block multiple addictions. Temperance does not work against true physiological necessities such as food (for mortals) or blood (for vampires).

Glossary

Blood Sacrifice introduces many new terms that derive from various cultural traditions. Most terms are defined within the chapters in which they appear. For convenience, however, we also define the most important terms here. This glossary also explains basic terms related to Thaumaturgy in general.

Akhu: Egyptian, "Spells," or the innate magical power possessed by the souls of the dead. The blood magic tradition of ancient Egypt, now practiced chiefly by the Followers of Set.

Amulet: A magical object that continuously and passively protects a person, place or thing.

Ashipu: Babylonian, "Magician." A practitioner of Dur-An-Ki.

Dur-An-Ki: Sumerian, "Master of Heaven and Earth." The Middle Eastern tradition of blood magic, derived from Mesopotamian, Persian, Jewish, Islamic and many other mortal religious and magical traditions.

Formula: The instructions for performing a ritual, plus any ingredients or incantations required by those instructions.

Hermetic: Pertaining to the tradition of Western ceremonial magic and occultism.

Incantation: Words that a magician speaks, chants or sings as part of magic. Incantations can include prayers, recitation of legends, commands, names of powerful spirits or unintelligible words.

Ingredient: A material item required to perform a ritual. The magic rite might consume the ingredient (like a sacrifice), but a magician can use some ingredients many times (like a magic wand). Sometimes also called a component.

Lector Priest: A practitioner of Akhu.

Nahualli: A practitioner of Nahuallotl.

Nahuallotl: A rare form of blood magic based upon Aztec, Maya and other native Central American religions.

Orisha: A Wanga term for the powerful spirits worshipped in voudoun, Santería and other Afro-Caribbean religions. Other terms include loa, saint, mystére, endoki and enkisi.

Path: A codified sequence of magic powers united by a shared concept. A path may focus on an effect (example: the Lure of Flames), a component (the Path of Blood), a purpose (Hands of Destruction) or any other ideal. Path magic usually requires little or no preparation or ingredients.

Relic: An object associated (perhaps loosely) with a saint or prophet that carries a bit of divine power because of its connection to the holy man.

Rite: The sequence of acts used to perform non-path blood magic.

Ritual: A sequence of actions that produce a magical effect. A ritual requires time to cast, as well as some physical component and (usually) an incantation to shape and direct the magic to a desired task.

Sadhana: Sanskrit, "Attaining." The Indian tradition of blood magic, chiefly from Hindu roots.

Sadhu: Sanskrit, "Achiever." A practitioner of Sadhana.

Sending: The magic that results from a ritual, especially when directed at a specific person, place or thing.

Sorcery: A catchall term for traditions of blood magic other than Tremere Thaumaturgy; thus, Koldunic Sorcery, Setite Sorcery, etc.

Subject: The recipient of a magical effect that does not cause direct harm.

Talisman: An object that confers some active, noncontinuous magical power on a person, place or thing. A talisman may be an ingredient in a ritual, or an item of "stored magic" that other people can use.

Target: The recipient of a magical effect, usually one meant to cause harm. Also called a victim.

Thaumaturgy: Greek, "Wonder Working." Loosely defined, any blood magic. More specifically, Thaumaturgy refers to the magical Discipline of Clan Tremere (and most other blood magicians in the Western world), or any of its paths and rituals. To avoid confusion, Blood Sacrifice usually calls the Tremere art Hermetic Thaumaturgy.

Tradition: A system or style of magical practice. A thaumaturge's tradition describes both the favored procedures of her magical style and the inner logic that explains the magic.

True Name: A name that holds the magical essence of a person, spirit or thing.

Wanga: A blood magic tradition inspired by voudoun and other African and Afro-Caribbean religions and magical beliefs. Also, this tradition's term for a spell or amulet.

Wangateur: A practitioner of Wanga. Some may call themselves houngans, bokkor, mayomberos or other titles.

Working: A less-used variant of sending, especially used for necromantic magic and magic with no clearly defined subject. For instance, summoning a spirit to attack an enemy is a sending; summoning a spirit to answer questions is a working.

Chapter One: Akhu: The Divine Image

Get back, you crocodile of the West, who lives on the Unwearying Stars! Detestation of you is in my belly, for I have absorbed the power of Osiris, and I am Seth.
— The Book of Coming Forth by Day, Spell 32

Not a few vampires know that the Followers of Set claim an ancient magic quite distinct from the Thaumaturgy of the Tremere. Most of these Kindred simply call this magic "Setite Sorcery." This magic art has an actual name of its own, though. The Setites themselves call it Akhu, and they are not the only only vampires who practice this art.

Unlike Europeans, the ancient Egyptians regarded magic as a profoundly legitimate art. A sorcerer did not blaspheme against the gods by casting spells: The Egyptian gods gave magic to humanity as a gift, and each spell reaffirmed this bond between the human and the divine. Priests doubled as community magicians. The Egyptians saw no fundamental difference between a rite conducted in a temple for the benefit of Pharaoh and the state and a spell cast at a client's house for personal benefit.

The ancient Egyptians also did not distinguish between "black" and "white" magic. All magic was ethically neutral. An Egyptian certainly did not like becoming the target of a curse, any more than a modern person likes being shot at; but an Egyptian responded to hostile magic by consulting his local priest-magician for spells to protect him — and to let him shoot back. Historians find only one record of an Egyptian trial for criminal sorcery, in the case of an official who attempted a sorcerous coup using magic books he stole from Pharaoh's library. The official's crimes, however, lay in the theft and the assassination attempt — not in the magic itself.

The Egyptians had several words for magic. The most important were Heka, "Magic," and Akhu, "Spells." The ancient texts use these words interchangeably. As early as 1000 BC, however, Egyptian vampires used Heka to refer to mortal sorcery and Akhu to refer to their blood magic. Except for the use of vitae, Heka and Akhu used much the same tools to cast similar spells.

Egyptian attitudes changed during Roman times. The Romans forbade priests to cast spells, though the practice continued in secret. Egypt's conversion to Christianity completed the transition. After centuries of decline among mortals, only vampires remembered and practiced the ancient sorceries. Heka apparently died, while Akhu went underground.

In the ancient world, Egyptian priests enjoyed a reputation as the world's greatest sorcerers. Thanks to Akhu, the Followers of Set inherited this reputation. Suspicion of the "pagan" Setites and of "Satanic" sorcery fed on each other in the Christian and Muslim world. Some undead historians argue that the Setites themselves came to believe the baleful rumors spread about them and their sorcery, and that many Setite practices grew from these centuries of propaganda.

In the Middle Ages and Renaissance, Clan Tremere replaced the Followers of Set as the leading purveyors of magic in Europe. A dreadful Inquisition in their native Egypt further reduced Setite power and destroyed most sorcerers from other clans. Egyptian sorcery became an increasingly

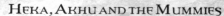

Heka, Akhu and the Mummies

Actually, Heka (or Hekau, the plural form) is not dead. The Egyptian Mummies, also known as the Reborn, preserve the ancient art in something close to its pure form. This does not mean that the knowledge is easy to acquire, though: Few mummies exist — though their numbers now increase — and they seldom become friendly with vampires. Thus hardly anyone else knows about mummy Hekau, and the mummies know little about vampiric Akhu. Because of their common roots, however, the two arts retain strong similarities despite thousands of years of separate development.

Interested readers can learn more about Hekau in **Mummy: the Resurrection**.

rare art. Relatively few Setites (or Egyptian vampires of other clans) bothered to learn Akhu — not least because so few Kindred could read the ancient papyrus grimoires.

In the 19th century, however, Champollion's translation of Egyptian hieroglyphics led to renewed interest in all things Egyptian among Kindred and kine. Some Tremere became interested in the magic of their old rivals and sought to learn Akhu. A large percentage of these Warlocks rebelled against their clan's hierarchy and became Set-cultists themselves. In 1930, the Council of Seven banned research into Akhu. In 1973, Muharram Rasul ibn Babar, Pontifex of Antioch, persuaded the Council of Seven to lift the ban. The Pontifex, known for his hatred of the Setites, argued that House and Clan needed to master the Serpents' magic in order to defend against it. The clan's elders, however, still look askance at any Warlock who shows too much interest in Egyptian magic. The Tremere have lost too many secrets because of defectors.

Magical Theory and Practice

From contact with the Setites and study of ancient papyri, Tremere scholars can reconstruct the Egyptians' theory of magic. Akhu seems to possess an almost uncanny continuity with the magic of mortal Egyptians. Even the obvious differences conceal subtle magical properties.

Images and Imitations

The Egyptians made great use of images, from the mighty statues in the temples to quick sketches drawn on a person's skin. They believed that a picture or statue held the essence of whatever it depicted. An idol carried the power of the god it represented. A tomb-painting of food became real food in the afterlife. Skewering a wax effigy of a person with needles inflicted a curse upon the actual person. A spell could bring a model animal to life to attack a magician's enemy, or a model ship could become a real ship. An image of the god Horus trampling upon crocodiles, snakes and scorpions protected the owner from those actual beasts.

The power of images reaches to the very heart of Egyptian magic and religion. Pharaoh was the living image of Horus and ruled in the god's name. Pharaoh was also arch-priest, but since Pharaoh could not conduct every rite in every temple, the priests conducted rites as the image of Pharaoh. In later millennia, when Romans and Christians suppressed the Egyptian religion, purely secular magicians cast spells and offered sacrifices in imitation of priests.

The gods themselves used magic. Thoth and Isis bore particular reputations as patrons of magic but the supreme god of magic was Heka, who personified magic itself. When a priest-magician cast spells, he identified himself with one or more gods in his incantation, usually including Heka. Many spells include a *historiola*, a brief recounting of a myth in which a god performed the same feat as the magician: "As Horus did thus-and-so, I do the same."

Words and Names

A name was another sort of image. Naming something gave power over it. The secret True Name of a person or thing gave *total* power over it. When a priest burned the written name of the chaos-serpent Apep, he burned Apep itself. When the goddess Isis extorted his True Name from the sun-god Ra, she took possession of his irresistible might.

The Egyptians also saw writing as intrinsically magical. Hieroglyphic writing was especially magical, because it consisted of pictures — combining the power of the Word and Name with the power of images. Hieroglyphics carried so much power that the Egyptians wrote the signs for evil powers such as Apep cut in half or pierced with knives, to render them less dangerous. Akhu practitioners claim the ancient title of "lector-priest" (*kher-heb*, literally "the one with the book").

Some spells owed their effect to being written. The funerary spells that guided the deceased through the Underworld and made him a god — from the early *Pyramid Texts* to the later *Book of the Dead* — needed no living person to read them. Their written presence in the tomb sufficed.

Every Akhu ritual, therefore, includes an incantation. Most rituals incorporate writing in some way: the written name of a god, a short incantation or command, or mystic words and symbols of obscure meaning.

The Multi-Part Soul

The Egyptians believed that the body, or *khat*, carried more than one spiritual force. Various parts of the soul not only powered magic, they could be affected by magic as well. These multiple souls (or aspects of the soul) performed various functions and separated from the *khat* at death. Kindred magicians interpret these ancient religious concepts in their own way.

• The *ka* is the "astral double" of the body — a ghost. The *ka* separates from the body at death. It also acts as the vehicle for consciousness during astral projection.

• The *ba* or "breath" is the life force animating the body. Vampires have no *ba*: they steal it from the living as blood.

• The *ab* or "heart" is the source of good or evil thoughts. The *ab* carried a record of all a person's deeds and moral character. The gods consulted the *ab* when they judged a person after death. Vampires consider this their "humanity."

- The *khaibit* or "shadow," however, was the self-destructive, evil aspect of the soul. Some Egyptian vampires call the Beast their *khaibit* (though some wraiths and practitioners of other magic arts say the Beast is actually a quite different psychic force).
- The *ren* is a person's true name, the essence of identity and existence.
- The *sekhem* is a person's spiritual vitality and magical power. Vampires have no *sekhem* of their own; as with *ba*, they steal it from the living.
- The *sahu* is the truly eternal soul, everlasting and incorruptible, which can ascend to Heaven and join the gods after death.
- The *khu* or "shining" is the aura, visible to beings with spiritual perceptions.

The Afterlife

To the Egyptians, as long as someone remembered the blessed dead and made offerings at their graves, the dead could return with blessings for the living — or curses, for mortals who mistreated them. The Egyptians buried food, furniture, household goods and treasures in their tombs because they expected the dead to use them, in the next world if not in this one.

The soul's free travel between the lands of the living and the dead depended, however, on preserving the *khat*. The cadaver's destruction brought true death to the soul, or at least rendered the *ba* and *ka* unable to visit the living world. Mummification preserved the body, ensuring the soul's immortality, and Egyptian aristocrats built hidden tombs in hopes of protecting their mummies from grave robbers.

The Egyptians believed in two realms of the dead. The Western Lands, or Amenti, received the souls that Osiris found worthy. The god Anubis conducted each soul to the judgment-hall of Osiris. There the deceased made the "negative confession," proclaiming his innocence of 42 standard crimes. Anubis weighed the person's heart, or conscience, against a feather that symbolized *Maat*, or truth, justice and the cosmic order. If the person's sins weighed more than the feather, however, a monster called the Eater of Hearts stood ready to devour him. If the deceased truly had a sinless heart — or if the proper spells jiggered the scales of judgment — the god Thoth wrote the person's name in the Book of Life. The soul then passed to the Western Lands. The afterlife in Amenti resembled life on Earth, but magic made it more pleasant. For instance, the deceased were obliged to plow-plant and harvest just as they had on Earth, but a magic spell could animate little statues called *ushabti* into laborers who did the work instead.

Before the Egyptians conceived of Amenti, however, they believed in a grimmer underworld, which they retained for the dead who failed the test of Osiris. The Egyptians believed that after it sailed across the sky during the day, the boat of Ra sailed under the Earth through the caverns of Duat, the River of Death. Serpents, monsters and demons haunted Duat; although parts of Duat burned, the nightly passage of Ra gave the only light. The dead consigned to Duat existed without food, light, air or motion. The most ancient spells and prayers sought to deliver the dead person from this bleak half-existence by adding them to the sun-boat's crew, who enjoyed an eternal afterlife with Ra.

CHAPTER ONE: AKHU: THE DIVINE IMAGE

Escape from Duat, passage to Amenti and visits to the mortal world all required magic spells. The dead needed spells to breathe, spells to eat, spells to take other forms, spells for everything the dead person might want to do or avoid doing. At first only the pharaoh received this divine privilege. He needed a pyramid with the requisite spells and prayers chiseled on the walls of the tomb chamber (the *Pyramid Texts*). When the Egyptians found pyramids uneconomical, they inscribed the necessary spells on the surface of the sarcophagus (the *Coffin Texts*). This practice never entirely died. In time, however, the Egyptians decided it was more practical to simply write all the spells and instructions for reaching Osiris in a scroll, and place a copy in the person's tomb. The Egyptians called this funeral text *The Book of Coming Forth by Day*. Modern folk often call it *The Egyptian Book of the Dead*. Each copy differs in its details, but the *Book of the Dead* remains the most encyclopedic guide to Egyptian magic yet known — to mortals, at least.

NATURAL MAGIC

Akhu also employs "natural magic" — the occult powers of herbs, stones and other substances. Many Akhu rituals use some sort of material object or ingredients. Most commonly, curse rituals require that the magician possess something that came from the victim's body, such as hair or spittle. Other substances bear traditional associations from Egyptian mythology, religion or funeral practice. For instance, the Egyptians favored green stone for amulets dedicated to Osiris, who began as a god of vegetation.

RAIDING THE WESTERN LANDS

Unfortunately for the Kindred, the Egyptian religion did not grant them the benefits of divine magic. Vampires lacked breath and vital force; their banishment from the sun's light proclaimed them anathema to the gods. No divine contract gave them the right to cast spells. Just as vampires stole blood from the living, however, the ancient Egyptian Kindred found ways to steal magic from the gods.

Even so, the Egyptian blood magicians drew their charter from a divine legend: the myth of Set and Osiris. When the sun-god Ra grew too old to continue as king of the gods and the world, he appointed Osiris as his successor. This decision outraged Osiris' brother Set. The warrior-god reminded Ra of his nightly service, battling the chaos-serpent Apep so the sun-boat could pass the gates of dawn, but Ra would not change his mind.

Set took revenge by murdering Osiris and dismembering his body. Isis, the sister-wife of Osiris, recovered his body, mummified it and magically conceived a son by her dead husband. This son, Horus, grew up to avenge his father and become the next king of the gods, while Osiris became the king of the dead. For a time, however, Set successfully usurped the powers of light and life.

In the same way, all blood magicians fuel their spells with the life force they steal from the living. Practitioners of Akhu go even further. They additionally steal power from the dead by re-enacting the dismemberment of Osiris, the greatest act of blasphemy in Egyptian legend. *The Book of Going Forth by Night*, — a text written by Set himself, according to legend — tells them how to do it. This power enhances their magic. Lector-priests can cast many spells without expending vitae, relying entirely upon the power stolen from the dead and from Osiris himself.

BLASPHEMY-SHRINES

As the Egyptians condensed their funerary magic from the *Pyramid Texts* to the *Book of Coming Forth by Day*, they allowed more people to enjoy the afterlife privileges once restricted to pharaohs. By Hellenistic times, the Egyptian priests opened the Western Lands to any commoner who could afford the mummification process and a copy of the *Book of the Dead*. All these people joined the kingdom of Osiris. By emulating the god's mummification, they mystically became Osiris.

Cultists of Set take this claim seriously. They interpret "becoming Osiris" to mean that these souls become extensions of the god and feed his power through a spiritual vampirism. Even tonight, they believe, souls can find themselves in Amenti and become the happy, deluded slaves of the god. The Egyptian religion may have died out, but people still seek immortality through extravagant burials, monuments or a cadaver preserved for the ages.

Since people pass to Amenti through obsession with their cadaver or the pomp of their burial, lector-priests free them from the Western Lands by reversing these conditions. They desecrate the body by breaking bones, splitting open the ribcage and using hooks and cords to pull the corpse into a torturous position. By mutilating the corpse, they imitate Set's murder and dismemberment of Osiris.

The Setite magician likewise mocks and perverts the grave goods. In a full Egyptian burial, the viscera went in four special "canopic jars" placed in a specific arrangement. A Setite reverses that arrangement, placing the northern jar in the south and the eastern jar in the west. Other grave goods join the tableau after suitable defilement. The magician might load a beautiful coffin with manure and turn it into a mushroom farm. Rich clothing becomes a rag-rug for the magician to wipe his feet upon.

Set's book supplies insulting uses for classically Egyptian grave goods such as amulets and jewelry, *ushabti* figures, furniture, weapons and vases for unguents. Setites dealing with latter-day burials must exercise their ingenuity. For instance, given a person who sought immortality by endowing a library, museum or hospital, a Setite might steal and defile the commemorative plaque, the official stationery and other objects from the building.

The Book of Going Forth by Night says that this desecration withers the soul in the Western Lands and inflicts eternal torment upon it. At least, part of the soul writhes and howls in pain. Some Setites believe that the wailing spirit is merely the person's *ka* or "astral double." The imperishable true soul, the *sahu*, slips free of the broken *ka* like a snake sloughing its skin, a second death to a genuine and transcendent new life. Other Setites omit this point of doctrine. They say that anyone who serves Osiris deserves a few millennia of torture. After all, the tortured cadaver eventually falls apart, no matter how carefully a Setite preserves it, and then the soul's torment ends.

Metaphysics aside, an Akhu practitioner absolutely must perform this rite of desecration in order to work magic. The broken cadaver and tortured *ka* pull magical power from Amenti to the lector-priest's ritual chamber. A lector-priest can perform magic elsewhere, but must conduct monthly rites to honor Set in the blasphemy-shrine. If some ill luck destroys the blasphemy-shrine, the lector-priest can no longer perform even the simplest magic ritual.

(The Setite Sorcery ritual of "Opening the Gate" permits a lector-priest to gain even greater benefit from a blasphemy-shrine. Once per night, the sorcerer can actually raise her blood or Willpower pool by drawing upon the stolen energy of Amenti. See the Setite Sorcery section of **Blood Magic** for the details of this ritual.)

The Book of Going Forth by Night

Set's book gives full instructions for "Opening the Gate." *The Book of Going Forth by Night* also tells how to inscribe a consecrated copy that makes other magic rituals more likely to succeed, and how to brew a vitae-laced sacramental beer (see below for a full description of these rituals.) *The Book of Going Forth by Night* contains no other rituals of Setite sorcery. Many Akhu rituals employ its legends and liturgies, though. Some sendings demand the physical presence of a copy. A tradition-bound Setite would insist upon a copy of *The Book of Going Forth by Night* written in hieroglyphics upon a genuine papyrus scroll. Less formal lector-priests accept printed copies bound as a modern book (scrolls are not very convenient), and written in hieratic, demotic or Coptic script. Setites have translated the book into Greek, Arabic, English and several other languages for their neonates to study, but these have no value in magic.

Tools and Techniques

In addition to the blasphemy-shrine, a lector-priest employs a wide variety of tools. Some are nigh-omnipresent in spells and Storytellers can assume their presence in nearly every ritual. Others are more specialized. Akhu practitioners not only use these tools in their rituals, they often enchant them as talismans. Egyptian magic also includes a variety of standard procedures that can appear in a wide variety of spells.

Amulets

The Egyptians surrounded themselves with dozens of different amulets, which they called *sa* or *meket*. Each amulet secured specific blessings for its owner. The most common amulets were the *ankh*, whose name meant "life"; the *djed* or "backbone of Osiris"; the scarab, a symbol of Ra; and the *udjat*, or "eye of Horus." They also used animal forms associated with various gods. Amulets generally bore hieroglyphic inscriptions. The Egyptians made many amulets out of gold and semiprecious stones.

Magic Rods

Egyptian magicians employed a variety of magic rods, and so do Akhu masters. The common rod with a twisted crossbar at the top, called the *uas*, began as a priest-architect's measuring-rod and became a general symbol of priestly authority. Priest-magicians also used square stone rods with figures of gods, animals and hieroglyphs carved on the sides, rods topped with the ankh or the djed, or rods shaped like serpents. Setite sorcerers combine the uas with the serpent-headed rod by having the crossbar clenched in the serpent's jaws. The magician commonly uses the rod to trace a magic circle before casting a ritual.

Writing Tools

A lector-priest uses a reed pen and a variety of colored inks to prepare amulets written on papyrus and to write words and names upon figurines. A priest also needs a burin and other tools to engrave words and symbols on amulets of stone and other tools.

Funerary Paraphernalia

Because stealing power from the dead plays such an important role in Akhu, its practitioners often employ funeral equipment in their spells. Canopic jars, miniature (or full-sized) sarcophagi, natron (a natural alkaline salt used in mummification), linen bandages and other paraphernalia may find use in rituals, especially for magic dealing with the dead.

Stelae and Other Monuments

A *stela* is a stone tablet carved with pictures and inscriptions. They commemorated everything from military victories to a deceased person. Stelae could bear spells as well. Magicians could also carve spells on a pyramidion (a miniature pyramid) or a miniature obelisk. In Hellenistic times, magicians built whole portable, miniature shrines to which they made suitably tiny, symbolic offerings.

Figurines

An Egyptian magician-priest must own icons of her favorite gods. The Egyptians placed magical figurines in their tombs and used statuettes as offerings. Whole paths of Akhu deal with the magic of images and figurines.

Sand

The Nile's inundation left banks of sand behind. Its connection with the Nile made this sand sacred. The Egyptians also used sand for scrubbing, making it a symbol of physical cleanliness as well as spiritual purity. The Egyptians strewed sand in their temples, and priest-magicians scattered sand to exorcise hostile spirits before casting their spells. Akhu practitioners do the same.

The Circle

Egyptian magicians often drew a magic circle to hold forces in or out. A lector-priest often walks around a circle: He imitates Ra, who circles the entire world in one day, and thus claims the god's mastery over all the forces of Heaven, Earth and Underworld.

Spitting, Licking and Swallowing

These related acts could either bless or curse. Ra spat out his first children, but spittle could also carry the poison of malice. Swallowing something could be an aggressive, threatening act, or a way to assimilate a divine or magical power. Some Egyptian spells involved drawing the figure of a god on one's skin, then licking it off. Magicians also wrote spells on papyrus that the recipient dissolved in beer and drank, or a person drank beer that the magician poured over a stela bearing the spell.

Notable Gods

A practitioner of Akhu must know about the Egyptian gods. That is no small feat. In the course of 3000 years, the Egyptians believed in many gods, with numerous local variations. To complicate matters even more, the priests often fused gods into composite deities — as when Hellenistic priests identified Osiris with Apis, an aspect of the artisan/creator-god Ptah, to create the new deity Serapis. We list only a few of the more famous gods, or those most often invoked in magic.

• **Ra**, the sun-god, was the most ancient ruler of the gods. The priests of Ra declared him self-begotten and ancestor of all other gods. Over the centuries, however, Ra became more distant and less active — a remote symbol of abstract, universal power — while other gods dominated daily life and Egyptian politics and religion. The Egyptians retained their fixation on the Sun as the source of life, however, and so Ra retained enough prominence that pharaohs routinely identified their favorite gods with him. For instance, the ram-headed war-god Amun, whose priests became extremely powerful in the New Kingdom, was often called Amun-Ra. Ra's totem animals include the falcon, the cat or lion, and the scarab.

• **Osiris**, originally a god of vegetation and fertility, became one of the most enduringly popular gods. After his murder by Set, Osiris became the king of the dead who promised a blissful afterlife and eventual bodily resurrection. Osiris is most often represented as a mummy holding a crook and flail. Setite sorcerers do not invoke Osiris, except to curse him.

• **Isis**, the sister and wife of Osiris, eventually became one of the most popular gods in the ancient world. She was both a mighty magician and a paragon of faithful wives. Isis regularly thwarted the schemes of Set. Setite sorcerers revile her as another enemy of their divine ancestor, but Tremere students of Akhu find that her mention in an incantation does not doom the spell to fail.

• **Horus**, the son of Isis and Osiris, avenged his father's murder and became the next king of gods and men. The pharaohs declared him the first pharaoh, and claimed descent from him. Mystically, the pharaoh embodied Horus in life and Osiris in death.

Confusingly, the Egyptians also believed in a second, older Horus — a sun-god like Ra. Horus the Elder was the patron god of Lower Egypt, while Set was the patron of Upper Egypt. Horus had many other aspects, too. Horus the Avenger was Set's implacable enemy, but Tremere experimenters find that they can invoke the god's other aspects in rites. Many of Horus' aspects use the falcon as their symbol.

• **Set**, also called Seth or Sutekh, naturally assumes a primary place in Setite sorcery. Only later in Egyptian history did Set become the god of evil. Early legends place him on the sun-boat with Ra, battling monsters so the Sun could rise each morning. He was the God of the Desert, however, and of storms, earthquakes, foreigners and everything else that could upset the peaceful order of Egyptian life. Mortal magicians regularly invoked Set in their exorcisms, on the principle that the Dark God was a fearsome enough deity to frighten any demon.

In his human form, Set had red hair and blue eyes, which the Egyptians considered strange and sinister. Set's totem animals included the hippopotamus, the crocodile, the black pig and the "Typhonic Beast," a strange creature with a long snout and square-topped ears.

• **Thoth**, the god of writing, the Moon, calendars and all scholarly arts, surpassed even Isis as a god of magic. His origin was obscure: The Egyptians sometimes described him as self-begotten, like Ra. His totem animals were the ibis and the dog-headed baboon. Although myths frequently show Thoth assisting Osiris, Isis and Horus, he is so central to Egyptian magic that the Setites could never excise him from Akhu. Many rituals invoke Thoth.

• **Heka** personified Magic itself. The god appears in incantations, but was so abstract that he never enjoyed much actual worship.

• **Ptah**, represented as a mummified man with a shaved head, was the god of craftsmen, engineers and artists. His home city of Memphis elevated him to creator-god, and all Egyptians regarded him as a great magician. In spite of Ptah's frequent identification with Osiris in later Pharaonic and Hellenistic times, Setite sorcerers invoke Ptah every time they craft and consecrate a magical tool.

• **Khnum**, another creator-god, became nationally prominent in the 26th dynasty. The Egyptians represented Khnum as a ram-headed man who shaped the bodies of the unborn on his potter's wheel. Lector-priests often invoke Khnum in spells that affect the body.

• **Amun**, the chief god of the New Kingdom, also looked like a ram-headed man. Amun largely replaced Ra as the god of kingship and the state; his priests identified Amun with almost every other god, as an all-purpose deity. Lector-priests invoke the authority of Amun in spells of command and mastery.

• **Anubis**, represented as a jackal or a man with a jackal's head, held an important role in all sorts of magic. He guided souls between the worlds of the living, the dead and the gods. Diviners appealed to Anubis for visions. Exorcists called Anubis to harry hostile spirits back to the Underworld; he could also release demons to plague and curse the living. For all his benign roles in many myths, the common Egyptians seem to have feared the Jackal at the Gates of Death.

Set's wife Nephthys bore Anubis, but Set was not his father… at least, not in the official legends. Myths say that Nephthys seduced Osiris by a trick; Anubis embalmed his illegitimate father as the first mummy. The Followers of Set dispute this story, but prefer to invoke the Jackal under the name of a similar god, wolf-headed Wepwawet, whom the Setites claim as Set's child (or childe).

• **Sebek** (or Sobek or Suchos) began as a crocodile-god of the Faiyum region, but became popular throughout Egypt.

Some *Coffin Texts* of the Middle Kingdom paint Sebek as an evil monster of the Underworld. In most periods, however, the Egyptians admired his ferocity. The crocodile-god even achieved identification with Ra or Horus. Setites prefer to emphasize Sebek's occasional identification with Set, based upon the crocodile-god's ferocity, totem animal, and temple at Set's "home city" of Ombos.

• The hippopotamus-goddess **Taweret** held associations with both childbirth and sorcery. The Egyptians knew the hippo as a dangerous beast. Exorcists invoked Taweret to drive away hostile spirits — but magicians could invoke her to lay curses, as well. Some legends make her a wife of Set, which added to her sinister reputation. The Setites claim her as one of Set's childer as well as his consort, and invoke her in many rituals.

• Magicians invoked **Bes**, a dwarfish god with a lion-like face, in exorcisms and all sorts of protective spells. He particularly assisted women in childbirth and protected newborns. He also became a god of music, dancing and revelry. Akhu sorcerers invoke him in all these roles.

• **Sekhmet**, a lion-goddess, presided over disease, war and strife. A special class of "Sekhmet-priests" worked as physicians and magical healers. Sekhmet could also cause disease, however: The Egyptians called plagues and fevers "the arrows of Sekhmet." Lector-priests call upon Sekhmet to cause or cure disease, or in spells of magical murder. She was the consort of Ptah.

• **Seker** (or Sokar or Socharis) was a very ancient god of death. He ruled the dark Underworld of Duat and fed upon the hearts of the dead; unlike Osiris, Seker offered no resurrection. The Osiris cult relentlessly absorbed every other death-god, including Seker, but the Followers of Set preserve the myths and rites of the bleaker, older god. The Egyptians represented Seker as a sparrowhawk or a hawk-headed mummy.

Not all Setite vampires actually worship Set directly. A large minority of Setites identify the Dark God with deities from other pantheons. One prominent cult, for instance, identifies Set with the Greek monster Typhon and the Roman gods Mars, Bacchus and Pluto. Another cult actually links Set to Jesus through some truly amazing "secret doctrines." A handful of lector-priests translate Akhu to exploit these other pantheons. Most Setites who learn Akhu simply move beyond the "mask" of the other pantheon to worship Set directly and use the old Egyptian forms. So far, no vampire from any other clan has learned any of these hybrid forms of Akhu.

Not all lector-priests come from the Followers of Set clan. They are all Setites in the sense of worshiping the Dark God, but a significant percentage come from other lineages — such as the Tremere defectors and their childer. Few Kindred of other clans adopt the Setite faith, but the Followers of Set teach them Akhu as freely as they teach their own childer.

DEMONS AND MESSENGERS

The Egyptians believed in several classes of spirits. The ghosts of the blessed dead were called *akhu* (singular *akh*). Spells sometimes appealed to them for help. *Mut* were evil or at least unredeemed ghosts. Gods could project spirit-images of themselves, called *bau* (singular *ba*), to serve as messengers and convey blessings or curses. Duat held a variety of demons and monsters. Apep, the Great Serpent of chaos, became the most notorious. Egyptian funerary texts describe other monsters too, though, such as Maka, a flint-armored and knife-slashing serpent 50 feet long. The lesser demons, called *sebau*, serve Set. Their chief, Seba, looks like a giant snake with 12 human heads sprouting from its body. *Sebau* look like serpents, crocodiles, or patchworks of these creatures with human parts.

The blessed souls lie beyond the reach of Akhu, but lector-priests can evoke *mut*, *bau* and *sebau*. Setite sorcerers greatly prefer the *sebau*: Some Setites believe that clanmates who suffer Final Death become *sebau*, transformed by the power of Set.

Storytellers can refer to the **Vampire: The Masquerade** (pp. 282-3) for "quick and dirty" wraith templates. These can also serve as models for *bau* and *sebau*. The Summon *Sebau* ritual evokes a demon comparable to the Recently Deceased wraith. Only the most powerful lector-priests can summon spirits comparable to the Old Soul.

Divine messengers possess Disciplines or Thaumaturgical paths suitable for the god that emanates them. A *ba* of Ptah might possess the Path of Conjuring, while a *ba* of Seker might know Necromancy paths, and the *bau* of a kingship god such as Ra, Amun or Horus would have Presence. All *sebau* have Serpentis 4 (as well as other Disciplines), and do not have to expend their analog of blood points to fuel these powers.

GAME MECHANICS

The game mechanics of Akhu differ from Hermetic Thaumaturgy in several important ways. Most immediately, Setite Sorcery paths do not all use a Willpower roll. Some paths call for an Attribute + Ability roll — always the same roll for each power in the path. All rituals use an Intelligence + Occult roll. Difficulties are usually the power or ritual's level + 3, to a maximum of 9. In some cases, however, a power or ritual might use the victim's Willpower as the difficulty instead.

Most Akhu path powers do not require expending vitae. The lector-priest draws upon her blasphemy-shrine's power instead. Vitae expenditures within Setite Sorcery often take the form of sacrifices to Set or another god.

A lector-priest character needs at least one dot of Occult and one dot of Linguistics to know the requisite mysteries of Egyptian myth, magic and language. Alchemical rituals demand that the magician possess at least one dot of Medicine or Science. If a character lacks at least one dot of Crafts, the difficulty of all rituals that involve written spells, engraved amulets or other inscriptions increases by one.

Storytellers may impose other difficulty penalties or bonuses upon a player's roll, depending on how thoroughly the character adheres to the full pomp of Egyptian priestly tradition. For instance, rituals that involve writing assume that the character employs an authentic reed pen, ink and papyrus. She could also draw her inscription on a moist clay tablet and bake it hard. Chiseling the spell into a stone stela and painting the hieroglyphs would merit reducing the difficulty by -1. Conversely, scribbling spells with a ballpoint pen on a three-by-five note card would increase the sending's difficulty by +1. Other factors that could reduce difficulties

THE BOOK OF THOTH

The Book of Going Forth by Night is not the only Akhu grimoire. The Setites have written many others, but all their grimoires pale before the *Book of Thoth*.

Egyptian legend describes the *Book of Thoth* as the mightiest grimoire in the world, written by the god of magic himself. No one ever copied the manuscript. The legends say that the spells inscribed in the *Book of Thoth* give power over life and death and all the powers of Earth and the spirit worlds. Anyone who read the book's hieroglyphic script could threaten the gods themselves.

The Followers of Set believe in the existence of the *Book of Thoth*. One Setite legend claims that Moses used the *Book of Thoth* to call the 10 plagues upon Egypt. Some believe it tells secrets from before the beginning of the world, from worlds and cycles of existence that died before the gods were born. These Setites add that the gods of these dead worlds still exist, in some sense, but that only a fool or a madman would call on these malign primordial powers.

Fortunately for the world, the *Book of Thoth* seems remarkably elusive. Both mortal and undead magicians have chased rumors of the famous tome for more than 3,000 years. For instance, the mortal priest Na-nefer-ka-ptah found the *Book of Thoth*, but lost his life. Centuries later the priest Setne Khamuas stole the grimoire from Na-nefer-ka-ptah's tomb, but the ghosts of the slain priest and his wife "persuaded" Setne to return it.

The *Book of Thoth* seems to reappear every few centuries. About half the time, the supposed grimoire turns out to be a hoax — the Setites' great temple archive at the House of the Eclipse holds no less than eight false *Books of Thoth*. Other times, the magician meets a grisly end and his book of magic disappears before anyone else can ascertain whether it was the *Book of Thoth* or not. Alleged *Books of Thoth* have been buried in landslides, fallen into the sea, and carried off by demons. Setite legend insists, however, that nothing can ever destroy the *Book of Thoth*. A few Cainite lore-masters, reviewing the history of disaster, death and madness that follow reports of the *Book of Thoth*, suggest that sorcerers should leave this grimoire alone. The Tremere chantry in Alexandria, however, offers a reward for any information about the *Book of Thoth*.

A rumor of the *Book of Thoth* makes an excellent hook to draw characters into a story, especially a story that involves travel. We encourage Storytellers, however, to keep the actual *Book of Thoth* out of characters' hands. Perhaps the dreadful book remains a rumor, its existence never firmly established. Alternatively, a Storyteller can use the *Book of Thoth* as a plot device to set great events in motion before it vanishes again and its owner meets a colorful doom.

---

include the use of genuine Nile water, ancient ritual tools or a congregation of fellow Set cultists (such as a personal blood cult). Negative factors include wearing synthetic or animal-derived fabrics (Egyptian priests wore linen), or improvised ritual tools. We recommend that Storytellers not adjust difficulties up or down by more than two.

Some Akhu paths require the use of a material focus. In most cases, the path requires only a small amulet or item of jewelry. A few paths require as much time and preparation as rituals — but they are so fundamental to Akhu that players spend experience points for their characters to learn them.

SETITE ALCHEMY

Akhu includes a subset of rituals that create magical salves, unguents and potions. These are collectively called "the Milk of Set." Unless otherwise mentioned, it takes one week per level of the ritual to brew a single dose of an alchemical preparation. The salve, unguent or potion retains its potency for a number of weeks equal to the player's successes on the Intelligence + Occult roll, and then becomes useless.

AKHU PATHS

Blood Magic: Secrets of Thaumaturgy presented two other paths of Setite sorcery: the Dry Nile and the Snake Inside. Akhu also employs its own versions of other paths presented in various **Vampire** supplements, but often gives them other names. Each path relates in some way to Set or Set-cultist activities. This list does not exclude Akhu versions of other paths, but we recommend that Storytellers not import too many paths from other styles, as this can dilute the mystique of each school of blood magic.

Alchemy (Alchemy): **Blood Magic: Secrets of Thaumaturgy**

Conjuring (Path of Ptah): **Vampire: the Masquerade**

Corruption (The False Heart): **Guide to the Camarilla**

Curses (*Sebau*'s Touch): **Blood Magic: Secrets of Thaumaturgy**

Focused Mind (Path of Thoth): **Blood Magic: Secrets of Thaumaturgy**

Mars (Valor of Sutekh): **Guide to the Sabbat**

Mastery of the Mortal Shell (Vengeance of Khnum): **Blood Magic: Secrets of Thaumaturgy**

Spirit Manipulation (Path of Anubis): **Guide to the Camarilla**

Weather Control (Breath of Set): **Guide to the Camarilla**

It's up to the Storyteller to decide whether these duplicated paths require a lector-priest to expend vitae. If you find it simpler to use each path exactly as written, then do so. If you find it less confusing to rule that the blasphemy-shrine's power removes the need for spending blood points, follow that plan instead. Discuss it with your players — and make sure that every lector-priest character in your chronicle follows the same rule.

DIVINE HAND

This path deals with sympathetic magic. What the magician does to a model of an object happens in truth to the real object. More frighteningly, the Divine Hand can affect people, too. The Divine Hand ignores distance: using this path, a magician can affect targets around the world.

The composition of a model object does not matter — cardboard works as well as anything — but the model should resemble the object as closely as possible. (Realistic scale model cars, trucks and other toys are a boon to magicians with Divine Hand.) The lector-priest must hand-craft models of people, animals or spirits out of beeswax. The magician inscribes words of power on the model while chanting invocations to the gods. What the magician then does to the model, happens to the real object within the next 24 hours. As a magician becomes more powerful, he can affect larger objects and a wider variety of victims.

Lector-priests typically use the Divine Hand to destroy or attack. For instance, burning a model of a house makes the actual house catch fire. Snapping off a doll's arm makes the real person break his arm. The magician can also cause instantaneous, "real time" damage to a target, but only if the magician can actually see the target.

The Divine Hand has more subtle uses, though. A magician could steer a truck off the road by pushing a model truck, or stop a damaged boat from sinking by supporting a similarly damaged model boat with his hand. A magician could even fix a damaged object by repairing a consecrated, identically damaged model.

System: Every application of the Divine Hand calls for a successful Intelligence + Occult roll (difficulty of the effect's level +3). The spell to activate the Divine Hand takes at least five minutes to cast.

Making an adequate model of a person or object calls for a Perception + Crafts roll (difficulty 6-8, based on the details of the target). The player needs a single success. If the model is especially good (many successes rolled) the Storyteller may grant a small reduction of difficulty to the roll for the actual spell. Conversely, if the magician did not try very hard to duplicate the target (for instance, not painting a cardboard model of a stone object) the Storyteller may raise the difficulty by 1.

• HAND OF PTAH

At first, the magician can affect only small objects with the Divine Hand — 200 pounds at most. Typical targets might be a wooden support beam, an item of furniture or a small motorcycle. The lector-priest identifies himself with the artisan-god Ptah.

System: The magician can inflict (or repair) two health levels of damage on the object, or exert a force equal to a Strength of 3.

•• HAND OF KHNUM

At this level of mastery, a magician gains the power to affect mortal beings — humans and animals — with the Divine Hand. The magician takes on the power of Khnum, divine shaper of life. Innately supernatural creatures such as vampires and werewolves, however, remain immune.

To cast the Hand of Khnum upon a mortal, the magician inscribes the person's name on the wax doll and incorporates bits of the person in the doll — a snippet of hair, say, or fingernail clippings. A supernatural "True Name" removes the need for body relics, but most modern people do not have a True Name, or at least they do not know it.

The magician can also affect more massive objects, up to 1,000 pounds, such as a telephone pole, steel support beam, large motorcycle or dumpster.

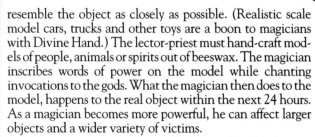

OPTIONAL: AKHU AND NECROMANCY

Akhu has strong necromantic aspects, but it is not a complete substitute for Necromancy. Practitioners who want to learn Necromancy Paths must learn them as a separate Discipline, not as secondary paths of Akhu. At the Storyteller's option, Akhu does include its own versions of particular Necromancy rituals; the Storyteller should increase a borrowed ritual's level by one, however, to reflect that Akhu isn't as good at death-magic as Necromancy itself.

System: For each success the player rolls, the magician can inflict one health level of lethal damage upon a mortal victim. Alternatively, she can exert Strength 2 against the person for each success rolled — for instance, the magician could wrap her hand tightly around a doll to immobilize the victim.

Against inanimate objects, the magician can inflict four health levels of damage or exert a Strength of 6.

••• HAND OF ANUBIS

At this level, the magician gains the power to influence corporeal supernatural entities: vampires, werewolves, changelings and other such creatures of mixed natures. The character calls upon Anubis, the mediator between worlds. He cannot affect wraiths or other sorts of spirits. As with the Hand of Khnum, the magician needs the victim's True Name or a sample of her body and her mundane name. The magician must make an extraordinary effort, however, to overpower the innate magic of the victim's being.

The magician can also now affect inanimate objects weighing up to 5,000 pounds, such as a car or a large speedboat.

System: To affect a supernatural victim, the magician's player spends two blood points and two points of temporary Willpower (that do not add successes to the dice roll). For every success rolled on the Intelligence + Occult check, the magician inflicts one health level of lethal damage to a supernatural target.

The magician can inflict up to six health levels of damage on inanimate objects, or exert a Strength of 9. This application does not cost vitae or Willpower.

•••• HAND OF THOTH

At this level of mastery, the magician can employ the Divine Hand against all sorts of spirits, including wraiths. Since spirits do not have corporeal forms, the magician needs the spirit's True Name or (in the case of wraiths) a relic of the deceased's khat or some object (called a Fetter) that was supremely important to the person in life. The lector-priest can also affect a spirit that she sees directly. The magic only affects spirits who manifest on Earth, or at least in the spirit world very close to Earth. The Hand of Thoth cannot reach spirits in their own realms.

At this level, the magician can use the Divine Hand against inanimate objects weighing up to 20,000 pounds, such as an armored limousine, a semi, or a Learjet.

System: The magician's player spends two blood points and two points of temporary Willpower to affect a spirit, and makes the Intelligence + Occult roll. For every success, the magician inflicts one health level of lethal damage to the spirit. The magic only affects spirits who manifest on Earth or in the Penumbra or Shroud.

The magician can inflict up to eight health levels of damage to an inanimate object, or exert a Strength of 12, without expending vitae or Willpower.

●●●●● HAND OF HEKA

A master of the Divine Hand can transmit magical powers to affect a target anywhere in the world by calling upon Heka, personified Magic itself. The transmitted magic can be a Discipline effect or another path or ritual power. For instance, a lector-priest could make a person fall in love with her by pouring a love potion over a consecrated doll, or by using the Presence power Entrancement upon the doll. The Hand of Heka cannot transmit purely physical effects such as a Feral Claws or Quietus attack, but the Hand can transmit non-physical effects to objects, mortals, supernatural beings and spirits.

At this level of mastery the magician can also damage or manipulate inanimate objects weighing up to 100,000 pounds. Examples include a small house (or a section of a larger building), a large yacht, a passenger plane, a boxcar or a good-sized tree.

System: The magician's player spends two blood points and two Willpower points to affect supernatural or spiritual targets. The player also expends whatever vitae the transmitted magic demands, and makes separate dice rolls for the Hand of Heka and the transmitted magic. Either the Hand or the other magic might fail. To influence mortal or corporeal targets, the magician needs the victim's True Name or something from the victim's body. Affecting spirits requires possession of the spirit's True Name, a body relic or Fetter for wraiths, or line of sight.

The magician can inflict up to 10 health levels of damage to an object, or exert a Strength of 15.

PATH OF DUAT

Through the Path of Duat, a practitioner of Akhu conjures the attributes of the Egyptian netherworld and inflicts them upon an enemy. The effects are mental and hypnotic rather than physical; an observer sees no physical cause for the victim's malady.

Each power within the path calls for a Charisma + Occult roll. Except for the last power, the effect lasts as long as the magician concentrates upon maintaining it. This means that the magician cannot engage in any violent physical activity, or employ other path or ritual magic. The character can, however, use passive amulets. None of the Duat powers cost blood points: The magician relies upon her blasphemy-shrine's power.

To use the Path of Duat, the magician must carry a talismanic gem of black onyx carved with the image of a mummified man — the form of Sokar, the god of Duat. A few minutes before using the path, the magician smears the talisman with a drop of her own blood as an offering to Sokar, and whispers a short prayer.

The hypnotic aspects of the Path of Duat mean that all powers operate at +1 difficulty if the lector-priest does not catch the victim's attention using the darkly glittering talisman on the turn when she initiates the magic. The victim does not need to see the magician on subsequent turns. If the character does not feel the need to attract the victim's attention, the Path of Duat can affect any victim that the magician can see with his own eyes. Once the magician can no longer see the victim, Path of Duat attacks end.

● A SENDING OF SERPENTS

Serpents, the spawn of Apep, haunt the 12 caverns of Duat. They swim in the river and coil about the limbs of the unredeemed dead. Through this power, the magician makes her victim hallucinate about snakes. The victim starts by seeing a single asp slithering nearby. No matter what the victim does, the snake comes closer. If he runs, another snake drops down before him or slithers from behind the furniture. If he attacks the snake, it vanishes but another serpent takes its place. Before long, more serpents appear, and one manages to coil around his body…. Although the snakes look real and deadly, they never actually bite. They can only frighten the victim.

Other people, of course, do not see these phantom serpents and might assume that a frightened victim is on drugs or has lost his mind.

System: The Charisma + Occult roll has a difficulty of 4, or 5 if the victim did not see magician and the talisman of Sokar when the attack began.

●● DARKNESS OF DUAT

The dead in Duat exist in darkness, relieved only by the nightly passage of the ship of Ra. This power casts the darkness of Duat into a victim's eyes, rendering him blind. The victim also hears the soft lapping of the River of Death as it flows through the Underworld.

System: If the Charisma + Occult roll succeeds, the victim sees nothing for as long as the magician concentrates upon her. Blinded characters are at +2 difficulty on Dexterity-based actions, or tasks that involve sight (such as searching for an object, typing at a keyboard, etc.). Those who attack a blind character receive +2 dice to their attack rolls.

●●● SUFFOCATION OF THE TOMB

Along with their other torments, the dead in Duat cannot breathe or speak. The "Opening of the Mouth" funerary ritual was meant to deliver the deceased from this unhappy condition. Through this power, a magician renders a victim as breathless and mute as the dead.

System: If the player succeeds in the dice roll, the victim can neither breathe nor speak for as long as the vampire concentrates upon her. For vampires, muteness is a minor inconvenience; they do not, of course, need to breathe. For a mortal, loss of breath can kill and deliver him to the netherworld in truth if the magician persists long enough. Mortals can survive a few minutes of suffocation, but immediately drop to Injured. For each turn of energetic action that a mortal attempts while suffocating, the player rolls Stamina + Athletics roll (difficulty 6). Failure means that the character suffers another health level of bashing damage. Once a mortal loses consciousness from this attack, she can live as many minutes as her Stamina Trait rating before suffocating to death.

●●●● THE NARROW HOUSE

The dead in Duat rest in coffins that open only when the sun-god Ra makes his nightly passage. At this level, the magician makes her victim feel that he is trapped in a coffin, unable to move.

System: A successfully paralyzed victim can take no action at all so long as the magician concentrates upon her, unless her player spends a Willpower point. In that case, the victim can act for that single turn, at a dice penalty equal to the number of successes the magician's player rolled. This power affects vampires, other corporeal supernatural entities and wraiths, but not other sorts of spirits.

●●●●● CONSIGNMENT TO DUAT

The ultimate power of this path sends the victim's entire consciousness to Duat. For a mortal, this means death. For a vampire, it merely means torpor — but since the victim is at the magician's mercy, in all likelihood Final Death soon follows anyway.

System: Unlike the other powers in this path, the magician's player spends a Willpower point. This does not add a success to the Charisma + Occult roll. The victim, feeling himself die, can also expend Willpower to stay active for another turn. While doing this, the victim suffers a -2 dice penalty to all dice pools, as if attempting to do two things at once. The victim's player spends another Willpower point each turn to keep the character alive (or undead, at least), but the magician's player does not have to expend more Willpower points to continue the attack. To survive the attack, the victim needs some way to break the magician's concentration or escape her line of sight.

Torpor induced by Consignment to Duat lasts the normal duration set by the victim's Humanity or Path of Enlightenment rating — barring further action by the magician.

USHABTI

The name of the path comes from the figurines that prosperous Egyptians had buried with them. In the Afterlife, these figurines supposedly became servants who would work for the interred person's soul. Images of objects also became real in the death-realm. Egyptian magicians also brought images to life in this world. One old tale tells of a magician who created a magical sedan chair and bearers who kidnapped a king from distant countries and returned him the same night. Vampire magicians cannot perform such magnificent feats, but masters of the *Ushabti* Path can still achieve many wonderful things.

Each use of this path requires a separate figurine. Thus, a magician who wants to create a crocodile fashions a model crocodile; to create a falcon, he uses a model falcon. Animal figures are as easy to animate as images of humans. A magician can use a figurine only once.

In every case, the magician makes the figurine out of wax or clay mixed with one blood point's worth of her own vitae. The lector-priest writes words of power upon the model, including its name in Egyptian hieroglyphics — "digger," "bullock," "guard" or the like. Then she bathes the figurine in honey and beer and fumigates it in the smoke of various herbs.

System: When activating an *ushabti*, the magician anoints the figurine with one blood point's worth of her own vitae and speaks an incantation. At this point, the player makes an Intelligence + Crafts roll to determine whether the magic succeeds. If the magic works, the statuette expands into a life-sized, animate figure. If the player rolls a botch, the statuette

animates but an evil spirit possesses the *ushabti* and sets about making the character's unlife miserable.

Ushabti creatures have Attributes and Abilities. Attributes are limited only by the magician's mastery of the path. A lector-priest cannot give an *ushabti* any Ability that she herself does not possess, and cannot grant an Ability rating above her own. Only at the highest level of mastery can an *ushabti* have Virtues, Humanity or Willpower, because they have no genuine minds or free will. Most *ushabti* can only follow orders. They cannot think for themselves, even to preserve their own existence.

An *ushabti* has health levels identical to a human or vampire. They soak both bashing and lethal damage with their full Stamina at difficulty 6. Although *ushabti* can possess the physical abilities intrinsic to an animal form, such as flight for a bird or a lion's claws and teeth, they cannot have any sort of magical powers.

Ushabti range from obvious animate mannikins to simulacra almost indistinguishable from life. The number of successes from the player's Intelligence + Crafts roll indicates the realism of the animate figure:

One success	Obviously clay or wax, crudely formed.
Two successes	A fairly realistic mannikin, like wax-works or a china doll.
Three successes	Moderately lifelike; could fool a casual viewer (Perception + Alertness, difficulty 6, to detect as false).
Four successes	Incredibly lifelike (difficulty 8 to detect as false).
Five successes	Indistinguishable from life.

An *ushabti*'s "realism rating" can never exceed the level of the power that created it. Thus, a Guard could never look more than moderately lifelike.

An *ushabti* creature remains active for one lunar month, so long as it has no contact with mundane humanity and stays within the vampire's haven. At the end of this period, the magician can extend the *ushabti*'s existence for another lunar month by feeding it another blood point. If an *ushabti* interacts with ordinary humans outside its creator's haven, the magic degrades rapidly: within an hour, the *ushabti* reverts to wax or clay and becomes a crumbling statuette again. A "slain" *ushabti* becomes a figurine at the moment of its "death."

Ushabti figurines are always made for use by a specific person; no one else can employ them. Most of the time, the magician makes *ushabti* for his own use, but she can prepare *ushabti* for another person to use at some later time. This costs the magician a point of Willpower. The other person activates the *ushabti* using the requisite magic words, but does not need to expend vitae.

● Laborer

At first, a magician can produce only simple, nearly mindless servants. These *ushabti* can perform simple, repetitive tasks such as digging, sweeping, pulling and carrying. Laborers cannot fight.

System: Whether human or animal, these basic *ushabti* have two dots in each Physical Attribute, one dot in each Mental Attribute and no dots in their Social Attributes. (*Ushabti* can be beautiful, if their maker fashions them so. A 0 Appearance represents an *ushabti*'s inability to perform any task requiring Social Attributes.) They have no Abilities.

●● Servitor

A more skilled magician can produce *ushabti* with greater intelligence and usefulness. Servitors can perform moderately complex tasks that require some small degree of common sense.

System: To the basic Laborer, add three dots of Attributes (but no Social Attributes, and no Mental Attribute can rise above 2). Also add two dots of Abilities. At this level, these cannot be combat Abilities.

●●● Guard

At this level, the magician can create *ushabti* with simulated minds that work quickly enough to handle combat. An *ushabti* created with this level of mastery does not *have* to be an actual guard, but it is a common application.

System: To the basic Laborer, add six dots of Attributes and four dots of Abilities. Guards can have Social Attributes, but no Social or Mental Attribute can have a rating higher than 2; neither can any Ability.

●●●● Overseer

A truly skilled magician can create formidable *ushabti* — powerful beasts, or servants more skilled than many humans. Such an *ushabti* can command lesser *ushabti*, and perform complex tasks without supervision.

System: To the basic Laborer, add nine dots of Attributes and six dots of Abilities. No Social or Mental Attribute can rise above 3 dots; neither can any Ability.

●●●●● Gift of Khnum

The ancient Egyptians believed that the god Khnum shaped human beings in the womb, as a potter shapes clay. A master of *Ushabti* can create servants of remarkable skill or power who are utterly loyal, but do not know that they are fakes. Even more remarkably, a magician can craft a body for a spirit and that spirit and body will truly live, as a free-willed being from then on. Through the Gift of Khnum, a blood-sorcerer can raise the dead — or release demons on the world.

System: To the basic Laborer, add 12 dots of Attributes and eight dots of Abilities. The *ushabti* also has Virtues, Humanity and Willpower like a starting **Vampire** character. It can think for itself, but remains emotionally bound to its creator as if blood bound. Alternatively, the magician can simply craft a body and infuse it with a pre-existing soul: either a wraith or some other sort of spirit. The *ushabti* then has whatever Abilities, Virtues and other Traits the spirit had. The magician can create whatever body he pleases, but the spirit must agree of its own free will to occupy the body.

The Gift of Khnum costs two Willpower points. The player can spend more Willpower Points for added successes on the Intelligence + Crafts roll to increase the chance of a highly lifelike *ushabti*, if she wants.

An *ushabti* created by the Gift of Khnum does not degrade in the presence of ordinary humans, or at the end of a month. It *will* degrade within minutes, however, if someone challenges its identity and convinces it that it is not a real person. One Setite legend tells of a faithful *ushabti* who served its creator for a hundred years before it saw its reflection and realized that it was just another one of its master's statues. Another story tells of a perfectly lifelike *ushabti* who married and bore children to her husband. She crumbled to dust, however, when her husband sought to discover her past and found that she did not have one.

RITUALS

LEVEL ONE RITUALS

TYPHON'S BREW

Most preparations of Setite alchemy begin with this magical, vitae-laced beer. A lector-priest who does not know how to create Typhon's Brew can forget about pursuing further knowledge of alchemy. This beer sustains ghouls as if it were true vampiric vitae. Vampires can drink it, too.

By itself, Typhon's Brew has no other properties. It cannot be used to Embrace a mortal, nor to blood bond the imbiber: The brewing process negates this aspect of vitae.

System: Brewing the Typhon's Brew takes a full month, beginning and ending at the dark of the moon. For every gallon brewed, the alchemist includes one blood point's worth of his own vitae. The brewing process multiplies the vitae, so that a ghoul can gain one blood point per quart of the magic beer. Vampires, however, gain only one blood point per gallon consumed — the same rate as in brewing the beer. For vampires, the beer's magic is limited to the fact that they can drink it at all without heaving it up seconds later. They can even get drunk on it, and suffer a hangover later.

INSCRIBE THE BOOK OF SET

Many Akhu rituals involve reading prayers from *The Book of Going Forth by Night*. For some purposes, the words themselves suffice. Powerful rituals, however, demand the use of a specially consecrated scroll. A sorcerer hand-copies the book in hiero-glyphic script, on a scroll of authentic papyrus, using vampiric vitae for ink. This generally takes a few years. No one else may handle the copy until it is complete, and the copyist must avoid dirt, stains, blots or other impurities. Consecrated copies of *The Book of Going Forth by Night* are worth large amounts of money or significant boons to a Setite temple.

Apart from their absolute necessity in some powerful rituals, a consecrated *Book of Set* increases a lector-priest's chance of success at other rituals through its mere presence. As a final magical effect, sunlight burns such scrolls to ash.

A sorcerer may also use this highly extended ritual to inscribe other texts. In this case, the resulting book burns in daylight but has no other magical properties. The Setites use this aspect of the ritual to keep their sacred texts out of mortal hands.

System: Inscribing the Book of Set requires the usual Intelligence + Occult roll (difficulty 4). Failure indicates that the character did not observe some ritual condition while copying the text, or made too many errors. The copyist does not have to use his own vitae, although this adds prestige to a copy.

SEAL THE GATES OF BLOOD

Egyptian doctor-priests prescribed an amulet of Set to prevent miscarriage and excessive menstrual bleeding, as the Dark God's brutal masculinity frightened the womb into shutting tight. Egyptian Setites still vend the charm, though they do not tell clients about one of its powers.

System: The amulet requires no special effort to scribe and consecrate. A woman who wears the amulet does not miscarry, and her menses are greatly reduced. The menstrual blood, however, actually passes to the lector-priest: one blood point, once a month, but never more than that. If the

recipient does not wear the amulet through one menstrual cycle, the spell breaks. The spell otherwise lasts one month per success rolled.

LEVEL TWO RITUALS

OPENING THE MOUTH

This magic ritual imitates one of the standard Egyptian rites performed before burial. The funerary rite enabled the deceased to breathe and speak in the Underworld. The Akhu ritual enables a dead person to speak through his own cadaver.

Opening the Mouth works only if the body retains an intact head and tongue. The magician sprinkles the cadaver with water and natron (a natural salt used in mummification), places three amulets on the body and recites a funeral prayer. At the end, the magician touches the cadaver's mouth with his ceremonial rod while commanding it to speak.

System: If the priest correctly performs the ritual, the deceased can hear and speak for one minute, but take no other action. The ritual does not compel the deceased to tell the truth; nor does the person know anything he did not know when alive. He cannot speak of the afterlife or Underworld, though. (If asked, he says that Osiris forbids him to speak of such things… even if the person never heard of Osiris in life. Magic is mysterious.) Opening the Mouth works only once for a particular magician upon a given person.

DREAMS OF DUAT

By invoking Set, the magician curses a victim to suffer terrifying dreams. The magician needs some part of her victim's body, such as hair or nail clippings. She seals them inside a wax figurine that she inscribes with the person's name (as closely as hieroglyphic script can approximate it). While reciting the curse, the magician bathes the figurine in water made bitter with natron and declared to come from the river of Duat. The victim then dreams of Duat's horrors.

System: Unlike most rituals, this one uses the victim's Willpower as the difficulty. For each night in which the magician successfully curses her with nightmares, the victim loses one point of temporary Willpower.

If the magician's player ever rolls a botch, the victim has a different dream. Into the nightmare of darkness, monsters and death sails a shining boat staffed by animal-headed men and women. An ibis-headed man — the god Thoth — tells the dreamer how the magician has cursed him, and gives the magician's name. (Religious magic has the problem that it goes wrong in religious ways. By accepting the reality of one god, Setite magicians also accept the power of other gods to interfere.)

LEVEL THREE RITUALS

LINKED SOUL ELIXIR

This magical drug consists of Typhon's Brew mixed with juices and resins from seven herbs, including hashish, opium and mandrake. Before administering the Linked Soul Elixir, the magician pours the brew over a stela bearing a spell-prayer to Anubis and collects the liquid in a basin. The prayer recalls the god's role in judging the dead and demands a similar power to see into the hearts of others.

People who drink the elixir feel each other's sensations and emotions, as long as they remain within line of sight of each other. It also renders the imbiber completely unable to resist any sort of mind control: The drug opens his soul and he can no longer tell which thoughts are his own. Vampires as well as mortals can drink Linked Soul Elixir.

System: Each preparation of the Linked Soul Elixir creates two doses. A person under the elixir's influence feels the pleasure, pain, thoughts and emotions of every other elixir-user within sight. For instance, if one elixir-user suffers a wound penalty, all the other elixir users suffer the same wound penalty. If one user's player must roll for the character to resist frenzy or rötschreck, all the characters' players must do so. On the other hand, all the characters joined by Linked Soul Elixir can use each other's Abilities as if they were their own.

An imbiber of Linked Soul Elixir cannot resist Dominate, Presence or any other sort of mind control magic. Every use of such Disciplines or magic on the target receives at least one guaranteed success that no number of 1s rolled can cancel out. The target's player cannot expend Willpower to resist the magic. What's more, every linked character receives the effect of the mind control magic. Every hour after drinking the elixir, a subject receives a Stamina roll (difficulty 6) to throw off the effects.

Scorpion Sending

Set dispatched a scorpion to sting the infant Horus. This ritual emulates the myth by creating a magical scorpion that attacks a single, predetermined victim. The scorpion's magical venom has an excellent chance of killing a mortal and can seriously inconvenience a vampire.

The magician makes a model scorpion out of wax, incorporating hair, nail clippings, spittle or something else that came from the victim's body. She writes the name of Set on the wax scorpion in green ink and recites the myth of the poisoning of Horus (though not the god's healing). Then she leaves the model scorpion in a place frequented by the victim. The next time the victim comes near the model, it becomes a real scorpion and stings him.

System: The scorpion's venom inflicts one health level of lethal damage every 15 minutes. The damage ends if the victim's player makes a successful Stamina roll at difficulty 7 (check at every increment of damage). The venom harms both mortals and vampires (although Kindred can expend vitae to increase their Stamina and heal the damage). It also affects Lupines, changelings and other supernatural races who have physical bodies.

The victim might see the scorpion before it strikes (a Perception + Alertness roll, difficulty 7 due to the scorpion's small size, or 9 if the victim-to-be is not actively looking). If the target kills the scorpion before it stings him, it reverts to a wax model. If the scorpion dies after stinging, it stays a real scorpion.

Level Four Rituals

Severing Sand

A handful of consecrated Nile sand can force all sorts of spirits to return from whence they came. Indeed, the Severing Sand possesses a limited power over all supernatural creatures. For instance, one magician used Nile sand to prevent a magical giant snake from re-joining its severed halves.

The magician must obtain authentic Egyptian river sand, washed absolutely clean and dried in sunlight. She sprinkles the sand with perfumes, natron and a few drops of her own vitae, and chants a litany of praise to the Nile.

When using the Severing Sand, the magician invokes an appropriate Egyptian god counter to whatever spirit or supernatural creature he faces. Against wraiths, a magician might call on Anubis to pull the ghost back to the Underworld; Ra or Set work equally well to banish the demons of Duat. Seker affects vampires. A wise magician intuitively knows what god works best for particular circumstances.

System: A magician may enchant Severing Sand in advance. The sand retains its power until sunrise. An exorcised spirit returns to its home; the magic sand works against all spirits, not just Egyptian ones. The spirit cannot return to Earth until the next nightfall.

A vampire, werewolf or other supernatural creature temporarily loses whatever healing powers it may possess. This effect lasts one minute.

Summon Sebau

A lector-priest can use a clay model to summon *sebau* — the demons of Duat — and send them to harry her enemies or perform other tasks. The magician must make the model with his own hands, using clay mixed with one blood point of his vitae.

System: If the ritual succeeds, the magician can command one service from the *sebau*-fiend that the demon can accomplish in one night. If the player rolls a botch, the demon attacks the magician. If the magician wants the *sebau*-fiend to attack a specific enemy, he needs the victim's True Name or some part of the victim's body.

Level Five Ritual

Warding Cippus

The ancient Egyptians prized stelae carved with the figure of the infant Horus trampling on crocodiles and strangling serpents or scorpions in his fists. Such statues — called cippi — served as amulets to repel these harmful creatures and, more generally, all the malign forces of the world. The Followers of Set still craft these cippi on rare occasions. Setites seldom use figures of Horus in their magic, but the power of an enemy is still power.

This enchanted stela protects against spirits, not material animals. A consecrated cippus bars all but the most powerful or determined demons of Duat from its proximity. The Tremere possess several Warding Cippi, and chantries compete for their possession in regions where the Setites are strong. The special cost of manufacturing a Warding Cippus in these latter nights ensures that the Tremere never have enough to go around.

System: Spirits of Duat cannot approach within 100 feet of a Warding Cippus. If they try, they vanish back to Duat.

No special conditions apply to the carving of the cippus. Enchanting the stela requires several hours of prayers, exorcisms with sand and water, incense, and bathing the stela in honey, beer and the blood of a crocodile, an asp and crushed scorpions. At the end, the magician lets the rising sun burn his hand to ash while it rests upon the cippus. Completing the final prayer while burning off one's own hand costs a point of *permanent* Willpower. Note that this also means taking one health level of aggravated damage. The Warding Cippus works by itself from then on, continuously. Some Warding Cippi are thousands of years old.

Level Six Ritual

Hybrid Mummy

A magician can stitch together parts of human and animal cadavers, mummify them and invite a spirit to occupy and animate the patchwork *khat*. Typical hybrid mummy forms included animal-headed men and women in imitation (or parody) of the Egyptian gods, or beasts given human heads and hands.

Creating a hybrid mummy requires suitable human and animal body parts and typical mummification equipment. The physical process takes 40 days, just like a normal, non-supernatural mummy, and includes various subsidiary rituals. At the end, the magician conducts an hour-long invocation to Apep and other dreadful, deathly powers of the Underworld while smoking the wrapped, patchwork cadaver over a noxious and stinking fire.

Few normal ghosts consent to occupy such a butchered, composite cadaver. Instead, debased lector-priests call upon evil and insane ghosts called specters who somehow escaped judgment and the Eater of Hearts, or demons of Duat that were never human at all. A few powerful Setite magicians employ hybrid mummies as their servants.

System: Although the Hybrid Mummy spell requires the normal Intelligence + Occult roll (difficulty 8) to succeed, the magician's player also spends a variable number of points of Willpower in the final rite. Hybrid mummies are more durable than Necromantic zombies: They can endure for thousands of years as long as they remain in subterranean crypts and labyrinths. Mercifully, they decay quickly when exposed to sunlight and an incredulous modern world.

The magician's player defines a hybrid mummy's Traits beforehand. A hybrid mummy starts with one free dot in each Physical and Mental Trait. A lector-priest can make a hybrid mummy with up to Dexterity 3, while Strength and Stamina can go as high as the magician wants: the sorcerer just uses bigger, stronger parts. Hybrids can also have up to two dots each in Intelligence, Wits and Abilities. (They have no Social Attributes, though.) For every three dots in Attributes or Abilities the hybrid mummy receives, the magician expends one Willpower point. A new hybrid mummies cannot have any Ability that its creator does not, or at a higher rating.

Hybrid mummies can learn through experience, however, and raise their Charisma, Manipulation, Mental Attributes or Abilities Traits. Raising a Trait costs four times as many experience points as it would for a vampire.

The hybrid mummy is a character in its own right. Its creator may bind its will with other spells or Disciplines, but the hybrid has a mind and interests of its own.

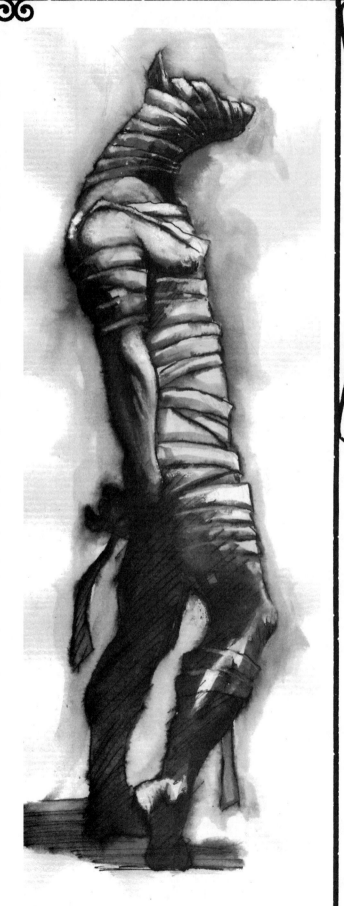

Chapter Two: Dur-An-Ki: The Demon-Haunted World

O evil Spirit, evil Demon, evil Ghost, evil Devil, evil God, evil Fiend!
Be exorcised by Heaven! Be exorcised by Earth!
— Babylonian incantation tablet

Dur-An-Ki means "Master of Heaven and Earth" in the tongue of ancient Sumeria, and this well describes the ambition of its practitioners. From Tashkent to Tangier, vampire sorcerers stand between the grave and the stars, drawing power from both. Through ancient spirit-covenants and ecstatic trances, they command the unseen legions of demons who plague the world. If they gain sufficient power, they may hope to storm Heaven itself and become prophets and saints to the Damned.

Practitioners of this ancient art call themselves *ashipu*, a Babylonian word for a sorcerer. Dur-An-Ki began in ancient Mesopotamia and draws upon the myths, gods and practices of Sumeria, Akkad, Assyria and Babylon. Mesopotamia, however, formed part of a wider network of Middle Eastern cultures. Millennia before written history began, people from towns such as Jericho traveled hundreds of miles to trade for sulfur, lapis and obsidian. Cultures traded ideas, too, and early *ashipu* borrowed practices from the Hittites, Egyptians, Greeks, Persians and other ancient civilizations.

When Alexander the Great conquered the entire Middle East, he forged even closer ties between the disparate cultures. In times of Roman prominence, people and religions traveled freely from the Atlantic to India. As a typical example, Roman soldiers worshipped the Persian god Mithras in a temple on the borders of Scotland. The classical era saw the genesis of many new religions — from mystery cults to

Christianity — and Dur-An-Ki borrowed from them all. When Islam swept through the Middle East centuries later, the *ashipu* likewise exploited this powerful new religion.

Islam, the Dark Ages and the Crusades progressively severed the links between the Eastern and Western worlds. Dur-An-Ki, which prior to that time had held undisputed prominence among the undead, was isolated and prevented from spreading to the west. This is why Dur-An-Ki did not become the magic of European vampires. Until recently, Western blood magicians had very few opportunities to learn about Dur-An-Ki.

In the 19th century, undead savants as well as mortal European scholars sought to learn the wisdom of the Orient; the mortals had better luck. Western archeologists unveiled Troy, Babylon and Ur of the Chaldees, but hard-line Assamites regarded any Western vampire in the Middle East as fair game. Other vampires, who held grudges dating back to the Crusades, assisted the Assamite hunters. The Tremere began a systematic effort to learn the secrets of Dur-An-Ki, but found that they had to do most of their work through mortal agents. Indeed, the Tremere researchers learned more about Dur-An-Ki in the British Museum than they did through their own fieldwork: At least researchers survived trips to the Museum. The British Tremere also learned a great deal from London's ancient Prince Mithras, who knew a great deal about Dur-An-Ki's Mithraic cult practices because he invented some of them.

In the 20th century, the Tremere succeeded in recruiting a few *ashipu* to their clan. The Assamites remained implacably hostile, but fortunately, not all modern *ashipu* come from the Assamites' sorcerer bloodline. Every clan in the Middle East can claim its own blood magicians. A few *ashipu* came to Europe along with mortal communities of immigrant laborers.

One of the greatest successes in the Tremere recruitment effort came in 1974. The French Tremere discovered Madame Yacine, a Malkavian sorceress dwelling among the Algerian community of Lyon. They persuaded her to ally with them, using the argument that while she obviously could not join *Clan* Tremere, *House* Tremere was another matter. Madame Yacine recently became a primogen in Lyon and is on remarkably sympathetic terms with the regent of the city's chantry.

When persuasion and favor-trading fail, the Tremere will attempt to torture secrets from captured *ashipu*. The clan also Embraces mortal practitioners of Middle Eastern folk-magic in hopes that they can adapt mortal occult beliefs into genuine blood magic. While this last method is the least popular, it is arguably the most common.

The recent schism among the Assamite clan lends fresh urgency to the Tremere's study of Dur-An-Ki. Dozens of Assamite sorcerers fled their Middle Eastern homelands to reside in Western cities instead, and even the ones who formally acknowledge the Camarilla by claiming membership don't like the Tremere very much. Many Assamites still hate and fear the Tremere for placing a curse upon them long ago. Several cities have already seen vicious contests of magic between Assamite and Tremere sorcerers. The Tremere leaders also want desperately to know how the Assamites broke that curse after 500 years. The Tremere have unprecedented opportunities to study Dur-An-Ki... and unprecedented need to understand the magic of these new rivals.

Magical Theory and Practice

Dur-An-Ki draws upon a dizzying array of influences, from Sumerian exorcisms to Platonic philosophy. Indeed, Dur-An-Ki shares many of the same roots as Hermetic Thaumaturgy: astrology, kabbalism, demonology, Greek mystery cults and many other elements besides. Dur-An-Ki, however, assembles these elements in a very different way. Where Hermetic sorcerers treat divine names and religious paraphernalia as abstract symbols of power, an *ashipu* believes that his magic depends upon the whims of spirits. He may master Heaven and Earth, but must constantly remind the spirits of their obligation to honor ancient covenants.

The Covenants

The idea of pacts between humans and gods runs through Middle Eastern religion and magic from the earliest times. Long before the covenants of Abraham, Moses, Jesus and Mohammed, the myths of Sumeria tell how the people served the god of their city-state, that the god might bless and protect them in return. Humanity's greatest defense against evil lay in covenants with gods. Every witch-hunter who ever brandished a cross at some night-creature follows a tradition more than five millennia old: Frighten the demon by proclaiming your tie to a greater, more powerful spirit.

Each covenant begins with a prophet's personal relationship to a god. Yahweh guided Abraham; Enki guided the Babylonian prophet Atrahasis. Sometimes a prophet forged a relationship that could endure after the prophet's death. Abraham pledged the loyalty of his descendants to Yahweh, while the Hittite king Hattusilis III dedicated his nation to the goddess Ishtar. The god promises that he or she will protect the people and promote their interests as long as they follow certain rituals and standards of conduct.

Covenants were not necessarily exclusive; the series of covenants that began with Abraham are somewhat unusual in this respect. A covenant with Marduk did not forbid honoring Dagon when that seemed prudent. Magicians keep this attitude in spades. Some Jewish, Christian and Muslim *ashipu* do retain their mortal piety. Fortunately for them, all peoples of the ancient Middle East believed in a universal and supreme deity, addressed only as "Lord" or "God." Muslim *ashipu* excuse calling upon Baal, Ishtar and other pagan gods by closing their incantations with *Insha'llah* — "If God wills it."

Scriptures

Ashipu call upon divine covenants through the holy books and symbols of mortal religion. Modern sorcerers make cautious use of the Koran, the Torah and the Gospels: The covenants of Abraham and his successors carry too much power of living faith for the Damned to use safely. The *ashipu* prefer to exploit older and more obscure scriptures, such as the *Zend-Avesta* of the Zoroastrian faith or the *Enuma Elish* epic of Babylon. The undead sorcerers can even draw upon myths nearly lost to mortal archeologists, such as the rites of the Hittites, the pre-Islamic Arabs and the Greco-Roman mystery cults. The mortals never wrote down many of their religious practices. Elder Cainites remembered them, though. Centuries later, vampires wrote down the faith's doctrines and rituals and passed the lore to their childer.

Not all scriptures come directly from religious sources. Greco-Roman sorcerers esteemed the *Iliad* and *Odyssey* as scriptures of Greek religion; a few sorcerers in Turkey still quote from Homer's epics in their spells. Other *ashipu* seek passages of magical power in Persian epics such as the *Shahnamah* of Firdausi, or the mystical verses of Rumi and other Sufi poets.

Relics

A prophet gains spiritual power through his contact with a god, and this power spills into everything he touches. The Christian traditions of pilgrimage and veneration of saintly relics are too well known to require explanation. Islam has similar traditions. Everyone knows about the *hajj* to Mecca, but devout Muslims also visit a wide range of shrines and tombs associated with the Prophet, his family and other saints of their faith. Every year, thousands of pious Muslims visit the tombs of holy men. They circle the tomb, touch it, and perhaps tie a votive ribbon to its railing or collect a pinch of dust from the floor as an amulet or magical medicine. In the same way, Jewish supplicants visit the tomb of Rabbi Meir Baal ha-Nes in Israel and pray to him for healing.

The *ashipu* fully believe in the power of such relics, and they steal it for their spells. The blood magicians of the Middle East conduct a thriving nocturnal trade in tomb-dust, leaves from trees where a holy man rested, and other such minor relics. Actual bone fragments or other body parts from saints, however, generally carry too much power of faith for undead sorcerers to withstand or control.

Anything associated with a bloody martyrdom carries special value for *ashipu*. For instance, sorcerers prefer to craft amulets and tablets from clay from the town of Kerbala, because Mohammed's grandson Husain was beheaded there. The earth of Kerbala still carries the spiritual essence of Husain's blood — a power that a sorcerer can usurp for his magic.

Sometimes, a sorcerer cannot obtain even a minor relic of a dead saint or prophet. Fortunately, the Middle East holds thousands of living relics: the *Saiyids*, or descendants of Mohammed himself. Those who carry the Prophet's bloodline command great respect in the Muslim world. A *Saiyid*'s blood suffices as a minor holy relic for lesser rituals. Jewish communities supply a more diluted sacred bloodline from the *kohanim*, a class of hereditary priests. Christianity lacks such a sacred bloodline, but apostolic succession and the Eucharist offer an adequate substitute. Jesus passed his divine power of salvation to his disciples, and gave them the right to pass it on to their disciples in turn. The bread and wine of the Eucharist, consecrated by a legitimate priest, convey the power of Christ to the worshipper. The actual blood of Christian priests carries no special power, but the Eucharist counts as a minor holy relic, equal to the blood of a *Saiyid*.

NIGHT SAINTS AND BLOOD IMAMS

Living prophets established the greatest pacts with the divine, but vampires can establish covenants as well. The Curse of Caine itself forms a baleful covenant: God's curse supplies the divine power behind all vampiric magic. Through the path of Spirit Manipulation, Kindred can make other deals with spirits, too. Indeed, the greatest masters of Dur-An-Ki — the true Masters of Heaven and Earth —establish such covenants as a means to power.

Paths and rituals often result from an *ashipu*'s covenant with a god or spirit. Dur-An-Ki practitioners, for instance, know the Path of Neptune's Might as the Path of Enki. They believe that an ancient blood sorcerer founded the path through a pact with the Sumerian god of waters.

The path of Spirit Manipulation lets a sorcerer negotiate more or less directly with a god to establish a pact, but this is not absolutely necessary. *Ashipu* can also form covenants through prayer and sacrificial offerings, and receive the god's messages through dreams or artistic inspiration. The best proof of a successful covenant comes from developing a path or ritual related to the god. Conversely, contacting a spirit does not excuse a sorcerer from the time and effort of researching a path or ritual — or excuse the player from spending the necessary experience points. An *ashipu* simply engages in different sorts of research and labor than a Hermetic magus.

Covenants by vampire-sorcerers, however, carry no power of faith. It is likely that no *ashipu* surpasses the power or pacts established by the Assamite Amr al-Ashrad, but no relic of his unlife or body would assist in any ritual. In faith, as in so many things, the undead are parasites.

DUR-AN-KI AND DARK THAUMATURGY

So how do the spirit covenants of Dur-An-Ki differ from the demonic pacts of Dark Thaumaturgy?

Not a lot. Some old paths and rituals appeal to evil gods such as Tiamat and Ahriman. Other magic calls upon Syriac and Phoenician gods such as Baal and Dagon, that modern infernalists know as demons.

These gods were not demons when the old *ashipu* codified the magic, though. More importantly, an *ashipu* does not offer eternal and exclusive servitude to a spirit. A spirit helps an *ashipu* learn a path or ritual, but does so because the sorcerer invokes covenants the spirit (or a more powerful god) made with mortals long ago. The *ashipu* says, in effect, "I met your conditions, now pay up!" An infernalist grovels and says, "I'll give you *anything*… master."

Ashipu can form long-term, personal covenants with lesser spirits. These are often mutual, however, or the magician dominates the relationship.

MESOPOTAMIAN STATE RELIGION

The temples and inscriptions of Mesopotamia come from state religions that deal with fertility, social order and war. The king needed to maintain order so he and his people could properly serve their gods. In return, they prayed for the gods to send them good harvests, abundant progeny for their animals (and themselves), and victory against their rivals.

The priests treated the statues of their gods as if they were living people. The priests "woke" the statue in the morning, dressed it and offered it food. The priests then ate the food offering as the god's "leftovers." On special occasions, they mounted the statue in a chariot to see and be seen by its people. Supplicants presented their requests to the statue, and brought a gift to show their respect. The priests did not own any of the clothes, furniture or other offerings made to the god; they merely had use of them as the god's live-in servants.

Gods also received sacrificial offerings of animals, fish or other things. Sacrificial methods varied, but often the priests burned sacrificed animals in a descending trench.

Mesopotamian religion certainly had a sexual element. The gods married just as mortals did, and their unions helped ensure the fertility of the soil, animals and humans. Statues of god and goddess made conjugal visits. Temple tablets also tell of ceremonial "marriages" be-

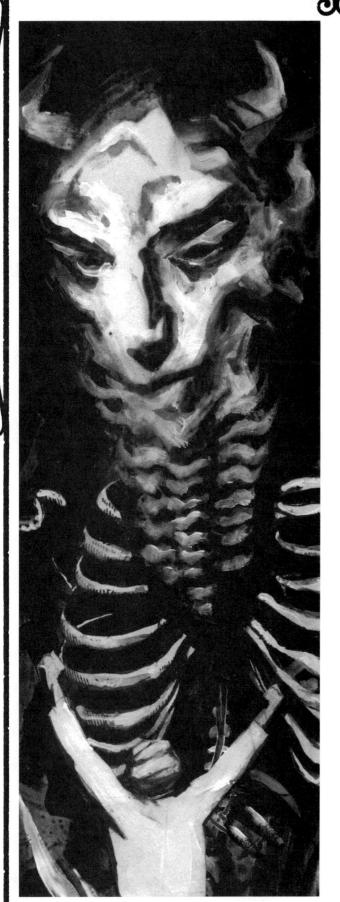

tween the king or high priest (standing in for a god) and the god's high priestess. In some cases, the participants may have consummated these sacred marriages. The Greek historian Herodotus claimed that an odd sort of sacred prostitution took place at the temples of Ishtar; kine archeologists doubt his account. Certainly some forms of ceremonial intercourse took place, but the Mesopotamian records do not discuss the matter in detail.

An *ashipu* who seeks to learn a path or ritual associated with a particular god spends a period propitiating that god in the proper ways. He makes a statue of the god, offers sacrifices and performs suitable rituals. Like a priest, he stands in for the god in some ceremonies, such as consuming blood offerings in the god's name. Of course a vampire cannot genuinely consummate a sacred marriage (as either king, priest or priestess), but he can go through the motions and that's enough for magic.

MITHRA AND MITHRAS

The most ancient Persian priests, called magi, propitiated numerous gods. Their religion greatly resembled that of their cousins the Aryans who invaded India. They worshipped Mithra as a god of the Sun and of oaths and the social order. Their rituals involved fire and drinking an intoxicating liquid fermented from the juice of a plant called *haoma*.

Some time between the 10th and 6th centuries BC the prophet Zarathustra, or Zoroaster, radically reshaped the Magian religion. Zoroastrianism demotes Mithra to a *yazata*, one of the second rank of spirits, after the *amesha spentas* ("immortal holy ones") who personify virtues, and *Ahura Mazda* ("Lord Wisdom"), the supreme deity of Light and Good. *Angra Mainyu* or *Ahriman*, the spirit of Evil, opposed *Ahura Mazda* from the beginning of time until its destined end. Zoroastrian worship continues to center on fire, as the earthly symbol of *Ahura Mazda*'s light. Holy books called the *Zend-Avesta* and the *Gathas* preserve Zoroastrian doctrine. The Muslim conquest of Persia in the 7th century nearly destroyed Zoroastrianism, but small pockets of the faith survive in Iran. India has another small community of Zoroastrians, called the Parsees, centered on Bombay.

The Parsees continue the Zoroastrian custom of exposing their dead on top of *dakhmas*, or "towers of silence," for vultures to eat. Contact with the dead would defile earth, fire or water — so Zoroastrians give their corpses to the birds of the air.

When the Persian Empire conquered the entire Middle East, it spread Zoroastrian ideas. Some of these surely influenced the Greco-Roman cult of Mithras, but archeologists cannot trace the line of influence with certainty. Classical Mithraism began in Asia Minor. It became a favored religion of Roman soldiers, who spread its subterranean temples from the border of Scotland to the Arabian Sea. Like other mystery religions, Mithraism had no written gospel or book of rituals. Believers learned its doctrines gradually, as they attained each of the faith's seven levels of initiation: Crow, Gryphon, Soldier, Lion, Persian, *Heliodromos* ("Sun-Runner") and Father.

The central rite of Mithraism consisted of the *tauroctony* or "bull-slaying," in which the blood of a sacrificed bull drenched an initiate who sat in a trench. Every Mithraic temple includes a depiction of Mithras stabbing a bull (a scene that occurs nowhere in Zoroastrian or known Magian mythology). This aspect of blood sacrifice attracted many Roman Kindred to Mithraism and ensured its status as an important source of Dur-An-Ki ritual.

Mithraism also bore a deep connection to astrology. Many Mithraic temples include symbols of Zodiacal constellations. A pair of heralds, one carrying a raised torch and the other a lowered torch — symbols of the equinoxes — frames the temple's *tauroctony* illustration. The *tauroctony* scene often includes stars; for instance, stars sometimes spangle Mithras' cloak. Mithras looks very much like traditional representations of Perseus, whose constellation hovers just north of Taurus, the Bull. The illustration also invariably includes a crow, a serpent, a dog and a scorpion — more constellations.

Some *ashipu* re-create the Mithraic mysteries and the *tauroctony* as part of their magic and training. A small school of Ventrue *ashipu*, for instance, lead student sorcerers through the Mithraic mysteries as part of their initial training. Their rank in the Mithras cult matches their level of Dur-An-Ki mastery.

The Mithraic mysteries (as well as the Isis cult and other mystery religions) hold a deeper significance as well for *ashipu*, a connection to the cosmos that promises not salvation, but godhood.

ASTROLOGY

From the beginning of recorded history, Middle Eastern folk placed gods in the sky. Most pre-Islamic Arab gods bear some relation to the Sun, Moon or the planet Venus. The Mesopotamians associated the Sun, Moon and planets with their leading gods. For instance, Marduk lived in his statue in his temple; but he also lived in the sky, as the planet Jupiter.

The Sumerians believed that the souls of the dead dwelled in a dismal realm underground. Later civilizations thought that the gods might pull favored souls into the sky, to live with them among the stars (think of Elijah, caught up to Heaven in a chariot of fire). This idea of a celestial afterlife became extremely popular in Greek and Roman times. The Neoplatonic philosopher Porphyry, for instance, suggested that souls dwelled in the Milky Way.

Anyone could see how the motion of the sun controlled the seasons, and how the moon ruled the tides. Mesopotamian astronomer-priests sought more subtle omens in the motion of the planets. They believed that the arrangement of planets in the zodiac revealed the will of the gods, and the configuration at a person's birth — his horoscope — foretold his life. Astrology promised to reveal a hidden order behind the chaos and suffering of human life, and provide warning and guidance.

Astrology forms an important part of Dur-An-Ki. *Ashipu* study the skies to find auspicious nights for their spells. The Mesopotamian lunar calendar supplies a 473,000-year cycle of lucky and unlucky nights.

Many Dur-An-Ki rituals have no fixed, immutable form. The sorcerer adjusts the ritual to take advantage of auspicious planetary positions and minimize the effect of baneful conjunctions. For instance, if Saturn's position in the sky interferes with a working, but Mars has a favorable placement, a sorcerer incorporates objects and symbols associated with Mars in her ritual but scrupulously avoids any element associated with Saturn.

Ashipu also seek portents to events on Earth. True astrology, however, demands intuition rather than calculation. Most mortal astrologers never look at the sky: They chart the planets using an *Ephemeris* — a book of tables of planetary positions. True sorcerers know that the celestial spirits do not speak through charts and numbers. The horoscope charts of conventional astrology have their place, but only a person who communes with the stars directly can truly read them.

An *ashipu* can use a person's horoscope chart as a sympathetic link to her. Some rituals require a target person's horoscope chart. In other cases, a sorcerer can use a victim's chart to target a long-range sending, instead of some other sympathetic link. Since a horoscope chart does not identify a person as precisely as an actual sample of their blood or body, any ritual targeted through a horoscope alone suffers a +1 difficulty penalty.

Kindred have two horoscopes: one for their mortal birth and one for their transition to undeath. These two charts together *do* uniquely identify a vampire out of everyone else in the world. An *ashipu* who knows the dates of a vampire's mortal birth and Embrace possesses as perfect a sympathetic link as a sample of the character's blood or her True Name. (See **Blood Magic: Secrets of Thaumaturgy** for a discussion of True Names.)

Modern *ashipu* face a quandary since astronomers discovered three more planets. They know that they used to cast perfectly adequate horoscopes without knowing about Uranus, Neptune and Pluto. Should they include the "new planets" now that they know about them? Elder sorcerers firmly say no. They insist that you cannot commune with the spirit of a planet that you cannot actually see in the sky. Some younger *ashipu* are not so sure.

CLIMBING THE LADDER OF HEAVEN

Astrology became wildly popular in the Greco-Roman age. Unfortunately, the motions of the heavens are too regular and predictable. The Babylonians, for instance, could predict eclipses far into the future. Did the relentless, unchanging machinery of the skies imply an equally relentless predestination on Earth? That was just as bad as chaos.

Classical astronomy described the cosmos as a series of concentric spheres. At the center floated the motionless Earth. The sphere of the stars formed its outermost limit. In between spun the invisible crystal spheres that carried the sun, moon and planets.

Mystics of many traditions supposed that each sphere and planet held its own spirit-realm, growing more blessed the greater their distance from Earth. Some mystics believed that a soul required special passwords and magic charms to climb through the spheres.

The philosopher Celsus described the path of ascent as "a ladder with seven gates and at the top an eighth gate" through the sphere of the stars to… beyond. If, as the astronomer-mystics said, the planets took their motion from the daily turning of the stellar sphere around the pivot of the Earth, what powered that outermost sphere? What but the Supreme God, the Prime Mover who could subdue the lesser gods of the planets and the Earth? Faiths as diverse as Judaism and the Cult of Isis taught believers to seek salvation from this transcendent deity. Whether through magic ritual, meditation, baptism or prayer, mystics sought to climb the celestial ladder and see the Almighty face to face. Success would mean liberation from the twin hells of chaos and predestination. You would be like unto a god yourself.

For more than two thousand years, *ashipu* sought to storm Heaven using every method humanity ever imagined, from prayer to flying machines. Over the centuries, they narrowed their quest to trance techniques. Modern science shows that the sorcerers cannot literally fly to Heaven. The Supreme God does not seem to answer their prayers. Baptism and other sacraments of mortal religions promise entry to Heaven only after death. In trance, however, the mind seems to journey into the spirit world. Through ecstatic trances, therefore, the *ashipu* set their souls climbing the Ladder of Heaven. They return with magic.

KALIF

Most of the Assamite sorcerers climb the Ladder of Heaven through a drug called *kalif*, hashish from marijuana plants mystically fed on vampiric vitae. Some sorcerers smoke the mystic resin themselves and force their blood to draw the drug from their lungs. Others have mortal servants smoke the *kalif*, then drink the servants' drug-saturated blood. A few simply powder the resin and mix it with a shot of blood, but most sorcerers feel that this method belittles a sacrament.

Kalif induces blissful hallucinations in untrained users. *Ashipu* know what to expect and shape the hallucinations into a visionary quest. Assamite sorcerers learn to follow a specific hallucinatory path.

BUT IS IT TRUE?

Most Assamite sorcerers experience the Ladder of Heaven as described above. Other *ashipu* do not, though themes of struggle and travel figure in all their trance-visions. The spirit-world has no fixed, objective appearance, and seekers tend to find what they expect. No model of the spirit world really offers much advantage over any other.

Most *ashipu* believe that in ancient times, some vampire sorcerers did climb Heaven's Ladder to the top and that they gained power surpassing the Methuselahs. Maybe so; but if they exist, these undead sages are as elusive as vampires in Golconda.

First the Assamite sorcerer sees the world fragment, recede and vanish into a chaos of whirling cones, spirals and other geometric shapes. Then they perceive themselves standing at the foot of an endless stairway. As they climb the stairs, they experience doubts and fears. This may take the form of actually re-living a traumatic experience from their past, or a hallucination of something that frightens them, or simply a wave of terror or despair.

As they climb, however, the sorcerer may find respites, which the sorcerers call "stations." These hallucinatory scenes may be as simple as a bare room with a person in a chair, or an elaborate fantasy-world. At each station, the *ashipu* can meet and bargain with spirits. The spirits seldom give straight answers, but after months of argument, cajolery, riddles, threats and tests, a sorcerer may learn some useful secret of magic — perhaps a path power, or the understanding of a ritual.

At the top of the stairway the sorcerers found the Station of Ultimate Rapture, a garden of unearthly delights whose pleasures never palled. They thought they had indeed stormed Heaven.

A few decades ago, some clever sorcerers asked themselves if the Station of Ultimate Rapture might be a devilishly clever trap. It seemed like Heaven, but *ashipu* did not return bearing new magic. These sorcerers resisted the station's pleasures… and found that it formed the base of a whole new stairway. In 2,000 years, their lineage had climbed only the first step of Heaven's Ladder. Prevailing opinion among the Assamites holds that the Station of Ultimate Rapture is the gate of the Lunar Sphere, a spirit-realm of treacherous illusions. As a reward, the sorcerers returned from the Station of Ultimate Rapture knowing the long-sought final power for the Path of Hunter's Winds: "Ghost Body," the power to become as insubstantial as a mirage.

Over the years, Assamite sorcerers struggled up the second stairway, encountered new stations and new spirits. Temptation, illusion and desire form the hallmark of this second stair. At the end they found another great station that offered the temptation of ultimate knowledge. To their astonishment, they found that the Sphere of Mercury connects them to the global communications network. In trance, they hear news updates from radio and TV stations, see images from spy satellites and glimpse the flickering lace of electronic fund transfers. Beyond the Station of Reading the Sky, as they call it, they find a third stairway that blocks their ascent with enigmas. The spirits of its stations teach magic to tap into a strange world of radio, computers and information, and powerful new rituals to twist space and annihilate distance.

And beyond? The sorcerers have yet to reach the spirit-spheres of Venus, the Sun, Mars, Jupiter and Saturn — let alone the Final Gate. The sorcerers press on, more drunk with new knowledge than with *kalif*, eager to storm Heaven at last.

DANCE

Not all *ashipu*, or even all Assamite sorcerers, fuel their visionary journeys with *kalif*. Indeed, most sorcerers practice several trance techniques, so as to understand trance and the spirit world more completely. Besides, *kalif* is not exactly easy to produce or use. When conducting rituals, *ashipu* prefer to enter a trance through some more convenient method.

Mystics around the world have danced their way to ecstasy. In the Middle East, the so-called "whirling dervish" sects seek communion with God in this manner. As the dervishes spin, they circle their teacher and master. At the climax of the dance, everyone leaps high into their air, seeming almost weightless in their flowing, skirted robes.

Many *ashipu* find trance-dancing a useful adjunct to rituals. They need nothing but their own bodies and some space. Through their training, with *kalif* or other trance techniques, they enter a trance more quickly than mortal dervishes can.

PAIN

Overwhelming pain and shock can push a person beyond torment into a strange, floating ecstasy. In India, both fakirs and ordinary worshippers show their holy immunity to pain by piercing their flesh with needles, hooks and metal rods. The Assamite clan's Indian wing and the far-wandering Ravnos introduced Middle Eastern blood sorcerers to these pain techniques.

The undead, however, take a tremendous amount of pain before they enter a trance. A few needles stuck through the cheeks won't do the job. Instead, an *ashipu* might flay himself and roll in salt.

Ashipu who know Auspex may deliberately heighten their senses before a ritual or a bout of self-torture, just so they can feel enough pain to push beyond it. Other sorcerers take a more dangerous course, and use the pain of fire to alter their consciousness, as part of Zoroastrian flame-rites. Only a sorcerer of iron will and awesome courage, however, can suppress Rötschreck reliably enough to make fire-torture a viable technique.

MEDITATION

Some mystics prefer to alter their consciousness through pure intellect. Jewish kabbalists search the Torah for esoteric meanings hidden in the text, in hopes of comprehending divine mysteries. A vision of the Throne of God provided the ultimate reward. Muslim mystical groups such as the Brethren of Abstraction performed similar meditations inspired by the Koran.

Most of these contemplative schools of mysticism draw heavily on the Greek philosopher Plato. In Platonic thought, the physical world of the senses echoes a true and perfect world of pure ideas. In Plato's most famous analogy, the material world is like a play of shadows on the wall of a cave. Through reason and meditation, Plato's followers hoped to escape the cave and see the real objects and the divine light that create the shadows.

Most *ashipu* believe that God dwells in this world of pure ideas. In classical times, Plato's followers thought that the realm of archetypes lay outside the shell of the stars. Modern sorcerers know that the relationship is not spatial, in the conventional sense, but still believe in an intellectual realm beyond the material world and the various spirit realms. Some, like many Assamite sorcerers, try to approach this archetypal world by stages. Others try to find the archetypal world directly through meditation.

Eloquence and Art

Music, poetry and other forms of art can affect the emotions so profoundly that they induce altered states of consciousness. Sufi mystics place great emphasis upon poetry and song as a vehicle for imparting mystic ideas and as a product of mystic awareness.

Middle Eastern peoples saw the fine arts as more than a trance technique, though. The poet, musician and painter held a dangerous, magical power over minds and souls. The Prophet Mohammed himself said that, "Verily, eloquence includes sorcery." The Arabs and Persians tell many tales of men and women who instantly fall in love with a beautifully painted portrait, or singers who cause listeners to faint from the beauty of their song.

This power of the arts has never sat easily with Islam, or with some Christians or Jews, for that matter. To many Muslim legalists and theologians, this mightiness of the artist challenged the Almightiness of God. It didn't help that in pre-Islamic times, the Arabs believed that poets received inspiration from *djinns*. If an artist's power did not come from God — why, it must come from the Devil!

Muslim mystics and poets argued that perhaps an artist could receive inspiration from God. Only the Koran counted as the true Word of God, but the arts could still carry a little divinity. A poet or artist could use symbols of the visible world to impart concepts of the invisible world. By leading the audience to perceive the archetypal world, the artist led people closer to God.

Many *ashipu* employ poetry, music, song, painting or sculpture in their magic. They pour the power of the Blood into their art, increasing the power intrinsic to a skillful performance. For mortal artists, "making the invisible visible" remains a metaphor. Sorcerous artists do this for real. At the same time, *ashipu* who feel the forbidden nature of their magic most keenly take comfort in the idea of the divinely inspired artist-magician whose magic serves the glory of God.

AMULETS AND TALISMANS

All the cultures in the Lands of Faith possess rich traditions of amulets and talismans.

The **cylinder seal** was Mesopotamia's most distinctive amulet. The ancient Mesopotamians wrote on clay tablets. To sign his name to a contract, a Mesopotamian rolled a little stone cylinder across a tablet, and the carved cylinder stamped the signature into the clay. Along with writing, cylinder-seals carried pictures of kings, gods, animals, spirits or whatever else struck the owner's fancy. The power of writing and the images of gods and spirits made these seals natural candidates for turning into amulets.

The type of stone could impart further power to the amulet. One tablet says that a seal made of hematite helps a man destroy his enemy; a seal of rock crystal makes him rich; a seal of red jasper brings the protection of the gods.

A cylinder seal can just as easily write out a short prayer or incantation. *Ashipu* use them for many purposes in their rituals. Tradition demands, however, that only cylinder-seals inscribed in authentic Mesopotamian language and script have any value in magic.

Incantation bowls come from Mesopotamian Jewish communities from the early centuries of the Common Era. Many Jewish homes from this period have clay bowls buried in their foundations. Each bowl carries a spell against evil spirits written in a spiral around its inside or outside. The spiral of the incantation helped to fascinate and confuse the spirits. The Jews of this period also buried such bowls in their cemeteries. *Ashipu* use them to trap, repel or mesmerize spirits.

Plaques and tablets of stone remain popular in the Middle East after 5,000 years. The Babylonians and Assyrians carved plaques with an image of the she-demon Lamashtu on one side and an incantation against her on the other. Many Arab and Persian amulets consist of a slice of agate etched with verses from the Koran, names or titles of God, intricate borders and geometrical designs. Similar amulets made of silver or brass also occur. Hebrew versions of these amulets resemble the pentacles of Western ceremonial magic. The owner might wear such amulets as a necklace or brooch, mount them on the wall of a house, keep them in her pocket or make them part of other objects. *Ashipu* sometimes turn other objects into talismans by incorporating these sorts of amulets. For instance, an Assamite warrior's enchanted sword might bear an inscribed agate plaque in its hilt: It does not matter if the blade breaks because the magic rests in the plaque.

Paper amulets consist of a strip or square of paper, parchment or gazelle-skin, ornamented with elaborate calligraphy, drawings of saints and other legendary figures, religious symbols, animals, signs of the Zodiac or geometrical figures. The amulet-writer often uses colored inks perfumed with musk, oil of roses or saffron, and embellishes the talisman with gold. The owner might use the amulet as is, or fold it up into a small metal or leather case, or roll it up into a tube. Metal amulet-cases may themselves bear magical figures and inscriptions. People sometimes make necklaces or bracelets of many such cases and tubes.

Holy books themselves can become amulets. The advent of photolithography made a complete miniature Koran, held in a golden case with a powerful magnifying lens, a popular Muslim charm. Not a few Christians carry tiny pocket Bibles. *Ashipu* can carry more esoteric scriptures this way without exciting comment.

The **rosary** is not a specifically Christian invention. Muslims and Hindus have their own versions. The rosary's groups of beads help a person keep her place in a long, repetitive series of prayers. The association with prayer makes the rosary itself a holy symbol. *Ashipu* may devise their own forms, such as a 50-bead rosary for the 50 titles of Marduk.

Figurines of clay, stone or wood found common use in Mesopotamian magic. For instance, an exorcist-doctor might drive a demon from a patient into a clay doll of the patient, then smash the doll to destroy the demon. Assyrians sometimes buried figurines of dogs in the foundations of their homes, to guard the house against spiritual intruders. The Mesopotamians used statuettes of animals, gods, spirits, monsters and demons as amulets.

Hands occur in many sorts of Middle Eastern amulets. They may be drawings or actual hand-shaped amulets. *Ashipu* take particular interest in the little silver or brass hands that Iranians wear to show fulfillment of a vow to God. For instance, a mother might promise God that if her sick son recovers, he will march in the next holy day parade. In the parade, the child wears the metal hand to proclaim the vow. These little amulets thus represent successful, personal covenants with God, making them minor holy relics. *Ashipu* steal hundreds of these hands every year.

Some *ashipu* themselves wear hand-amulets to boast of favors successfully bought from spirits and vows honorably completed. Junior sorcerers may brag that their master has "70 hands." These trinkets, however, have no power in magic. Kindred magicians consume spiritual force more easily than they create it.

Middle Eastern folk employ many other sorts of amulets. Any sort of jewelry can become an amulet, though rings seem especially popular. Gnostic amulets usually took the form of cameo or intaglio gems bearing magic words and figures of strange gods and spirits. Beads, tassels and brasses protect man and beast from the Evil Eye. Animal claws and teeth have a long history as amulets, too. Some people prepare actual "charm bracelets" or necklaces bearing many sorts of simple amulets.

OTHER TRADITIONAL TOOLS

The spells written on Mesopotamian clay tablets often do not call for fancy amulets or special ritual implements. Many spells employ everyday materials: a stove or brazier; a flock of wool, perhaps dyed red; goat's hair; onions; a branch of dates; a tamarisk branch; reeds or reed matting; cedar or juniper wood; salt; sea water. Magicians used flour to draw magic symbols, as an offering to gods and spirits, as a base for medical pastes, or in dough for making images. In many rituals, the magician stands within a magic circle of flour, whitewash or darkwash.

Sweet odors mollify the spirits, so magicians often burn incense or aromatic woods in their rituals.

Pictures of benevolent spirits often show them holding a bucket and a large fir cone or date-palm spathe. Priests used these implements to sprinkle a person or area with pollen or holy water.

Medical magic employed a wide range of herbal poultices, potions, ointments and enemas.

Priests anointed sick people with blessed oil — a rite that still survives in Roman Catholic and Orthodox Christianity. Anointing a king with oil conferred and confirmed his divine right to rule. Magicians sought visions by gazing in a handful of oil, a salt crystal or a large, polished seed.

The Mesopotamians practiced many other sorts of divination, too. Diviners could seek portents through smoke, the entrails of sacrificial animals, through geomancy (tossing a handful of sand or flour and interpreting the patterns formed on the ground), or drawing lots. Most of these customs still survive. Modern folk also perform divination through dice. For immediate advice, Middle Eastern people sometimes turn to bibliomancy. The querent opens the Koran or the Bible at random and takes the first verse that catches her eye as an omen or advice.

Middle Eastern folk, like people in many other parts of the world, believe in the magic power of knots and cords. A sorceress tried to curse the Prophet Mohammed by tying knots in a cord.

Middle Eastern tradition ascribes great power to spittle, both to bless and curse.

Ashipu also draw upon the Middle East's tradition of alchemy. The medieval Arabs and Persians developed the art to a high degree. Some sorcerers still study the texts of medieval alchemists such as Jabir and Rhazes. They stock their labs with athanors, alembics and all the other classic paraphernalia. A few neonate *ashipu* seek to incorporate modern chemical equipment and techniques into Dur-An-Ki alchemy. They remain far behind Hermetic thaumaturges in this, however, and these modern *ashipu* sometimes try to steal the secrets of Tremere alchemists.

The number seven has great value in Middle Eastern magic: seven astrological planets (counting the sun and moon); a necklace with seven kinds of beads; a cord with seven knots, or of seven colors of thread; blowing seven times; seven prayers; seven spices; a spell using seven scraps of cloth, begged from seven homes; and so on. Three has less value (except when a Christian sorcerer draws parallels with the Trinity). Twelve connects a ritual to the signs of the Zodiac and the months of the year. Forty and 70 frequently appear as conventional ways of saying "many"; for instance, raining 40 days and 40 nights, or 40 keys attached to a bowl.

MIDDLE EASTERN SPIRITS AND DEMONS

In the course of millennia, Middle Eastern cultures have believed in many sorts of spirits, but some traditions continue from earliest Sumeria to the present night. Evil spirits haunt dirty, desolate or subterranean places, and filth attracts them. Other spirits act to help or harm at whim, or depending on whether mortals offend or propitiate them.

The *djinn* hold a prominent place in Arab and Persian folklore. God created the *djinn* out of black, smokeless fire. *Djinn* come in several tribes or nations, each with their own king. Mohammed himself converted the two kings Abdur-Rahman and Abdul-Kadir. The king Masidus rules over the Christian *djinn*, while Tututash rules the Jewish *djinn*. Other kings include Malik Afshan, Masitash and Talu Khush. Eblis rules the evil *djinn*; he rebelled against God when he refused to bow before Adam, a creature brought to life from clay. Legend says that most *djinn* dwell

on or beyond the Mountains of Kaf that encircle the world, but some make their home in ruins, tombs, or the deep desert, where they appear as dust-devil whirlwinds.

Djinn can change their form. Their favorite forms include black and white cats, or solid-colored or spotted dogs. They can also make themselves tiny and disguise themselves as a hair in food. They turn invisible, but children, religious devotees and sick people can see them. In their true forms, *djinn* have cloven feet, triangular eyes and long, unkempt hair. They may have blue or green skin. As the *Thousand and One Nights* show, *djinn* can materialize treasures (or nearly anything else) and move people, objects and themselves around the world in an instant.

The evil *Divs* of Persian legend have powers much like *djinn*. They are larger than humans, and have the tails, horns and hooves of cattle. If that is not enough, one can recognize a *div* by his protruding forehead, round, deep-set eyes, large nose, thick lips and spotted skin.

Mesopotamian legends and incantation texts mention a prodigious variety of spirits and monsters. Generic terms for spirits include *Maskim*, *Rabishu*, *Gallu* and *Utukku*. The earliest accounts describe these spirits as indifferently good or evil. Later Mesopotamians regarded these spirits as evil and prone to cause storms and disease.

The strange *Girtablullû* or "Scorpion-People" have a human head and torso, the hindquarters and talons of a bird and the tail of a scorpion. They guard sacred places and drive away other spirits. Other benign spirits include the seven *Apkallu* or "Sages," who look like aged men dressed in fish-skins; the *Suhurmashu* or "Goat-Fish," associated with Enki; and the male *Shedu* and female *Lamassu,* who can appear as humans or as winged, human-headed bulls or lions.

Several other sorts of spirits look like mixtures of human and animal parts. The *Ugallu* ('Great Storm Beast') has a human body with a lion's head, donkey ears and bird feet. The *Uridimmu* ('Mad Lion') has a human head and torso with leonine legs, hindquarters and tail. Mesopotamian art and figurines also show mermaids and mermen, bull-men, winged centaurs, lion-centaurs, snake-dragons and lion-fish.

Jewish tradition adds the *Shedim*, malevolent powers of the air that cause disease and all manner of evil. The *Lilin,* demon offspring of Lilith, prey upon children like their mother. Not all demons kill, however. One tribe of demons does nothing but pass along gossip.

GAME MECHANICS

In rules terms, Dur-An-Ki greatly resembles Hermetic Thaumaturgy. All Dur-An-Ki path powers call for a Will-power roll. All rituals use the usual Intelligence + Occult roll. Powers and rituals have a difficulty of 3 + the power or ritual's level, to a maximum of 9. All Path powers cost vitae. Dur-An-Ki demands no other special condition, in terms of game mechanics, from *ashipu*.

Optionally, Storytellers may rule that an *ashipu's* level of Dur-An-Ki mastery cannot exceed her Stamina Trait.

Many of the trance techniques used by these sorcerers place great strain on undead bodies. Conversely, long practice at dancing, self-torture, extended meditation and keeping a clear head despite intoxication can justify a vampire developing a higher Stamina. This optional rule plays up the physical as well as mental challenge of Dur-An-Ki. It also renders Hermetic Thaumaturgy slightly superior to the older art, emphasizing the Tremere's status as the premier thaumaturges of the World of Darkness.

Personal Covenants and Spirit Allies

Through the Path of Spirit Manipulation or various rituals, *ashipu* can forge long-term pacts with minor spirits. A sorcerer might win spirit minions through a relationship with some greater spirit, or she might bind spirits and force them to serve. Some spirits serve a sorcerer willingly in order to gain some special favor. The Amr al-Ashrad, for instance, commands a cadre of powerful *afrits* and *djinn*.

Spirits kept "on call" as minions count as Retainers. Spirits that assist an *ashipu* in lesser ways may become Allies or Contacts. For instance, a clairvoyant seer-demon that a magician can summon and consult without danger would make a fine Contact. A greater spirit that willingly advises an *ashipu* can become a Mentor.

Storytellers should remember that characters never gain long-term spirit allies easily. Gaining a spirit ally or minion can become the focus of an entire story. First the character has to find the spirit. Then the test truly starts, as the character matches wits and will with the spirit. The magician can try to trade favors and services, or browbeat or bully the spirit to serve. Perhaps the magician must outright defeat the spirit in battle and make it fear for its existence. Some spirits set tests and demand peculiar gifts and services before they accept a pact.

Storytellers should also remember that spirit Allies, Contacts and Retainers have personalities and wills of their own — just like any other Ally, Contact or Retainer. Spirits can have very strange priorities by mortal (or even Kindred) standards….

Paths

The Masters of Heaven and Earth know their own versions of common Tremere paths such as Lure of Flames, Spirit Manipulation and Conjuring. These come from a common heritage of sorcery. Indeed, an *ashipu* might learn any path not specifically described as a Tremere invention and limited to that clan. Millennia of contact between the Middle East, Egypt and India result in a few *ashipu* knowing versions of the Path of Duat (see Chapter One) or the Path of Blood Nectar (see Chapter Three). See also the distinctively Assamite paths of the Hunter's Winds in **Blood Magic: Secrets of Thaumaturgy**, Awakening of the Steel in **Clanbook: Assamite**, and the astrological Whispers of the Heavens in **Libellus Sanguinis 3: Wolves at the Door** for **Vampire: The Dark Ages**.

Just because these sorcerers as a whole know a wide variety of paths, however, does not mean that any particular sorcerer can learn any path she wants. Many paths are

very rare and held in strict secrecy, known only to one master and his immediate disciples or childer. Even al-Ashrad, arch-sorcerer of the Assamites, could not list every path known to his own clanmates — let alone all those known to all *ashipu*.

Middle Eastern blood sorcerers often give paths other names than the ones Western magicians know. We list some typical paths, their names in Dur-An-Ki, and the supplements where players and Storytellers may find them.

Path of Blood (Life's Water): **Vampire: The Masquerade**

Conjuring (Jinn's Gift): **Vampire: The Masquerade**

Father's Vengeance (the Ailing Jackal): **Guide to the Sabbat**

Lure of Flames (Hand of the Magi): **Vampire: The Masquerade**

Neptune's Might (Covenant of Enki): **Guide to the Camarilla**

Spirit Manipulation (Suleiman's Laws): **Guide to the Camarilla**

COVENANT OF NERGAL

In Babylonian myth, the war-god Nergal and his wife Ereshkigal, queen of the dead, had special command over plague-demons. Through this path, an *ashipu* claims this baleful power over disease. The path also grants limited powers to abate sickness. All the powers of this path affect Cainites as well as mortals, which gives the path an evil reputation among the undead.

Notes: Fortitude does not afford its normal defense against most Covenant of Nergal attacks. Each dot of Fortitude, however, gives the afflicted Kindred's player one more die on any rolls to resist Nergal's Wrath or Ill Wind. Covenant of Nergal attacks also do not work against vampires who have a higher rating in the path than the attacker.

Most of the powers in this path reduce a victim's Physical Attributes. If either Strength, Dexterity or Stamina drop to 0, the character is immediately Incapacitated regardless of her actual health levels. Strength or Dexterity cannot drop below 0. An attack that would reduce a victim's Stamina below 0 kills a mortal or drives a Kindred into torpor.

Most Covenant of Nergal attacks do not accumulate with each other, and higher-level powers supersede lower-level powers; Ill Wind forms the exception. For instance, Maskim's Touch and Breath of Ereshkigal cannot affect a victim already suffering from Nergal's Wrath. The last-named power would affect a person who already suffered from the lower-level powers, but its effects would not become noticeable until they exceeded the lesser power's effects or the lesser power's duration ended.

Of all the powers, only the Breath of Ereshkigal can cause an increased effect from multiple uses. Covenant of Nergal powers do accumulate their effect with other attacks that cause Attribute loss, such as the Quietus power of Scorpion's Touch.

• MASKIM'S TOUCH

By touching the subject — or at least getting near enough to touch — the magician causes effects much like influenza: fever, nausea, sore joints and the like. This makes the target slower, weaker and more frail.

System: If the Willpower roll succeeds, the victim loses one dot each from his Strength, Dexterity and Stamina. This loss lasts for one scene. Multiple Maskim's Touch attacks do not accumulate effects, either with each other or with higher-level Covenant of Nergal attacks. Effects will accumulate, however, with deleterious effects produced by other Disciplines, such as the Scorpion's Touch power of Quietus.

•• BREATH OF ERESHKIGAL

Simply by drawing a breath and exhaling in the victim's direction, a vampire can inflict disease upon her target. The sickness can affect victims some distance away. Unlike the Maskim's Touch, a vampire can use the Breath of Ereshkigal more than once upon a target.

System: The magician can attack anyone within about 50 feet. If the attack succeeds, the Breath of Ereshkigal reduces each of the victim's Physical Attributes by one. The number of successes determines the duration of the magical sickness:

1 success	One scene
2 successes	One night
3 successes	Two nights
4 successes	Four nights
5 successes	One week

Multiple attacks can accumulate, further reducing the victim's Physical Attributes, but only if the subsequent attack has at least as many successes as the previous attacks. Thus, if a vampire's player rolled three successes for the *ashipu*'s first attack, a second attack would strip another dot from each Physical Attribute only if the player rolled three or more successes for its effect. If the player rolled four successes on the second attack, subsequent Breath of Ereshkigal attacks would need at least four successes to increase the effect.

A vampire or ghoul can raise Physical Attributes by expending vitae, and so counter the Breath of Ereshkigal. Raising all three Attributes back to their starting value completely cures the magical illness. Then, however, the attacker can start over again. Mortals must simply wait for the curse to run its course.

••• NERGAL'S BLESSING

This power cures mild diseases, and at least reduce the effect of severe disease. The user touches the target for about a minute. Nergal's Blessing completely heals any health or Attribute loss from the Maskim's Hand or Breath of Ereshkigal. It partly negates the effects of higher-level Covenant of Nergal powers.

The Hand of Nergal cannot cure non-pathogenic diseases such as allergies, deficiency diseases, cancer, arthritis or genetic disorders, although it alleviates their effects for a day. It also does nothing for purely mental illness (though it may help in cases of mental illness with organic causes).

In countries that lack modern hospitals, *ashipu* still use Nergal's Blessing to buy favors and goodwill from mortals. In "developed" countries, *ashipu* find fewer truly desperate clients — but they do find them. AIDS is not the only disease that modern medicine cannot yet cure.

System: Nergal's Blessing can cure ordinary infections, from acne to pneumonia, with a single use. Notably severe or chronic disease like hepatitis or malaria might require two uses of this power, at the Storyteller's option. Really nasty or intractable diseases like ebola or AIDS require three uses to cure. A single use of Nergal's Blessing always suffices for illness caused by other powers in this path.

Successful use of Nergal's Blessing keeps the subject alive (or undead) for another night, no matter how severe the disease, and palliates the symptoms. This applies to non-pathogenic illness as well. Although the magician can never produce a true cure in such cases, Nergal's Blessing may keep a sick person alive long enough for the target to heal on her own.

●●●● Nergal's Wrath

This ghastly power induces severe disease in the victim. This is real infection — the appropriate microbes appear in the victim's body — but the disease progresses with unnatural speed. If the ravaging plague takes the form of gangrene, leprosy or some other relatively slow infection, its acceleration baffles and terrifies any doctor.

A vampire who achieves this level of path mastery selects a disease as his personal form of Nergal's Wrath. An attack from one vampire might take the form of cholera, while another uses yellow fever to kill.

System: Nergal's Wrath works by touch. For each success the attacker's player rolls, the victim suffers five hours of the curse's effect. A botch means that the caster suffers the curse's effects instead, for five hours per 1 rolled, on top of the usual Willpower loss. Of course, the magician can use Nergal's Blessing to try curing herself.

For each hour of the character's illness, the victim's player makes a Stamina + Survival roll (difficulty 8). Failure means that the character loses one health level and one dot each from Strength, Dexterity and Stamina. If the victim receives medical care, the doctor can substitute his Medicine Trait for the victim's Survival Trait, but only the victim's Stamina matters in either case. If the victim can accumulate five successes before dying, Nergal's Wrath ends.

A vampire can counter the effects of the curse by expending vitae to heal the damage. That can mean expending a good deal of vitae — and Nergal's Wrath will not stop just because it's daytime and the vampire must sleep.

●●●●● Ill Wind

A master of Nergal's Covenant simply walks by a location and people get sick. The disease appears natural. It will not progress any faster than normal, but the illness may be unusually virulent, and it can affect Kindred too. The Ill Wind ignores most mundane barriers. Only magic or an air-tight chamber can protect against the curse.

The Ill Wind always takes the form of a disease that could plausibly occur in the area where the magician uses the curse. Thus, an *ashipu* could attack a New York dinner party with ptomaine, E. Coli or even legionnaire's disease, but not smallpox (extinct) or bubonic plague (not native to the area). The Ill Wind's user has no control over what disease he calls, but every victim contracts the same disease.

System: The Ill Wind costs the magician's player one Willpower point in addition to the usual blood point. The number of successes rolled by the *ashipu*'s player determines the number of people affected:

1 success	Four people
2 successes	Eight people
3 successes	12 people
4 successes	20 people
5 successes	Everyone in the vampire's immediate area (an entire auditorium, a mob)

If an area holds more people than the vampire can affect, the Ill Wind infects the people with lower Stamina Traits first. The Ill Wind does not harm the magician herself.

The disease takes effect slowly (growing to full strength at about one day per dot of Stamina for a victim). Once the curse takes effect, the victim loses three health levels and three dots from each Physical Attribute, to a minimum of 0 — at this stage.

A victim has a chance of recovery for each day of bedrest, or sleep for Kindred. The victim's player makes a Stamina + Survival roll (difficulty 7). If the roll succeeds, the victim recovers one dot of each Physical Attribute. Failing the Stamina + Survival roll means losing another dot of Stamina. The curse ends when the victim recovers all her Physical Attributes. As with Nergal's Wrath, the player of a victim under medical care can add the character's Stamina Trait and the doctor's Medicine Trait.

Unlike other attacks based on Nergal's Covenant, Ill Wind does not protect a victim from the lower-level powers. A sick victim can suffer further Attribute loss from Maskim's Touch, Breath of Ereshkigal or Nergal's Wrath.

The Evil Eye

Middle Eastern people have feared the Evil Eye since time immemorial. To look upon a person or object with malice or envy may inflict a curse upon them. Surprise or admiration may have the same effect, and so a person who delivers praise exorcises the potential evil with an exclamation of "God is great!" or "What God wills!" Some people possess a powerful Evil Eye whether they want it or not. Such persons can kill animals with a careless word or glance, shatter stone, or in extreme cases make a person's eyes explode out of their head.

Naturally, vampire sorcerers had to claim such a formidable power. The Path of the Evil Eye inflicts a variety of calamities upon its victims. Although the powers take little time to use, the effects may take hours or nights to manifest, and the sorcerer often does not know or control the exact nature of the curse.

The powers of this path do not cumulate. While affected by a curse, a victim becomes immune to further use of that specific power by that specific vampire. For instance, if a magician inflicted a Peril on a victim, he could not curse that person with another Peril until the first had run its course. He could, however, still attack that victim with a Loss or any other Evil Eye power. Likewise, another *ashipu* could impose his own Evil Eye curse (making a very unlucky victim.)

The victim also has ways to remove an Evil Eye curse before it runs its course. People with True Faith can remove the Evil Eye's effect through religious ritual and prayer. Occultists can work out rituals to weaken or void a curse with a Wits + Occult roll (difficulty 8). Each success rolled by the player cancels out one success of the Evil Eye attack. For some powers, however, the exorcism works only if performed very soon after the *ashipu* lays the curse. No exorcism can restore what the victim has already lost.

• Humiliation

With a venomous glance, the vampire inflicts bad luck upon his victim. This bad luck attacks the victim's social standing. The victim suffers some terrible embarrassment within the next few nights. Neither victim nor attacker knows what form this embarrassment will take, so the victim has no way to defend against it. Will you say something incredibly stupid? Will a waiter trip and drench you with soup? Will a childe or ghoul commit some hideous blunder? You have no way to tell. The Humiliation inflicts no real harm, but can ruin a person's prestige or credibility for a while.

Humiliation works well against Camarilla vampires, especially if the local Kindred include a few really vicious harpies, but Sabbat vampires can suffer humiliation too. Besides the obvious physical embarrassments, a Sabbat might inadvertently help an enemy, or seem to act "too human."

System: The attacker's player makes the usual Willpower roll. If the roll succeeds, the victim suffers humiliation some time within the next week. If the Storyteller uses the optional Prestige Background, the victim might lose one dot of Prestige for every two successes rolled (round up), until she does something to restore her reputation.

•• Loss

This curse affects the victim's property. Within a few nights of the curse, the victim loses both real wealth and some possession of emotional value (assuming the victim has such a thing). Lost property does not magically vanish; some "natural explanation" (such as a fire, accident, theft, confiscation or unexpected legal fees) causes the loss. Even the sorcerer who casts the curse has no idea what form the loss may take. Loss is permanent, barring special exertions by the victim. Lost money and possessions do not magically reappear, either.

System: If the Willpower roll succeeds, the victim loses one dot of Resources within the next week. The Storyteller decides what sentimental loss the victim suffers. If all else fails, the victim might lose a Retainer or a dot of Herd. Even if a victim completely lacks Resources, the curse still finds *something* to strip away. Perhaps the victim loses his wedding ring, the last memento of a happier life, or an abandoned building used as a Haven might burn down.

••• Peril

This power puts the victim directly in danger. Over the next few nights — neither victim nor attacker knows precisely when — the victim finds herself in dangerous situations. The victim might cleverly escape the danger, and Kindred can probably survive even the worst Perils. Then again, they might not.

System: The number of successes on the Willpower roll gives the number or severity of the perils:

1 success	One mild Peril (Example: a mugger)
2 successes	Two mild to moderate Perils (a car crash)
3 successes	Three mild to moderate Perils
4 successes	Three moderate to severe Perils (a collapsing building, locked out of haven near sunrise)
5+ successes	Three Perils, one catastrophic (meet a Lupine pack, haven catches fire during the day)

Each night is 50% likely to bring a Peril, and the curse continues until all Perils have occurred (or the victim finds a way to lift the curse).

•••• Enemy

This level of Evil Eye has the most far-reaching effect on a victim. Friends turn away; enemies appear (and may be former friends). Perhaps the victim can recover lost allies and placate new enemies, but the Storyteller should not make it easy.

System: For each success on the attacker's Willpower roll, the victim either loses one dot of Allies, Contacts, Influence or Retainers, or gains an Enemy worth one point (as the Flaw; see **Vampire: The Masquerade**, p. 300). For instance, with four successes on the roll, the victim might lose two dots in Allies and gain a two-point Enemy (perhaps a former Ally). A victim never gains more than one Enemy from the curse; more points of Enemy indicate a more dangerous foe. No one ever lose more than two dots from any single Background.

Imposing an Enemy takes time. The attacker might spend several hours in places where the victim has interests and connections, for example, spreading insults and innuendoes — just like a normal smear campaign, but the curse makes sure the smear campaign really works. The effects manifest within a week.

••••• Chashm Zakhm

The "Eye that Wounds" represents the most immediately dangerous use of the Evil Eye. Unlike the other powers, this power acts immediately. The magician expresses fulsome praise, vicious insult or utter astonishment at the target person or object—and on the next turn, something *really bad* happens to the target.

System: If the player's Willpower roll succeeds, the target person or object suffers one health level of aggravated damage per two successes rolled (round up). The magician's speech shapes the form of the damage. For instance, saying nasty things about a person's car could make the engine explode, while praising a person's tennis backhand could make her arm instantly wither. Mortal victims generally suffer some permanent maiming. Animals affected by the Chashm Zakhm usually drop dead on the spot.

MUSIC OF THE SPHERES

The Neoplatonist philosophers taught that planets radiated musical pitches as they circled the Earth. Ordinary people could not hear this "music of the spheres," but highly spiritual people could. The medieval Arabs joined this idea to music's uncanny power to influence the mind and soul. In their quest to reach Heaven through trance, Assamite and Toreador sorcerers listened to the music of the spheres. They learned occult melodies that powerfully affected the emotions of listeners. The effects resemble a specialized version of Presence.

So far, no vampire has ever been known to have learned both the Music of the Spheres and the "Melpominee" Discipline of the small and obscure Daughters of Cacophony bloodline, but it's bound to happen eventually. The path and Discipline powers cannot add to each other's effects.

System: This path calls for the usual Willpower roll, but the character requires a Trait rating of 3 in Performance — either singing or playing some sort of instrument — to cast the Music of the Spheres. The magician can activate the Music of the Spheres through a single turn of melody, but everyone nearby can sense the occult power in the music. The magician can conceal the celestial melody within ordinary music, but this requires that targets hear the music for at least a full minute. Listeners also receive a Perception + Occult roll (difficulty 5 + the number of successes the performer's player received on the Willpower roll) to detect the unnatural force within the performer's music.

Each power affects a variable number of targets depending on how many successes the magician's player rolls, as noted on the chart below. If more people are present than the character can influence, the Music of the Spheres affects those with lower Willpower scores first.

1 success	One person
2 successes	Two people
3 successes	Six people
4 successes	20 people
5 successes	Everyone in the vampire's immediate vicinity (an entire auditorium, a mob)

The Music of the Spheres does not enchant people who hear it in a recording, or transmitted by telephone, television or other electrical or mechanical means.

If two characters use the Music of the Spheres against the same target, the character whose player rolls the most successes has her effect take precedence.

• SONG OF MERCURY

The music of Mercury, the planet that rules abstract thought, deadens emotions. The swift cascades of notes distract listeners and calm their souls.

System: In game terms, the Song of Mercury negates the effect of other Music of the Spheres powers *while the music continues*. The power costs one blood point to activate, but the effect continues as long as the character keeps singing or playing. The Song of Mercury lacks sufficient power to counter frenzy or Rötschreck.

•• SONG OF VENUS

The sweet music of Venus inspires feelings of affection that an occult musician can direct as she wills. The character can make people like her, or anyone else she chooses — for a while.

System: This power acts like the Presence power Awe, but the magician can direct the victims' warm feelings toward anyone she wants, to make someone else seem incredibly charismatic. The magician needs some way to indicate the recipient of the magical charisma, whether by words, admiring glances or other means. The effect lasts the rest of the scene. Affected people can resist the Song of Venus by expending one Willpower for every turn they remain within the target person's supernatural charisma. When a character's player spends a number of Willpower points equal to the successes rolled, the character shakes off the Song of Venus completely.

••• SONG OF MARS

The harsh chords and driving rhythms of Mars inspire feelings of anger and aggression. The magician can make his audience hate a particular target or actually drive listeners to fits of rage.

System: This power can have two effects. The magician can make an audience despise a target person or organization — like Awe in reverse. The target does not have to be present. This effect lasts a scene. Players can spend Willpower to have their characters resist the supernatural anger for a turn. If the *ashipu*'s player additionally expends a Willpower point, affected Kindred enter frenzy unless their players succeed at Self-Control rolls (difficulty 7). This augmented power can induce frenzy-like rage in mortals as well, but mortals resist at difficulty 5.

•••• SONG OF JUPITER

The strong, steady chords of Jupiter, the planet of power and status, boost courage and strength of purpose. Listeners feel resolute and fearless, like unto kings.

System: This power renders listeners immune to all attempts to use Presence *while the music continues*; it does not negate Presence uses that have already taken place. Any other mind control (such as Dominate, other Music of the Spheres powers, mortal magic or the powers of other supernatural beings) against an audience member suffers a +2 difficulty penalty (to a maximum of 10) for the rest of the scene.

The Song of Jupiter also strengthens the Man to resist the Beast. For the rest of the scene, characters resisting Rötschreck or frenzy have the difficulty of their Virtue rolls reduced by 2.

••••• SONG OF SATURN

The menacing chords of Saturn, planet of death and restriction, inspire terror in those who hear them. People affected by the magical music need all their courage and will to resist the urge to flee or surrender.

System: Affected Kindred immediately enter Rötschreck unless their players succeed at Courage rolls (difficulty 7). Mortal listeners feel the same blind fear (and have the same difficulty to resist it), but their terror may

take other forms than flight, depending on each individual's Nature.

RITUALS

Many of these rituals do not list specific components. In these cases, *ashipu* are free to select their own components, tools or methods from the traditional elements described above. Masters of Heaven and Earth do not have to use the same components each time they cast a ritual, either.

LEVEL ONE RITUALS

EXORCISE FEVER

This ritual exorcises the spirit of fever from a sick person, thus curing the disease. It only works against diseases that cause fever, though. *Ashipu* have other rituals for other common sorts of Middle Eastern diseases. Old forms of this ritual that appeal exclusively to ancient gods no longer work. The magician uses the old incantations, but must back them up with a minor holy relic from an Abrahamic faith.

System: A single success suffices to cure comparatively mild fever-causing diseases such as common influenza. More lethal and tenacious diseases such as scarlet fever or typhoid may demand two or three successes to exorcise.

HOROSCOPE

By inspecting the positions of the stars and planets at a person's birth (or Embrace), the magician can obtain simple information about that person.

System: For each success, the astrologer discovers one fact about the target, such as her Nature, great aptitudes (such as Traits rated 3 or higher) or (in the most general sense) tragedies in her past. A Horoscope provides no specific details about a person's history or goals, but can suggest routes for mundane investigation.

WARDING BAPTISM

Based on an Iranian rite to protect children from disease, this ritual involves baptizing a subject with blood and water, poured from a metal bowl with 40 keys attached. For the rest of the night, the subject becomes immune to one Thaumaturgical path, designated by the magician.

System: The *ashipu* does not have to use her own blood; animal blood will do. The ritual protects only against path magic that directly affects the subject. For instance, it would not protect against the Lure of Flames because the magical fire targets a place, not the person who happens to occupy that place. A person cannot receive more than one Warding Baptism at a time.

LEVEL TWO RITUALS

ASTRAL PORTENT

By inspecting the state of the heavens at a person's birth (and/or Embrace) and at the present, a magician can discover the most powerful forces at work in a person's life. The subject can ask for a general forecast, or seek more specific advice about his financial future, love life, a planned journey, etc. The astrologer can also ask such a question about a subject who does not know he is being studied.

System: Each success rolled indicates one significant fact about the person's near future — either in general or in relation to a particular topic. Clues should be short and somewhat vague.

Example: A mortal asks about his amorous opportunities. The astrologer's player rolls three successes. The three clues are "Travel by water," "Heaven favors boldness," and "Venus is unfavorable." From this (and discussions about the client's income and lifestyle), the astrologer might suggest that the client take the ferry to work instead of driving, aggressively pursue any hint that a woman likes him, but not to expect a happily-ever-after this time around.

This open-ended ritual carries risk for abuse. Storytellers should never give precisely detailed information — only clues that characters can follow up on their own, or warnings to keep an eye out for significant events in the near future. An Astral Portent is especially useful when characters simply have no idea what to do next. The heavenly portents will not give them an answer on a silver platter, but they can point the way to something interesting.

A character can receive only one reading of portents per story. By acting on their horoscopes, characters change their potential futures in every way. The mysterious web of Fate takes some time to adjust to the altered circumstances.

Note: More powerful versions of this ritual enable an astrologer to cast horoscopes for larger groups. A Level Three ritual lets a sorcerer read the portents for a corporate body, such as a coterie or a small business. A Level Four version produces a horoscope for large institutions such as a large business or a city. A Level Five version reveals clues to the future of an entire nation. National events have so much momentum, and result from such broad causes, however, that the stars rarely give better information than a decent economist or political analyst.

These rituals also have variant forms that employ other divination methods, such as reading entrails, dream interpretation or geomancy.

Bind the Heavens

This curse inflicts a month of drought upon an enemy's land. The magician paints a donkey's skull in gaudy colors, wedges papers bearing vituperative curses and the victim's name between its teeth, and throws it down a well — preferably the well of the victim. This offends the spirits of the land and water, who respond by steering the rain away from the victim's land.

System: Using a well that is not actually on the victim's land increases the ritual's difficulty by 2. If the ritual succeeds, however, no land owned by the victim receives any rain for one month per success rolled by the magician's player.

Earth's Blood Cry

Middle Eastern tradition holds that a murdered man's blood cries out from the earth demanding vengeance, as Abel's blood cried out against Caine. An *ashipu* can mold a tablet of clay and a murder victim's blood, and enchant it to scream when the murderer touches it.

System: The magician needs at least one blood point's worth of the murder victim's blood, collected after death (it's no good having someone store a pint as a hedge against the possibility of murder). Once crafted, the magic tablet retains its enchantment for one month, or until the murderer touches it. The tablet cries out only once.

Level Three Rituals

Bull of Heaven

The goddess Inanna (also known as Ishtar) once sent an enchanted bull to kill the hero Gilgamesh. To grant the bull supernatural power, she bathed it in precious oils and coupled with it. An *ashipu* can similarly enchant any animal (not just bulls), although instead of sex he bites the animal while feeding it some of his own vitae. The animal not only gains a ghoul's strength, the magician gains a psychic link to the animal for the rest of the night.

System: The animal becomes a normal ghoul, with one dot of Potence and one dot of another Discipline (either Fortitude or one possessed by the magician, at the magician's option — though no animal is wise enough to Dominate its foe or cast a Thaumaturgical ritual upon it, for example). For the rest of the night, the magician can use the animal's senses and direct its actions whenever she wants. This ritual's effect resembles the Animalism power Subsume the Spirit, but has much less power.

Portrait of Passion

This ritual makes real the Middle Eastern tales of people who fall in love with a portrait and obsessively seek out the real person. The magician paints a portrait, mingling her own vitae and a small sample of the intended victim's blood or spittle in the paint. If the ritual succeeds, when the victim sees the portrait he feels compelled to seek the person pictured, who for a while seems like the most important person in the world.

System: A magician requires a Trait rating of at least 3 in Crafts (Painting) to perform this ritual.

For each success rolled, the victim spends one week obsessed with the subject of the portrait. She spends every spare moment seeking the pictured person, and may neglect job, friends or family for the quest. If she succeeds in her search, she spends as much time as possible with the person. The attraction may take the form of love, friendship, admiration or any other form that seems suitable.

The victim can resist the compulsion for 24 hours by expending a Willpower point, but needs a pretty good motivation to do so.

The magician has no control over what happens when the magical compulsion ends. Both victim and the pictured person may find the experience baffling or even revolting; then again, it may be the start of a great love affair.

Sometimes a cruel *ashipu* paints an imaginary person. Either the magic fails outright, or the victim actually finds a person who matches the portrait! *Ashipu* find this mysterious, but sometimes useful.

Level Four Rituals

Kudurru

The Babylonians used carved stone stelae called *kudurru* to mark boundaries and record land grants. An *ashipu* can enchant a set of *kudurru* to mark his domain. The magic stones establish his claim over the domain, rendering all his activities a little bit easier.

The magician needs to procure at least five matching stelae carved with symbols representing himself and rulership. He may crib images from any culture that suits him. The magician hides four *kudurru* along the boundaries of the territory he wants to claim, and hides the fifth within a church or temple of some sort within that domain. The actual ritual costs a permanent Willpower point, and requires the use of at least three minor holy relics (such as a consecrated Host, *kohanim* blood and dust from an Imam's tomb).

System: A magician suffers no difficulty penalties due to the environment when he attempts a task in his *kudurru*-warded domain. For instance, if he fought someone in an alley crowded with piles of slimy refuse, his opponent would suffer difficulty penalties for bad footing and a narrow space, but the sorcerer would not. The magician can establish this magical dominion over an area equal to several city blocks.

The *kudurru* warding lasts until someone finds and breaks one of the stones.

Kudurru wardings cannot overlap. If a magician tries to claim any territory already claimed by another sorcerer, the working fails.

Tamimah

Tamimah is an Arabic word for an amulet or talisman. To *ashipu*, it refers to a specific kind of amulet that they can make. A *tamimah* carries a vampiric Discipline. Any Cainite or ghoul who wears the *tamimah* has that Discipline. To craft a *tamimah*, however, the *ashipu* must successfully diablerize a vampire who knows that Discipline to the desired level. The Assamites once created many *tamimah*, but could not do this for the centuries of the Tremere's curse. Now that they can make *tamimah* again, they find the art almost lost among their clan.

System: An *ashipu* can enchant a *tamimah* to carry any Discipline, but not paths of Thaumaturgy (whether Hermetic or any other form of sorcery). A *tamimah* can carry two fewer dots of a Discipline than the magician's Dur-An-Ki mastery. For instance, a character with a Trait rating of 4 in Dur-An-Ki could enchant *tamimah* carrying two dots of a single Discipline.

Tamimah do not cumulate with a character's existing Trait rating in a Discipline. For instance, if a vampire who had Dominate 2 wore a *tamimah* that carried Dominate 3, she would gain Dominate 3, not Dominate 5.

A sorcerer who successfully enchants a *tamimah* cannot reduce her generation from that particular diablerie. All the vampiric unlife-force goes into the *tamimah*.

LEVEL FIVE RITUALS

APSU PORTAL

The people of southern Mesopotamia believed that all lakes and rivers connected to an underground ocean of fresh water called *Apsu*. Their temples symbolized these life-giving waters with a large tank of holy water, which they also called an *apsu*. Sorcerers can exploit this myth of the connection of all fresh waters to travel around the world.

System: This ritual requires an *apsu* tank, properly consecrated through prayers and sacrifices to Enki, the god of the subterranean sea and master of all magic. In the ritual itself, the magician pours a pint of rose oil and one blood point's worth of her own vitae into the *apsu*. She also adds a phial of water from another body of fresh water anywhere in the world. Then one person (the magician or anyone else) can jump into the *apsu* and instantly emerge from that other body of fresh water. The Assamites like to tell the story of an assassin who reached a well-guarded victim after he bribed a pool-cleaner to bring him a sample of water from the elder's subterranean swimming pool.

LILITH'S VENGEANCE

One ancient and disputed legend among the Kindred says that Caine gained his first Disciplines through a covenant with the primal demon-queen Lilith — a covenant that Caine then broke. This ritual calls upon Lilith. It reminds her of Caine's treachery and grants her permission, in the name of all the gods of law and magic, to strip a given Kindred of the power he inherited from Caine.

System: This ritual requires the use of five separate holy relics, which the magician consumes in the course of the ritual. For instance, an *ashipu* might swallow a consecrated Host, a leaf from a tree where Mohammed rested, blood from a *kahane*, and a small tablet of Kerbala clay stamped with the image of Marduk by an authentic Babylonian cylinder-seal. Directing the power of Faith against oneself this way inflicts one health level of unsoakable aggravated damage upon the magician, whose player additionally spends a Willpower point and rolls for the character to resist Rötschreck. The magician must endure the torment, however, to atone for Caine's crime and assume (albeit falsely) the power of the Almighty. The *ashipu* also requires a strong sympathetic link to the target Cainite, such as her True Name, a bit of her hair, fingernails or vitae, or the horoscope charts of both her mortal birth and her Embrace.

For every success the *ashipu*'s player rolls, the victim loses one dot off a single Discipline of the sorcerer's choice. If the *ashipu* happens to name a Discipline that the victim does not possess, she wasted the ritual. The victim's Discipline remains reduced for a full month. An *ashipu* can curse a victim this way only once at a time. The sorcerer cannot curse the victim again until the first curse wears off.

LEVEL SIX RITUAL

JACOB'S KISS

An old Middle Eastern legend says that one can capture a dying person's soul in his last breath and take on his power and knowledge; that's why Jacob kissed his dying father Isaac. With suitable preparation of trance and prayer, an *ashipu* can perform this feat. Of course, the easiest way to be on hand when a person dies is to kill her yourself.

System: The magician can maintain the special trance state for up to an hour, but no longer, and must kiss the target *exactly* on his last breath. If the ritual succeeds, the *ashipu* captures and eats the target's soul. Jacob's Kiss works only upon victims who breathe, so a sorcerer cannot consume the soul of a just-destroyed Cainite.

The magician gains a reserve of "spare" Willpower points, equal in number to the target's Willpower Trait. Any Willpower expenditure comes from this pool, as long as it lasts; these points never recover. The magician also gains *all* the target's Abilities, for as long as the pool of stolen Willpower lasts.

LEVEL SEVEN RITUAL

TURN BACK THE SKIES

The constellations symbolized within the bull-slaying scene in a Mithraic temple all seem to connect to the precession of the equinoxes — specifically, the transition from the Age of Taurus to the Age of Aries. A few powerful *ashipu* can use the Mithraic mysteries to send a soul back in time, from the present Age of Pisces to the twilight of the Age of Aries. This requires the sacrifice of a ram in an authentic Mithraic temple, and an armillary sphere (a device that depicts the constellations and the zodiac, celestial equator and other map-lines of the heavens). These *ashipu* send minions back in time to seek long-lost secrets. Each use of the ritual can send several people back in time — a whole coterie of characters, in fact.

System: The magician's player spends a point of permanent Willpower while the ram's blood falls onto the subjects, and then turns the armillary sphere from the current heavenly configuration to the sky of the desired time. The souls of the subjects flash back in time and possess the bodies of mortals undergoing Mithraic initiation in that temple. Mithraism flourished from 68 B.C. to early in the 5th century A.D. so a sorcerer can send people to any time in that span. Those *ashipu* who continued to practice the Mithraic mysteries after the decline of the mortal faith may provide limited access to other times, at the Storyteller's option. The time travelers spend one lunar month in their stolen bodies before automatically returning to their own time. If a time traveler dies in his borrowed flesh, his soul never returns.

Time travelers have no supernatural powers (they are mortal now, after all), but retain all their Abilities. A time traveler can also call upon one dot of any Abilities the possessed person had that he does not. (This incidentally lets the interloper speak the possessed person's language.)

Any *ashipu* who know this spell warn time travelers to avoid changing history. Causality can adjust to a few knocks, but murdering famous historical figures or teaching the Maccabees how to make gunpowder destroys the foolish character. If a time traveler deliberately tries to cause such a drastic change to history, the character's soul instantly snaps back to his body, which then explodes and burns to ash.

Storytellers should not take these "rules" too seriously, though. Turn Back the Skies is so powerful — and beyond the reach of typical **Vampire** characters — that Storytellers can treat it as a plot device that follows whatever rules their story demands. For instance, if a character does something by accident that could change history, you could let the player devise a plan to put history back on track. Suppose, for example, that a time traveler accidentally kills the young Nero before he became emperor. The players might suggest finding a double to take Nero's place. The characters have the rest of the month to find a lookalike before a vengeful History destroys them. Given a choice between killing characters and shunting them into a thrilling new story, we recommend the story.

Chapter Three: Sadhana: A Meditation Upon Blood

That death which has fettered thee at thy birth with a firm rope, Brihaspati with the hands of the truth did strip off from thee.
— Atharva-Veda

Few lands are so steeped in magic as India. Thousands of self-proclaimed swamis, yogins, fakirs and other miracle-mongers travel from city to city and village to village, showing off their powers. In the absence of modern medicine, poor folk flock to temples in hopes that a magic thread can heal them. Government ministers kneel before god-men who bless them with sacred ash. Ancient superstition and squalid poverty coexist with refined philosophy and cutting-edge science.

India's obsession with magic extends to its undead. Two of India's major vampire clans teach blood magic to many of their members. Other vampires study the art as well. When the Tremere traveled to India with the trading ventures of the early modern age, they found a sorcerous tradition as rich and potent as their own… and immensely older.

India's blood magicians describe their magic using the same words as mortal self-proclaimed sorcerers. They call themselves *sadhus*, who practice Sadhana, "Gaining," to procure magic powers called *siddhis*, "achievements." Rituals are *tantras*, "instructions." When they distinguish themselves from mortal magicians, they use the prefix *rakta*, "blood." The *rakta-sadhus* share many beliefs with their mortal counterparts, and Sadhana's development parallels the history of mortal magical beliefs.

The Kindred have dwelled in India from time out of mind. The Indian Kindred trace their descent from ancestors whom they call *pitris* or "fathers." Western Kindred suppose the *pitris* to be Antediluvians (when they choose to acknowledge such), but the Indians do not know or accept the legend of Caine. Instead, India's vampires hold several myths about the origins of vampirism, few of which they consider mutually exclusive. One legend describes the *pitris* as sons of Yama, the god of death, who offended their father so greatly that he cursed them neither to live nor to enter his kingdom. Another legend explains the first vampires as demon princes slain by various gods, who retained a half-life because they had tasted the Nectar of Immortality. Some origin myths account for all vampires; others grant separate origins to the various clans. Most Indian explanations of vampirism, however, describe the Kindred as demons who incarnate as mortals and regain their supernatural power through the Embrace.

India's first known cities began in the Indus Valley of modern Pakistan and flourished before 2000 B.C. The writing of Mohenjo-Daro, Harappa and other cities defies translation. The Indian Kindred do not know any more about these ancient cities than do the mortal archeologists: All the vampires who survive from this period now sleep in torpor or hide themselves very well.

At about 2000 B.C., tribes who called themselves Aryans invaded India from Persia. These barbarian nomads worshipped gods of the sky, the sea, fire and other natural phenomena. Their chief deity was the sky-god Indra, an idealized warrior who rescued the cloud-cattle from Vritra, the serpent-demon of drought. The Aryans honored their gods with sacrifices of animals and the intoxicating liquor called *soma*. The most ancient text of Hinduism, the *Rig-Veda*, consists of more than a thousand hymns that celebrate the deeds of the gods and tell how to worship them.

In this early Vedic period, anyone could perform religious ritual. The Brahmin caste merely specialized as professional priests. As the Aryans settled down, however, the Brahmins elaborated the ritual of sacrifice and warned of the dire consequences should the slightest error creep into the rite. This trend climaxed in the *Yajur-Veda*, a manual containing the most lengthy and detailed religious rites of all time. The Brahmins declared themselves greater than the gods — because their rituals *forced* the gods to grant them anything they wanted. The divisions between castes hardened, too, as the Brahmins cemented their religious monopoly. The earliest known blood magic follows the Brahminist model of elaborate sacrificial rites.

The arid ritualism of the Brahmins eventually provoked a reaction. Ascetic magicians claimed that their meditation, fasting and other austerities granted them so much merit that they gained magic powers. Like the Brahmins, they could extort boons from the gods. Most importantly, anyone could practice asceticism — even demons. Indian legend offers many instances of demons who gained so much merit through their austerities that they challenged the gods. This period saw Sadhana's most rapid development.

The ascetics eventually provoked a reaction of their own. From the 8th to the 5th centuries BC, India saw a wave of new religions and philosophical movements. Buddhism became the most successful. Buddhism rejected the ritualism of the Brahmins and the self-torture of the ascetics. Instead, Buddhism offered serenity, wisdom and compassion for others as religious goals. Although a Buddhist monk might gain magical powers through the force of his enlightenment, he should not seek such powers, for attachment to power inhibits further spiritual development.

The wave of religious reform became a political conflict as well. India's secular princes — the Kshatriya caste — adopted Buddhism (and Jainism) as a way to curb the powers of the Brahmins.

Although Buddhist notions and other philosophies from this period deeply affected India's Kindred, they did not significantly alter the practice of blood magic. At least, no one can now find evidence of any impact. As mortal Brahmins slowly regained their dominance over Indian society, so too did undead Brahmins purge the temple libraries of heretical texts of blood magic. Waves of Muslim invaders churned Indian undead society, but did not change Sadhana.

When European merchants established trading posts such as Goa, European vampires came to India as well.

Like the mortals, most Western Kindred sought wealth and power in India. Few Western vampires sought to study the Indian Kindred themselves.

The Tremere became a notable exception. In the 16th century, Vienna sent its first cabal of scholars to study India's potent blood magic. These explorers relentlessly petitioned India's *sadhus* for teaching; sometimes they stole scriptures and talismans for their European colleagues to study. The Tremere also Embraced mortal sorcerers and ascetics and demanded that they adapt their former arts to undead use, just as the Tremere founders themselves had done centuries before.

Through the late 19th and early 20th centuries, increasing numbers of Indians sought freedom from Western colonialism. The undead acted more militantly and successfully than the living Indians. This period saw a veritable war between Indian and European Kindred. By 1930, few Western vampires remained in India beyond old colonial enclaves such as Goa, Calcutta and Bombay.

The Tremere endured. To this night, the clan has a significant and growing presence in India. Many Indian Tremere now come from mortal Indian stock. Several Indian cities host Tremere chantries with native regents and even lords. They pay little attention to the pontifices sent from Vienna, and even less to the councilors who ostensibly lead the clan.

The Indian Tremere profit from the caste restrictions that the native clans place upon would-be blood magicians. Most *sadhus* come from two clans, the Daitya (Indian Followers of Set) and Danava (Indian Ventrue). Both of these clans consider themselves Brahmins, and they teach Sadhana only to other undead Brahmins. Vampires of other lineages who want to learn Sadhana — and India holds many such Kindred — seek gurus among other

THE INDIAN MASQUERADE: LOST IN THE CROWD?

Most of India's wonder-workers wield no more real magic than a telephone psychic in America. They provide great cover, however, for the undead. Compared to an ascetic who spends his entire life standing in a river, or holding his arm in one position until the muscles lock, a fellow who only comes out at night and never eats in front of anyone else does not seem so strange. Indeed, an Indian Kindred had better act a bit peculiar if he wants mortals to mistake him for a holy ascetic.

Fortunately, a vampire can put on a good show with his supernatural powers. A Kindred can perform feats of unnatural strength, hold his nonexistent breath as long as he wants, or thrust needles through his dead flesh without worrying about infection — that's not even using Disciplines. In some cases, an actual undead *sadhu* can practice his magic arts openly… and it all helps the Masquerade because Indians associate such magical feats with living yogis, not animate, blood-drinking corpses.

lineages… and the Indian Tremere sometimes oblige them. The "Trimira" willingly teach other vampires who accept a blood bond and other oaths to renounce any former allegiances. Thus, an Indian "Tremere" may actually be a Nosferatu, Ravnos or some other lineage by blood.

MAGIC THEORY AND PRACTICE

Sadhana changed through the millennia. Most rituals reflect the Brahminist stage of Hinduism, while Sadhana paths reflect the ascetic stage. A Hindu blood sorcerer works magic through sacrifices to the gods, meditation and a wide variety of austerities.

Hindu beliefs are immensely complex, diverse and often contradictory. The religion sets only one test for orthodoxy: acceptance of the Vedas as the divine basis of all knowledge. The "commentaries" of later theologians, philosophers and magicians travel far indeed from these ancient collections of ritual, myth and liturgy. Thus, Hindu blood magicians do not regard their practices as blasphemous — and technically, they are not.

The doctrine of *maya* holds that the ordinary world is an illusion. All material things pass away and become something else. True reality lies in Brahman, the eternal, transcendent soul of the universe. The essence of Brahman consists of pure, objectless consciousness. Because the entire universe is a collective hallucination, an ascetic who merges his consciousness with Brahman can, in theory, change the universe any way he wants. After all, he *is* the universe.

Karma traps people in the cycle of reincarnation, called *samsara*. Every deed demands an equal and opposite compensation. The man who beats his wife in one incarnation, for instance, becomes a battered wife in a later incarnation. A person's balance of good or bad deeds determines their status in their next life. A person who accumulates enough merit can win reincarnation as a Brahmin, or even a god. A person who accumulates bad *karma* reincarnates as a pariah, a foreigner, an animal or a demon — perhaps a demon in mortal flesh, fated to receive the Embrace. A person does not need to perform good deeds in order to accumulate "good *karma*," though. Constant thoughts about a god, sacrifices and ascetic practices also confer merit. Indeed, holy men can transfer *karma* from one person to another.

The mystics define the goal of their studies as *moksha*, "liberation" from illusion, reincarnation and the limits of mortal existence. Some Hindus seek liberation through salvation by a god. Others regard *moksha* as a state of perfect intellectual clarity achieved through logic and philosophy. Still others strive to annihilate an ego they regard as an illusion.

Most undead *sadhus* seek a simple, straightforward liberation: They want to achieve godlike power. The vampires of India regard themselves as demons — and like all Indian demons, they seek to overthrow the gods and take their place. Indian myths present their goal as something eminently feasible.

SACRIFICIAL RITUAL

Sadhana includes many elaborate sacrifices. An aspiring *sadhu* studies the *Yajur-Veda* and Hinduism's first grimoire, the *Atharva-Veda*. Indian sorcery imitates the classic sacrificial rites described in these ancient texts. Sadhana demands great courage as well as great memory from its practitioners, because a Hindu sorcerer must pour the sacrificial offering into a blazing fire.

THE CATHAYAN CONFLICT

India falls between two realms. To the west, the childer of Caine stalk the night. To the east dwell an entirely different sort of vampire. These eastern vampires call themselves *kuei-jin*; western vampires call them Cathayans. The Kindred of India call them the *asuratizayya*, the "demon horde." Both sorts of vampires have haunted India for millennia, and for most of that time they fought.

You can find almost as many reasons for the war as you can find Indian vampires. The rationales boil down to competition for resources and fear of the alien. The powers of the *asuratizayya* differ from those of Cainites far more than the different Kindred clans differ from each other.

In their long struggle to dominate the Indian night, the Kindred and Cathayans learned a great deal about each other. The *rakta-sadhus* devote considerable study to the powers of their adversaries. They possess paths and rituals that emulate some Cathayan powers, and that counter others (India's Cathayans, of course, know just as much about fighting Sadhana and other Kindred powers). As the *kuei-jin* follow mortal Asian diasporas around the world, they clash with local Cainite populations. Very probably, Western vampire princes shall seek the help of *sadhus* against these invaders. The Tremere do not wait: The Council of Seven has already charged the Goa Chantry to prepare a document on the Cathayans, based on what they can learn from other *sadhus*.

In a small irony, both the Indian Kindred and at least some *kuei-jin* believe that they are demons in undead bodies. The differences between them prove, however, that they are not at all the same kind of demons.

They also differ in their attitude to the divine order of the world. As far as the Indian Kindred can figure out, Cathayans believe that the gods called them back from Hell for a purpose, and if they fulfill that purpose the gods may redeem them. The Daitya and Danava *sadhus*, on the other hand, seek to destroy the gods and take their place as masters of a darkened world. Far more *sadhus* pay lip service to this grim ideal, however, than actually work toward ruling the universe.

Many blood *tantras* call for an offering of the magician's own vitae, or some other sort of blood sacrifice. Archaic Hinduism specified the horse as the most precious and powerful of all offerings. Several powerful rituals employ a horse sacrifice. Other rituals may instruct the *sadhu* to offer a dove, a chicken, a cow (despite, or perhaps because of, their sacred and inviolate status within Hinduism) or stranger animals. The magician cuts the animal's throat, collects the blood in a bowl, and pours the blood into the fire. Most rituals also demand an oblation of milk, *ghee* (clarified butter) or, less often, curds.

The Vedas often speak of offering *soma*, an intoxicating sacred drink that gave gods their immortality. The Vedas do not clearly state which plant the ancient Aryans used to make *soma*, but most scholars think that they pressed the sacred juice from the ephedra plant. Fig wine is another popular guess. Sadhana tradition describes *soma* as ephedra juice fermented with figs and vitae.

The *Vedas* also direct celebrants to offer a sort of rice porridge to the Brahmins who officiate at a sacrifice. The dregs of this porridge find use in many Vedic spells. Many spells also require the dregs of a *ghee* offering. A sacrifice feeds the gods; the dregs become the gods' own leftovers, touched by their divinity, and that makes them powerful in magic.

A comparative few rituals demand other sacrifices. Offerings range from common foodstuffs such as millet cakes or candy, to merely expensive substances such as musk or pearls, to the truly bizarre such as tiger urine or juice from orchid flowers. Unusual offerings typically refer to some obscure myth or legend. A *sadhu* must discover the rationale for the offering before she can fully learn the ritual.

As a general guideline, powerful rituals demand greater sacrifices. The precise execution of the ritual matters just as much as the offering itself, though. The blood of a hundred horses, sloppily offered, gives no magical benefit at all. A single bowl of milk can shake the pillars of heaven if a Brahmin offers it at the climax of a truly complex and demanding ritual. A *sadhu* strives to execute offerings flawlessly, without mispronouncing a single word or performing a gesture a second too late.

Brahminist tradition holds that such a letter-perfect sacrifice compels the gods to work the *sadhu*'s will. The god has no choice in the matter: The sacrificial spell works as mechanically as starting a car. The Mimamsa school of Hinduism claims that a religious rites possesses power of its own — whether to save souls or work magic. The god does not even have to exist. Nevertheless, most blood *tantras* demand the presence of a god's idol to receive the sacrifice, and some sort of altar for the sacrificial fire. Pious Hindus offer garlands of flowers to their god's statue or anoint it with oil and colored powder. These play no role in Sadhana, but some *sadhus* make these offerings anyway out of piety.

ASCETICISM

Hinduism offers a wide variety of ascetic practices for spiritual development. Most of these are called *yogas* ("zeal, hard work"). The *yogins* who bend and twist their

bodies in odd postures practice *hatha yoga*. Other yogas include *bhakti* — making every action a prayer to a god; *dharana* — focusing attention; *dhyana* — controlling the mind to clear away distractions; and *pranayama* — breathing exercises. Ascetics also expose themselves to heat or cold, lie on beds of nails, stand in streams for months at a time, or inflict other obscure torments on themselves.

Undead *sadhus* engage in long meditation and grueling austerities to unlock the mystic power of the Blood. They practice most of the conventional yoga exercises — with special undead twists.

Raktayana

Hindu magicians believe in a subtle magical energy called *prana* ("breath") that permeates all existence. Magicians accumulate *prana* through special breathing exercises called *pranayama*. Vampires, however, have no *prana* of their own. They take *prana* from the living, as blood. Since the Kindred do not breathe, they cannot use *pranayama* to convert blood into magical energy. Instead they practice an art called *raktayana*. The ascetic practices moving blood through his body, while performing various yoga postures. This transforms the *prana* into a form the magician can use. The mystical energies accumulate at the base of the spine. As a student *sadhu* performs stronger austerities, a stream of magically potent vitae trickles up her spinal column, energizing mystical power-centers called *chakras* as it goes. When the *prana*-inbued blood reaches the seventh and last *chakra* at the crown of the head, the student gains the power to perform paths and rituals.

Dietary Restrictions

Hindus also believe they can gain merit through what they eat. A vegetarian, for instance, possesses greater ritual purity than a person who eats meat, because she avoids the *karma* of causing the death of animals. A period of fasting confers merit; so does eating a limited range of foods for an extended period.

The resemblance to Ventrue feeding restrictions should be obvious, and the Danavas gain prestige through more limited prey profiles. *Sadhus* believe they gain power through unusual feeding restrictions. For instance, a vampire who strives to learn a new ritual might feed only from barren cattle, or vegetarians, or only from the left arm of his vessels. *Sadhus* also practice fasts. Several potent rituals require that the magician fast almost unto torpor.

Mantras

A *mantra* is a magic formula or incantation, or phrases or syllables used in meditation. The famous *mantra* "Aum" is an example of a "seed syllable": a single syllable that represents a phrase that itself encapsulates whole volumes of mystic doctrine. "Aum," for instance, stands for *Aum Mani Padme Hum*, "Ah! The jewel in the lotus, amen!" Not only does a sorcerer meditate upon *mantras*, he may unleash his sendings through the powerful syllables.

Mantras gain much of their power through repetition. Hindu magic texts promise that a person can gain one power through 10,000 repetitions of a *mantra*, another through 20,000 repetitions, and so on. A sorcerer who learns a new ritual spends much of his time dutifully chanting a *mantra* thousands of times, building up the merit needed to work the sending.

A magician would not want to lose count of his *mantra* repetitions. To this end, Hindus employ a sort of rosary in their prayers.

Mudra

A *mudra* is a gesture. Like *mantras*, a magician often performs a *mudra* over and over again — perhaps tens of thousands of times in the course of learning a ritual or mastering a path. Some *mudras* call for the manipulation of a sacred or symbolic implement such as the *dorje* (thunderbolt-scepter), *kapila* (skull-cup), rattle or drum. Many implements symbolize divine powers, as shown in a god's pictures and idols. Vishnu, for instance, holds a discus, a conch-shell, a mace and a lotus-flower. As part of a ritual that invokes Vishnu, therefore, a sadhu might gesture with one of those implements.

Meditation

Blood magic demands great concentration, and the *sadhus* have spent millennia perfecting their techniques for developing the will and focusing the imagination. A magician must keep his mind on his work: In Sadhana, a single extraneous thought could ruin the performance of a sacrifice or disrupt the flow of magically charged vitae in the magician's body. A would-be sorcerer learns to exclude random thoughts from his mind, and to hold a single thought or image for a long time. Perfect concentration also demands an ability to ignore external distractions. *Sadhus* often display remarkable feats of mental and physical self-control, even to ignoring ghastly wounds.

Tapas

All these practices result in an ascetic gaining spiritual energy which gods feel as *tapas*, "heat." The longer and more extravagant the austerities, the greater the heat an ascetic generates. Not only can an ascetic discharge this spiritual energy himself to work magic, the gods may feel such intense heat that they offer magical boons to the ascetic if only he will stop!

The demon king Ravana, for instance, spent 12,000 years standing on his heads among five blazing fires. At the end of each millennium he cut off one of his heads and threw it into a fire as an offering to Shiva. As he was about to cut off his 12th and final head, Shiva appeared and offered him anything he wanted. *Anything*. Ravana asked to become invulnerable to gods, demons, beasts and all the powers of nature — and Shiva had to grant him this, through the force of Ravana's *tapas*. (Ravana scornfully declared that he did not need magic to protect himself from humans, though, giving the gods a loophole by which they could destroy him. See the *Ramayana* for details.)

Most Indian Tremere do not entirely believe the *tapas* theory. None of them have ever forced a god to appear through sheer force of their austerities. They do report, however, that *raktayana* and other ascetic practices confer a remarkable command of the body's vitae. This exquisite control extends to the magical force within vitae as well as its physical substance. *Sadhus* do seem to impart radically new powers to the Blood itself, at least on a temporary basis.

Stage Magic and *Maya*

Entertainment plays an important role in Indian magic. Most of India's mortal wonder-workers simply provide entertainment for money. On the other hand, even the greatest sages have produced spectacles to amuse and edify the public. Sadhana follows this tradition. A blood magician sees nothing strange about also learning sleight of hand and other conjuring techniques. All is *maya*, illusion: Blood magic and stage magic simply facilitate the illusion in different ways. If a sorcerer can achieve the result she wants through conjuring tricks, that conserves precious blood.

Sadhus also practice an intermediate form of magic that creates illusions in the minds of an audience. The magician hypnotizes the audience so that they see what he wants them to see. Mortal magicians supposedly use the same "power of suggestion" to perform the Indian Rope Trick and other famous illusions.

Indian Kindred know this power of illusion very well indeed, as the Ravnos clan's characteristic Discipline of Chimerstry. Many *sadhus* try to study Chimerstry as well as Sadhana. The sorcerers also know a special class of *maya* rituals that create effects like Chimerstry, but require much more time to perform.

Indeed, Indian sorcerers may mix conjuring tricks and *maya* with their paths and rituals. Some rituals begin with a stage trick, then add magic to make the trick happen in truth — or as much truth as anyone can have in a world of illusion.

Defilement

Paradoxically, the austerities practiced by *sadhus* often include elements that Hinduism normally defines as defiling a Brahmin's ritual purity. Normal rules, however, do not bind

Caste and Dharma

Hinduism divides humanity into five classes technically called *varnas*, "colors," but more often called castes. Not only does Hinduism forbid intermarriage between castes, people born into a particular caste can perform only certain types of work. Other occupations defile them. Each *varna* includes numerous specific castes and sub-castes. Some represent occupations, while others began as tribes, religious sects or other divisions.

Priestly Brahmins perform the sacrifices and claim most of the educated professions for themselves.

Kshatriyas were the land-owning, warrior aristocracy of old India, and rivals of the Brahmins as India's ruling caste. After centuries of religious and political conflict the Brahmins eradicated the old Kshatriya families. Over the centuries, however, the Brahmins awarded Kshatriya status to one conquering military elite after another, as a way to curry favor with the new ruling class.

Vaisyas began as farmers and tradesmen. They eventually claimed many of the middle class, mercantile and artisan occupations.

Sudras are peasants and menial laborers.

The Pariahs or Untouchables consist of all the people (and their descendants) who fell off the bottom of the caste system: aboriginal tribes; non-Hindus; criminals; slaves; the offspring of forbidden, inter-caste unions; and people who perform jobs the Brahmins thought especially degrading, such as sweepers and garbage-men. The very lowest castes defiled higher-caste people through proximity ("Unapproachables") or merely being seen ("Unseeables," who wash the clothes of Untouchables).

Brahminism defines separate and distinct codes of conduct and ethics, called *dharmas*, for each of the castes. A Brahmin who acts like a Sudra sins as greatly as a Sudra who acts like a Brahmin. Indeed, deviation from caste duty threatens the very order of the cosmos.

Jainism, Buddhism and ascetic Hinduism, on the other hand, all posit *universal dharmas*. These codes of conduct, ethics and supernatural merit apply to all people, regardless of caste. Anyone can renounce the world and live in the forest as an ascetic… and if a hermit moves far enough from his home village, who knows what caste he once held? Jainism proposes *ahimsa*, "nonviolence," as a universal virtue; Buddhism proffers the Noble Eightfold Path as a guide to enlightenment. Even demons can gain merit as ascetics, or convert to Buddhism and turn their violent natures to good use as "Wrathful Protectors" or "Guardians of the *Dharma*."

Indian Kindred possess their own versions of the mortal castes. Ancient codes decree that only Kindred from Brahmin lineages can study Sadhana. The ascetic tradition, however, opens Sadhana to any vampire — as long as that vampire renounces all ties of clan, caste and brood and becomes a hermit or wandering holy man. Indian mortals call forest-dwelling ascetics *sannyasas*, and Indian Kindred use the term for their undead renunciates. Lower-caste *sadhus* become honorary Brahmins — but many real Brahmins claim a right to destroy any *sannyasa* who involves herself in the affairs and intrigues of other Kindred.

That's the tradition, anyway. In the modern nights, the Brahmins can no longer enforce this rule of destruction. Many *sannyasas* now move into cities to meddle in mortal politics and business and sell their services to other Kindred. The Indian Tremere in particular defy the old caste system, and in so doing they implicitly invite other Kindred to defy it too. The Daitya and Danava high priests excoriate the Tremere as Untouchable foreigners, but the "Trimira" continue to attract disciples.

ascetics. They do things for different reasons. This goes double for undead sorcerers. As demons, they have a divine mandate to engage in behavior forbidden to mortals.

Needless to say, many of these practices require some alternate form of morality, or at least the strength of purpose to maintain a dwindling *humanitas*.

CORPSES

Indians normally avoid contact with the dead. Cremation, however, constitutes one of the most sacred rites that a Brahmin performs. Buddhism teaches students to meditate upon images of rotting corpses as a way to break attachment to life and fear of death. The Aghora and Kapalisa ascetic sects go considerably beyond mere images — and so do Sadhana practitioners.

A student *rakta-sadhu* spends many nights in the burning-ground. He smells the fire consuming the bodies. He hears the skulls pop, and the sizzle as the boiling brains spill into the flames. He sees how the rich man's corpse burns just like the pauper's, and tastes stale, dead blood imbibed from a scorched human skull.

Thus does a *sadhu* lose the emotional snares of mortal existence. She overcomes repugnance, forgets fear and pride and shame, and learns to love the gods who shall deliver her Final Death, as they bring inevitable death to all things. She herself becomes Death, the destroyer of worlds. As brother to demons and sister to gods, with Shiva and Kali at her back, shall any lesser power break her will?

UNCLEAN DIET

As blood-drinking demons, undead *sadhus* cannot become vegetarians or engage in the same dietary rituals as mortals. Sometimes a sorcerer seeks blood from the most degraded and degrading vessels: fresh corpses, Untouchables and "unclean" animals. For instance, Hindu dietary laws say that you cannot sink much lower than a "dog-cooker." Therefore, a *sadhu* might feed only upon the blood of dogs for an extended period. Depending how you look at it, such deliberate self-humiliation serves either as penance for the crime of existing, or as a way to establish credentials as an enemy of the gods.

OTHER TOOLS AND PRACTICES

MANDALA

Any sort of picture can serve as a *mandala*. Examples include the geometric diagrams called *yantras* and simple colored shapes called *tattwas* upon which an ascetic meditates. Sadhana rituals often employ more elaborate illustrations that combine concentric circles, squares and other forms with mystic symbols and figures of gods, demons, Buddhas and other creatures. These symbolize the powers that the *sadhu* invokes and directs. A sorcerer draws especially potent *mandalas* using colored sand or flour, and destroys them at the climax of the ritual to release the sending.

ALCHEMY

India has its own ancient tradition of alchemical transmutation and medicine, called *rasayana*. Sadhana itself does not include conventional "magic potions" or other sorts of alchemical talismans. Instead, *sadhus* combine Indian alchemy with the traditions of Indian medicine. Sorcerers drink concoctions of blood, herbs, mercury, sulfur and other minerals as part of their exercises. Advanced *sadhus* consume potions that would sicken even the undead, but transform the toxins through their spiritual force to increase their magic even further. Ascetic tradition includes transmutation as one of the great *siddhis*, however, and not a few undead *sadhus* learn paths with alchemical effects.

GIFTS

Mortal Brahmins never receive a salary for their religious or magical duties. That would make a Brahmin a mere hireling — no better than a ditch-digger. Instead, a client gives a Brahmin a gift, called *dakshina*. Vedic tradition lists clothing, gold, cattle and horses as the four proper gifts, but anything valuable will do.

Indian vampires expect their *sadhus* to follow the same tradition. Any hint of commerce destroys the magician's ritual purity. Sadhana rituals inevitably fail if the *sadhu* works for a contract or negotiates a fee. A would-be client can offer a gift, which the sorcerer accepts or declines, but the *sadhu* cannot dicker.

ASTROLOGY

India also has an astrological tradition. Indian astrology ignores Uranus, Neptune and Pluto, but lays great importance on the 28 lunar houses, called *nakshatras*. Sorcerers may engage in routine fortune-telling, but they chiefly employ astrology to determine propitious times for their exercises. Overall, astrology remains a minor part of Sadhana.

JEWELS

India has many legends of magical jewels. Both gods and demons sought a "Wish-Granting Jewel" at the world's beginning. Another legendary jewel enables a person to fly. Although *sadhus* place less reliance upon talismans than Hermetic or Middle Eastern sorcerers do, once in a while a sorcerer imbues a jewel with magic powers.

NOTABLE GODS

Hinduism takes an uncommon approach to its gods in that the faithful do not have to believe that their gods really exist. Hinduism's high philosophy teaches that the gods and spirits are masks or emanations of Brahman that only imagine they possess independent existence through the play of *maya*. *Bhakti yoga* teaches followers to devote themselves to a god: first to identify themselves with it, then to move beyond and use the god as a vehicle to identify themselves with Brahman itself. Other schools interpret gods as personified conditions or aspects of consciousness.

Most Hindus, however, take their gods literally. Their religion gives them no shortage of deities to worship. What's more, the major gods often exist in several avatars or aspects. For instance, Hindus can worship Vishnu the

Preserver in his own person, or as his mortal avatar Rama or his divine avatar Krishna.

Modern Hinduism elevates three gods above all others: Brahma the Creator, Vishnu the Preserver and Shiva the Destroyer. India's numerous followers of Vishnu and Shiva identify themselves through marks drawn on the forehead. A Vaishnavite wears a dot on her forehead; a Shaivite draws a V-shape with the point at the bridge of the nose. The three gods together are called Trimurti, "Three Faces." Most *sadhus* worship Shiva above all other gods, and carry his symbolic trident.

VISHNU AND LAKSHMI

Vishnu is the master of *maya*. Many times in Hindu legend, Vishnu uses his powers of shape-shifting and illusion to trick the demons who otherwise would seize rulership of the universe. Vishnu has manifested as a fish, a tortoise, a wild boar, a lion-man, a dwarf and several heroes and sages. When humanity becomes totally wicked, Vishnu shall appear as Kalkin, riding a white horse and wielding a flaming sword, to destroy the world so that new creation can take place.

Sadhus invoke Vishnu in order to borrow his powers of *maya*. Any magic of illusion or transformation falls under Vishnu's purview.

Vishnu meets and marries his wife Lakshmi in every one of his incarnations. Lakshmi, the Goddess of Fortune, bestows all the good things of life upon humanity: luck, happiness, food, children, everything. The undead do not invoke her, for all her gifts are denied to them.

SHIVA AND SHAKTI

Shiva and his wife Shakti, or Parvati, occupy central roles in many Sadhana rituals. Shiva began as a pre-Aryan god called Rudra, a deity of storms, wild animals and the hunt. Over time, Shiva gained more philosophical aspects. He governs all chaotic and catastrophic phenomena, from natural disasters to the flash of enlightenment that destroys illusion. He is the supreme guru and ascetic. Even the ghosts and demons worship Shiva.

Sadhus particularly revere two aspects of Shiva. Bhairava embodies the god's more concrete aspects of destruction. His name means "The Terrifier." Mahakala is Death itself, and Time that destroys all things. Parvati becomes Mahakala's female counterpart Kali, the dark mother who brings the death of self.

During their stay in the burning-ground, student sorcerers perform a rite called the *shava*-Sadhana to propitiate Kali and Mahakala. The *sadhu* fills the mouth of a corpse with oil and floats a wick in it to make a lamp. The *sadhu* then kneels upon the chest of the corpse and spends the rest of the night in prayer.

LESSER GODS

• Despite the cosmic roles of Brahma, Vishnu and Shiva, the fire-god Agni surpasses all other gods in magic because he is the sacrificial flame itself. He receives all offerings; every Sadhana ritual demands his presence.

• Elephant-headed Ganesha also holds a prominent role in Sadhana. He is a binding and loosing god, a creator

and remover of obstacles, and a god of knowledge and practical wisdom. Just as Hindu scribes invoke Ganesha at the start of books, sorcerers often invoke Ganesha before rituals to ensure their success — or they ask Ganesha to make their enemies fail.

• Varuna, one of the old Vedic gods, lost his original status as world-creator but retains importance as the king of the sea and master of magic. Varuna enforces the cosmic and moral order, but he does so through the subtle influence of magic and curses. He knows all the secrets of destiny.

• Kubera rules the nature-spirits of Hindu myth: the *yakshas*, *guhyakas*, *kinnaras* and others. He is also the god of wealth and mythic owner of all precious metals and gems. Ravana was his half-brother. Mortals do not worship Kubera, but *sadhus* must propitiate him if they hope to command his subjects.

• Many Vedic prayers beg Nirriti, the goddess of misery and destruction, to ignore the faithful. On the other hand, curses often invoke Nirriti to do her worst to the enemies of the magician.

• The *Rig-Veda* describes Brihaspati, god of the planet Jupiter, as the magician-vizier of the gods. Rituals often invoke Brihaspati along with other divine patrons of magic.

SAINTS AND SAGES

Primal holy men called *rishis* play as great a role as the gods in Hindu belief, for the *rishis* revealed the Vedas to humanity and the gods. Various *rishis* also fathered gods and demons. For instance, Ravana and Kubera were grandsons of the *rishi* Pulastya.

In its original form, Buddhism does not so much deny gods as deride them. The Buddha, Gautama, surpassed all gods by achieving perfect enlightenment; he taught that everyone could achieve enlightenment and salvation without the need for gods. Nevertheless, folk Buddhism turned Gautama and his disciples into quasi-deities, and invented mythological Buddhas to fill out the pantheon. Buddhist mythology also includes *bodhisattvas*, sages who achieve enlightenment but turn back to the world to teach and help humanity, and *arhats* or saintly monks.

Jainism supplies the *tirthankaras* or "precursors," 23 legendary ascetic sages who preceded the religion's founder Vardhamana. Much of Jain legendry concerns the *tirthankaras*, and Jain temples hold statues of them.

Each Buddha, saint or sage has his (or less often, her) own mythic attributes. Just as Catholics might appeal to saints, a Buddhist or Jain might pray to a particular *bodhisattva* or *tirthankara* who seems particularly associated with her occupation, problem or desire. Undead *sadhus* do the same. For instance, Vairocana, the fourth Buddha of meditation, presides over autumn (the season of dissolution) and represents the concept of pure forms or archetypes. Thus, a sorcerer conducting a ritual to dispel a supernatural force might draw a *mandala* with Vairocana at the center.

DEMONS AND SPIRITS OF INDIA

Indian myth describes a wide variety of spirits — far too many even to list. Few spirits are wholly benign. Even spirits who serve the gods may turn mischievous or rebel against their duty. On the other hand, individual demons can display many admirable traits of ascetic self-control, religious devotion, honor and generosity. For instance, the demon king Bali nearly conquered the universe through his overwhelming virtue, then surrendered it, and his life, to Vishnu rather than break a promise.

The demons called *asuras* oppose the gods themselves. Indian blood magicians seldom deal with such powerful spirits. As *asuras* in flesh themselves, however, they sometimes — in fits of hubris — believe that they possess a right to treat with their powerful cousins.

The *rakshasas* and *yakshas* threaten mortals. *Rakshasas* can look like humans or various animals. In their natural form they have blue, green or yellow skin, and eyes turned vertically in their faces. Everything else varies: *Rakshasas* can be tall or short, thin or fat, have one, two or more legs, or even multiple heads. They are the most consistently malevolent of demons. *Yakshas* seem more like nature spirits. They generally look human, and several heroes married female *yakshinis*, but they too can change their form and cast illusions, as well as command natural phenomena such as trees and water.

The loathsome *pisachas* threaten the dead. These demons possess corpses. In these stolen bodies they commit all sorts of vicious mischief. In 1999, India suffered a tremendous invasion of *pisachas* that just about every other supernatural faction seeks to abate. With them came many of the malevolent ghosts called *bhut*. According to legend, burning turmeric drives away *bhuts*.

Other spirits ostensibly serve the gods. The *apsarases* are heavenly maidens, like the *houris* of Islam. Although promiscuous lovers, they sometimes provide great assistance to mortals whom they favor. In particular, they can make a person lucky. The *apsarases'* male counterparts, the heavenly musicians and *soma*-guardians called *gandharvas*, frequently lust for mortal brides but these couplings tend to end badly for the women involved. Both sorts of spirits look like gorgeous humans, but can change their shape and create illusions.

The *kinnaras*, who have human bodies but horse heads, sing and play before Kubera. Other servants of Kubera, the *guhyakas*, guard the treasures of the earth. Warlike storm-spirits called *maruts* and *rudras* patrol the sky; they serve Rudra and another god called Marut and join the gods in their battles against the asuras.

As a complication, some Indian Kindred lineages take the names of demon types. Most notably, the Daitya and Danava clans take the name of *asura* tribes. Even the vampires sometimes fall prey to the resulting confusions and ambiguities.

GAME MECHANICS

Sadhana paths all call for Willpower rolls. A *sadhu* evokes all path magic by sheer force of will because that's how she believes ascetic magic works: If you gain enough merit through your austerities, what you wish comes true.

Most Sadhana rituals call for an Intelligence + Occult roll from the player, just like every other style of Thaumaturgy. The exceptions, the *Rakta-Maya* rituals of hypnotic illusion, are noted above and described below.

Unlike a Hermetic magus, a *sadhu* needs to learn an additional Ability besides Occult. Sadhana's austerities demand that a practitioner also develop the Secondary Skill of Meditation (see the **Vampire Storytellers Companion**). A sorcerer cannot employ path magic at a higher level than her Meditation Trait, though she may perform rituals of higher level. She still knows her primary path to the level of her full Thaumaturgical mastery; she simply lacks the spiritual force or focus to use it. When her player raises the character's Meditation Trait, she can use the path to the higher level.

Meditation has many uses in its own right, in accordance with an Indian adept's overmastering will. At the Storyteller's option, a *sadhu*'s player can substitute an Intelligence + Meditation roll for a path power's Willpower roll — but at the cost of the power taking as much time as a ritual of the same level. Meditation is not quick.

PATHS

Sadhus independently developed some versions of well-known Hermetic paths. Contact with the Middle Eastern ashipu inspired other paths. Ancient contact between the Daitya and their Setite cousins in Egypt led to a Sadhana version of the Path of Duat. This "Path of Yama," named after the Hindu King of the Dead, employs a Willpower roll instead of a Charisma + Occult roll, and does not require any sort of talisman.

Many Indian path names include the suffixes -*Raja*, "Rulership, Mastery" or -*Vidya*, "Lore."

Alchemy (Rasayana): **Blood Magic: Secrets of Thaumaturgy**

Conjuring (Brahma-Vidya): **Vampire: The Masquerade**

Elemental Mastery (Yaksha-Vidya): **Guide to the Camarilla**

Focused Mind (Echo of Nirvana): **Blood Magic: Secrets of Thaumaturgy**

Hands of Destruction (Hand of Mahakala): **Vampire: The Masquerade**

Movement of the Mind (Rishi's Hand): **Vampire: The Masquerade**

Oneiromancy (Lakshmi's Wishes): **Blood Magic: Secrets of Thaumaturgy**

Snake Inside (Temptation of Mara): **Blood Magic: Secrets of Thaumaturgy**

Spirit Manipulation (Asura-Raja): **Guide to the Camarilla**

THE PATH OF BLOOD NECTAR

Amrita is the Nectar of Divinity that grants perfect bliss and immortality to all who drink it. At the creation of the world, the gods needed the help of the asuras to obtain the *Amrita*. The demon-gods demanded a share of the nectar, but cunning Vishnu tricked them out of their portion. Those demons who became incarnate as Kindred eventually learned to create their own nectar of divinity. All Kindred can confer a fraction of undead power upon mortals by feeding them vitae, turning them into ghouls. Through the Path of Blood Nectar, an undead *sadhu* can do much more — turning her blood into a potion that briefly confers any one of her powers on a mortal or another vampire.

A few sorcerers of the Assamite clan also know this path, and find it a useful adjunct to Quietus. Other practitioners of Dur-An-Ki have not yet learned to produce Blood Nectar.

System: Blood Nectar requires one minute of concentration per level of the potion created. In this time, the vampire engages in yogic and vitae-shifting exercises and meditation. The character's player needs a single success on a Willpower roll, at the usual difficulty for a path power. At the end of this period, the alchemist opens a vein to release the blood nectar. Another person must drink the blood nectar immediately to gain its effects: The nectar loses potency within one minute of leaving the sorcerer's body.

Unlike most paths, Blood Nectar costs one blood point per level to use.

Each dose of Blood Nectar confers one of the *sadhu*'s powers upon the imbiber for a single scene. The sorcerer can confer either Disciplines or Thaumaturgical path powers, but not the effects of rituals. Of course, a sorcerer cannot impart a Discipline at a higher level than she herself knows.

Someone who imbibes a Blood Nectar gains that Discipline or path, up to the level the sorcerer chose to store. For instance, a level three nectar of Dominate would enable the imbiber to use the first three powers of that Discipline. If the imbiber already knows the Discipline to as high or higher level than the potion carries, the Blood Nectar has no effect except to grant the person one blood point's worth of vitae. Each dose of Blood Nectar counts as one blood point, no many how much vitae its creation consumed.

A person who drinks Blood Nectar does not gain any of the sorcerer's Abilities, so he might not be very good at using the powers gained. On the other hand, he might possess more innate talent (represented by a higher Attribute + Ability pool) than the *sadhu* herself.

Only one path cannot be stored as a Blood Nectar potion: the Path of Blood Nectar itself. The inscrutable God of Logic, before whom even gods, demons and Buddhas bow, forbids it on grounds that it could create an infinite regress.

A character can also wield the effects of only one Blood Nectar potion at a time. If a person imbibes a second nectar, the higher-level potion instantly cancels out the lower-level potion. Nectars of equal level cancel each other out, leaving nothing.

The enchanted vitae does not lose the power to turn a mortal into a ghoul, or to forge a blood bond. Anyone who plans on "borrowing" powers through Blood Nectar had best keep careful track of how often they imbibe potions, and from what *sadhu*.

As mastery of the Path of Blood Nectar increases, a sorcerer can store a Discipline to higher levels:

- •   Confer one level of a Discipline or path.
- ••   Confer two levels of a Discipline or path.
- ••• Confer three levels of a Discipline or path.
- •••• Confer four levels of a Discipline or path.
- ••••• Confer five levels of a Discipline or path.

THE PATH OF KARMA

Knowledge of other people's pasts is one of the most common powers claimed for Indian magicians, even to knowing a person's previous incarnations. Any mystic worth his title can remember his own past lives. Knowledge of the future is nearly as easy. Through the Siddhi of Karma, an Indian sorcerer can learn many secrets about another person's life, both past and yet to come. At higher levels, a *sadhu* can call upon the Abilities from his past lives. A true master can wrench control of the cycle of reincarnation to change destinies in this life and beyond.

Each power requires the expenditure of one blood point.

• THREADS OF THE PAST

The first *siddhi* of this path is knowledge of the important events of another person's past — the events that made her who she is tonight, and brought her to her present place.

System: For each success rolled by the player, the character receives one brief impression of an important event in the target's past. As a guideline, the Storyteller should describe each impression in one short paragraph of pure description, like a snapshot. The *sadhu* does not receive these impressions in any particular order; he can only guess at their interpretation. If the *sadhu* uses this power on a Kindred, however, the list of impressions always includes the subject's Embrace as the single most important event in that person's existence. The sorcerer also learns the target's common name (though not his True Name).

•• WEAVE OF THE FUTURE

The *sadhu* can receive brief impressions of potentially important events within the next year of the subject's existence. The events may be good or bad, dangers or opportunities. A person can try to avoid foreseen dangers, but this is never reliable. Sometimes the very action taken to avoid an event causes it to take place.

A *sadhu* can use this power for his own benefit, but only rarely. He cannot learn about events from his own future until all the events previously foreseen either have taken place or he has successfully avoided them.

System: For each success the player rolls, the *sadhu* sees one brief scene from the target's future (or his own). Again, the Storyteller should describe these in one image, like a snapshot, with no explanation of context or meaning, though the character can see if the subject faces obvious danger.

••• CERTAIN FATE

At this level, a *sadhu* can see farther and pick out the events, people and forces that inexorably shape the person's future. The magician gains more detailed knowledge, but the subject has less chance to change the future: The events grow from the whole shape of the person's life and, Hindus believe, past lives. Once again, these aren't necessarily bad things, but the Certain Fate often presents dire but obscure warnings. A *sadhu* cannot use this power on herself.

System: For each success rolled, the character receives one fact about the subject's entire future existence; for instance, an important conflict he will face, or a person who will become important to him in some way. As is the way with prophecies, the sorcerer sees the setup of future situations but generally not how they turn out. If the *sadhu* receives three or more successes, the visions include a scene of the subject's most probable death and whether or not a mortal subject is destined to become a Kindred, wraith or *kuei-jin*.

•••• PAST LIVES

At this level, a *sadhu* obtains moderately detailed, capsule biographies of a person's previous incarnations. A sorcerer can examine her own past lives, too. In India, people believe that events in this life reward and punish their deeds in past lives, so knowing previous incarnations can help one cope with this life's trials. The sooner you expiate your sins, the sooner you can accumulate merit for a better life in your next incarnation.

On a more practical level, a *sadhu* can use this power to temporarily gain Abilities that she knew in her past lives. She can thus gain virtually any skill she wants.

System: Each use of this power provides an overview of one of the subject's past lives. By itself, this has no immediate, practical benefit, but it's a great way to impress one's aptitudes on other people: They instinctively know that the *sadhu* tells them the truth.

A *sadhu* can also use this power to "remember" Abilities from her own past lives. For each success her player rolls, the *sadhu* gains one dot to place in any Ability she wants, subject only to the limitation that she cannot raise any Ability above three dots. The Abilities last a single scene. Note that the Ability comes from a past life, and are thus limited by the age of the Cainite in question. For example, a thousand-year-old *sadhu* would not be able to call upon her past lives for potential with the Computer Knowledge.

••••• MASTER OF SAMSARA

Samsara is the cycle of birth, death and rebirth. A master of *Karma* can not only look ahead to see a person's next incarnation, he can shape that incarnation to some degree. Even more amazingly, he has a limited power to reverse the wheel of *samsara* and briefly restore people to a previous incarnation.

System: All applications of this power require only a single success on the player's roll, but demand that the player spend one point of *permanent* Willpower. For this, the *sadhu* not only receives a capsule description of the person's next life, he can perform one of the following feats:

• Ordain one fact about that person's future life (nearly anything, comparable in power to imposing a Dark Fate but it could just as easily be a good thing).

• Preordain that a person becomes a wraith or Cathayan vampire upon death… or not.

• Transform a mortal (not a vampire) into whoever or whatever she was in a previous life for one scene. The target character retains only a dreamlike awareness of her "current" self. The subject temporarily becomes a different character. The *sadhu* can choose among the incarnations revealed by the Past Lives power, transform the subject in her immediately previous incarnation, or leave it all to chance and the Storyteller's whim.

• Transform a mortal (not a vampire) into whoever or whatever he will be in his next life; or

• Set the circumstances of his own next incarnation.

An undead *sadhu* can view and select his own future existence after his destruction as a vampire, but cannot use any of the other powers on himself. A *sadhu* who uses Master of Samsara often takes a rather casual attitude to the prospect of Final Death, since the *sadhu* has already selected a comfortable next incarnation… possibly including revenge on his enemies.

PATH OF PRAAPTI

Many Indian manuals of magic promise to teach Praapti, the power of instantaneous travel. The *sadhus* developed a path devoted to this power. At low levels, a sorcerer can travel only short distances, but at the higher levels of mastery a practitioner can move hundreds of miles. Some Cathayan vampires command a magical power to teleport long distances along lines of mystical force; Indian Kindred needed some way to match their mobility.

In legend, a master of Praapti could travel to the moon. Three centuries ago, the sorcerer Raivata devised an ancillary ritual that enabled him to perform this feat… but Raivata was a better mystic than astronomer. He forgot that he could see his lunar destination because it was in sunlight. No sorcerer since then has performed Raivata's ritual.

The Indian Tremere helped their European colleagues develop a Hermetic version of this path, called the Path of Mercury.

System: Individual levels of the Praapti Path do not require special description. The chart below describes the path level needed to teleport a given range.

To use this path safely, the *sadhu* must see his destination or know it very well. She can use a telescope, but TV images or magazine pictures will not suffice. If the character can distinctly see the target location, a failed roll results in nothing worse than some wasted vitae (and a lost point of permanent Willpower, if the player rolls a botch). Likewise, a magician faces little risk in teleporting to the other side of a wall.

When performing a long-distance "blind teleport," however, rolling a botch means that the character succeeded in working the magic… but reappeared interpenetrating a solid object. This inflicts one health level of aggravated damage to the vampire for every "1" rolled. Losing three or more health levels indicates that so much of the sorcerer's body fused with other objects (usually the ground) that she can free herself only with

great difficulty — if at all. Fortitude enables a vampire to soak damage from a botched blind teleport.

Blind teleports can modify a Praapti power's difficulty depending on the thaumaturge's familiarity with the target location:

Familiarity	Difficulty Modifier
Intimately familiar (own haven)	-1
Moderately familiar (visited regularly)	+0
Unseen, but an understood spatial relationship ("On the other side of this wall")	+0
Not very familiar (visited a few times; hazy on spatial relationship)	+1
Unfamiliar (a point on a map)	+2

Even if the Willpower roll succeeds, a blind teleport rarely lands a sorcerer exactly on target. Accuracy varies with the number of successes. Four to five successes means arriving exactly on target, while one success gives an error of 10% of the distance traveled, in any direction. For instance, a teleport of 400 miles could result in an error of up to 40 miles.

•   Teleport up to 10 yards.
••   Teleport up to 50 yards;
•••   Teleport up to 500 yards;
••••   Teleport up to 5 miles;
•••••   Teleport up to 500 miles.

RITUALS

LEVEL ONE RITUALS

ARMOR OF DIAMOND SERENITY

This *tantra* beseeches Shiva, the demon king Bali or some other ascetic god to purge the magician's mind of all the snares of mortal passions. This foretaste of Enlightenment temporarily grants a will as unyielding as diamond.

System: If the ritual succeeds, the magician becomes immune to frenzy and Rötschreck for the rest of the night. The character also receives -2 difficulty on Willpower rolls, while attacks that use her Willpower as the difficulty receive a +2 penalty to their difficulty (to a maximum of 10). On the other hand, the magician cannot expend vitae to raise Physical Attributes while the ritual remains in effect.

RAKTA-MAYA RITUALS

This label covers numerous rituals. Each ritual enables a magician to hypnotize a willing audience into seeing one specific illusion. For instance, one *maya* ritual makes an audience see the Indian Rope Trick. Another ritual makes the audience see the magician levitate. A third produces the hypnotic illusion of maidens leaping out of a basket, dancing for the amusement of the crowd, then vanishing into the basket once more.

System: Unlike other rituals, these illusions call for a Charisma + Performance roll (difficulty 4), as the magician persuades the audience to accept wonders. These rituals can affect several dozen people, whom the magician sets apart from the mundane world through an enclosure scratched on the ground.

WATER WALKING

Through a sacrifice of porridge and *ghee* to Varuna, the god of waters, the *sadhu* gains the classic holy man's power of walking on water.

System: If the *tantra* succeeds, the magician can walk on water. The power lasts a full scene. If something should knock the sorcerer off his feet, however, the magic ends and the *sadhu* splashes into the water.

LEVEL TWO RITUALS

ANIMAA

This ritual grants one of the classic *siddhis*, the power of clairvoyant shrinking or microscopic vision. The magician can see tiny things clearly, as if he were the size of a bird, a mouse, an ant, a grain of dust, or even smaller.

System: For each success in the ritual, the magician gains x10 magnification on her eyesight. She concentrates and closes her eyes. Then she imagines opening her eyes, and finds herself apparently shrunk to the appropriate size. The power is entirely clairvoyant, though; the magician does not physically shrink.

ASH OF AGNI'S CURSE

The magician burns an offering to Agni, god of fire and the sacrifice, while beseeching the god to withdraw his favor from the fires of the magician's enemies. The magician then gathers the ash of the sacrifice and stores it in a box or jar. A handful of the ash, scattered on a fire, extinguishes any mundane blaze.

System: For each success rolled by the magician's player, the magician gains one dose of magic ash that she (but no one else) can use later. Each dose of ash extinguishes 100 square feet of flame.

GARIMAA

This ritual grants another classic *siddhi*, the power of becoming "immovably heavy." For a time, the magician becomes almost impossible to lift, knock off her feet or push in any direction she does not want to go.

System: If the ritual succeeds, an effective Strength of 8 resists any force that attempts to move the magician against his will. The *sadhu* does not personally gain a higher Strength Trait; he cannot lift boulders or crash through walls. The magical force acts in a purely passive way, to resist other forces.

LEVEL THREE RITUALS

DESTINY'S CALL

Indian magicians have a reputation for weaving the strands of fate. This *tantra* enables the magician to meet a person having whatever qualities she wants. Somehow, coincidence brings the magician and the target together — although the magician does not know in advance precisely who comes at Destiny's Call.

System: This ritual acts like the Presence power of Summon, but instead of a specific person known to the sorcerer, Destiny's Call draws in an unknown person who meets three conditions set by the magician. The *sadhu* can set physical conditions, such as "an old man with green eyes" or "a blonde virgin girl"; or mental conditions, such as "a person interested in Ming pottery," "a skilled mathematician" or "a person of absolute honesty"; or social conditions, such as "the richest man in Benares" or "a recently jilted lover." He cannot set supernatural conditions, such as "a werewolf" or "a Methuselah." Since the sorcerer cannot specify every aspect of who comes, he must stay alert to recognize when the desired person appears. Sometimes the *sadhu* calls a person who fits all the conditions, but who proves surprising in other ways.

Destiny's Call dissipates at dawn. The desired person might not appear by then: This may happen if the only person who fits the conditions started at a great distance. The magician can perform the ritual again on subsequent nights, until the person appears or the *sadhu* gives up. The target feels drawn to the sorcerer's location without knowing why, and may well resist the call even though outrageous coincidences help her along her way.

LEPER'S CURSE

The *Atharva-Veda* includes several charms to cure leprosy… but a Brahmin can reverse a sacred rite and turn it into a curse upon an enemy. To curse a mortal with leprosy, a *sadhu* calls upon Agni, Indra and other gods of light and life to deliver the victim unto Nirriti, the goddess of misery and destruction.

System: If the *sadhu* performs the curse correctly, the mortal victim contracts leprosy within a week. This is true leprosy, not a magical simulation. The leprosy-curing spell from the *Atharva-Veda* can remove the curse, however, if the victim uses it within one month of contracting the disease.

MILK OF PUUTANAA

Indian legend tells of a demoness called Puutanaa who kills infants by suckling them with her poisoned milk. Undead *sadhus* can call upon Puutanaa, by their family connection as fellow demons, to poison a child of their choice. This baleful spell shocks even vampires with its viciousness. Daitya legend says that a *sadhu* created the ritual at the behest of a king's junior wife, who wanted to discredit her rival and clear the way for her own child to inherit the throne.

System: The *sadhu* needs a sympathetic link to the victim, consisting of the child's name and the names of the child's parents. The next milk that the child drinks carries Puutanaa's venom, which always kills. The curse cannot affect anyone after his first adult tooth grows in.

LEVEL FOUR RITUALS

AURAVA

Some Indian sorcerers can conjure *aurava*, a magical fire that burns under water. *Sadhus* have learned to imitate this feat. *Aurava* has some practical uses; for instance, one sorcerer used *aurava* to kill a Cathayan who slept in a

water-filled cave. More often, however, *sadhus* create the magical golden flame simply as a wonder to impress other Kindred. The ritual involves drawing a *mandala* on a golden tray underwater, placing an offering at the center, and challenging Agni to claim his due. When the offering bursts into flame, the magician can carry the tray about and use the *aurava* to set other things on fire.

System: The magical golden fire burns on the tray for a full scene. Substances that would be flammable in air can catch fire from the *aurava*, and they burn until the magic fire runs out of fuel or something other than water extinguishes them.

WARDED WOMB

The Indians have a story about a snake-demoness who destroys a pregnant woman's embryo and replaces it with one of her own spawn, so the woman gives birth to a snake. Through an oblation of milk and *ghee* and an amulet of lead, a *sadhu* can ban the snake-demoness from a woman's womb and guarantee that she delivers a safely human child.

System: Correctly performed, the ritual protects a pregnant woman against miscarriage and guarantees an easy delivery of a healthy child. It also eradicates any supernatural taint from the infant. Progeny of werewolves, werecats or (most particularly) the weresnakes of India do not inherit any supernatural heritage (though Storytellers using **Werewolf: The Apocalypse** are advised to either increase this ritual's level or remove it altogether). The ritual also negates the condition of being born a revenant and the potential for any other innate supernatural talent other than True Faith.

LEVEL FIVE RITUAL

TRANSCENDENTALLY SATISFYING BODY-FILLING

In Sanskrit, this powerful *tantra* has the sesquipedalian name of *parapurakayapravesa*. It enables a magician to enter and possess the body of another person. The sorcerer can then "learn his mind, understand his experiences, and even enjoy his wives." Although the sexual possibilities are not lost on *sadhus*, they also find more practical uses for the ritual. For instance, this ritual enables an undead *sadhu* to live again in another person's body, if only for a short time.

The *tantra* requires a drum made from the top of a human skull, the sacrifice of a horse to Shiva, an oblation of *soma* and finally drinking the *soma* dregs mixed with the horse's blood. The spell also requires something that came from the mortal victim's body, such as hair or feces, which likewise burns in the sacrificial fire. The *sadhu* vanishes and merges with the victim, wherever he may be. The *sadhu* performs the ritual at a shrine to Shiva previously consecrated by the magician and used for worship for at least a year.

System: The ritual works only on mortal humans (not anyone with any sort of supernatural powers), but they cannot resist its power — assuming the *sadhu*'s player makes a successful roll. The ritual works no matter how great the target's distance.

The effect resembles the Dominate power of Possession, but with certain advantages and limitations. The possessing *sadhu* can act freely during the day — her own body doesn't have to stay awake because it doesn't exist — and she can riffle freely through the victim's memories and use his Abilities as if they were her own. If she wants, the sorcerer can simple "ride along" and share the victim's mind and experiences while remaining hidden. On the other hand, the possessor cannot use any Disciplines at all. The possession ends at the next sunset, when the *sadhu* reappears in his own body at the site of the sacrifice. The *sadhu* can voluntarily end the body-filling before then, but had best be sure that her shrine is not then in daylight….

When the possession ends, the victim regains control of his mind and body. The effect on the victim depends on the Storyteller's discretion. If the magician passively "rode along," the victim might suffer nothing worse than a few nightmares. If the *sadhu* engages in abhorrent crimes and degradations while in the victim's body, the spiritual violation might place the victim in a coma for days, or even have accompanying Humanity problems.

LEVEL SIX RITUAL

LOOM OF VISHNU

This potent *tantra* enables a magician to usurp the god Vishnu's power of cosmic illusion. The magician burns an oblation of milk, *ghee*, *soma* and her own vitae within a special *mandala*, then burns a picture of a scene she wants to create. That scene then appears in solid form — real to every test that mortal senses can devise.

System: The zone of *maya* lasts until dawn. At the sun's rising, it vanishes like a dream.

This power of illusion has three limits:

• The illusion has a maximum diameter of 60 feet (although it may seem much larger from inside). If a person steps outside the illusion's actual boundary, he returns to normal reality.

• The illusion cannot cause real harm to anyone who enters it. The magician can set whatever rules he wants for this pocket of altered reality: People can fly, they become rotting animate corpses, *anything*, but the maya itself cannot inflict real damage. If a person does something stupid and hurts himself, however that's not the illusion's doing.

• The zone of *maya* must include the magician's sacrificial fire. The magician can place it in some context that hides its significance, such as placing it in a fireplace or disguising it as a campfire. Extinguishing the fire instantly breaks the illusion.

Auspex hints at the falsity of the scene. To Heightened Senses, everything in the scene looks a little too regular, without the fine detail of real things. Illusory creatures lack auras; the Spirit's Touch detects no psychic impressions on objects. The Storyteller should not come out and tell players that their characters have entered an illusion; let them figure it out for themselves.

LEVEL NINE RITUAL

EYE OF MAHAKALA

This ritual, one of the most powerful known to India's vampires, invokes Shiva as Mahakala, Lord of Time and Final Destroyer, to annihilate a small part of the world's illusion. What the magician commands Mahakala to look upon, ceases to be and never was. Everyone except the *sadhu* himself forgets the target's existence, because they never knew about it in the first place.

System: This ritual requires that the magician fast in the midst of an elaborate *mandala*. As the character starves past the Incapacitated health level, the player spends a permanent Willpower point for the character to hold off torpor for a few minutes. Only then, when the *sadhu* hovers at the brink of death, can she see Mahakala's face and guide the Destroyer to his target. A wise *sadhu* keeps an acolyte on hand with blood to revive her after this most fearsome sending.

Mahakala's glance can unmake anything up to the size of a skyscraper, or any one person. The magician needs the victim's full name and the full names of both parents. The few *sadhus* who even know of this ritual's existence also say that it probably cannot unmake gods or creatures of commensurate power, such as the vampire *pitris*.

The world adjusts to conceal whatever Mahakala destroys. Unmaking a skyscraper does not leave a big hole in the middle of a city. Someone would have built *something* there, so that plot of land holds another building instead, or a park.

People have become much more difficult to unmake in the last century. Modern folk spread causal links around the globe, from mortgage payments to Internet chats, and the weave of *maya* tries to preserve as much as it can. If a person has too many connections to too many people and events, even Mahakala cannot remove them from reality; or perhaps reality replaces the person with someone almost identical. If a character becomes a target of Mahakala's Eye, the player rolls a dice pool of the character's two highest social Backgrounds (Allies, Contacts, Fame, Herd, Influence, Resources or Status) at difficulty 9 to resist annihilation.

CHAPTER FOUR: WANGA: LEGACY OF THE CARIBBEAN

"I am sending you to find [my enemy]. Rid me of his head, rid me of his memory, rid me of his thought, rid me of his house, rid me of all my enemies, visible and invisible, bring down on them thunder and lightning."
— Portion of a prayer invoking Saint Expedit to slay a foe

Like the land from which it hails, Wanga is a mystery to the Western world and the Western Kindred alike. It is a study in contradictions, both ancient and relatively new, neither wholly African nor wholly anything else. More than a mere path of magic, it is a religion and a system of belief that would seem inaccessible to the vampires who practice it. It venerates life, calls upon spiritual beings and divine emissaries who do not take kindly to frivolous requests. Yet as the Final Nights approach, more and more of the descendants of Caine search for something, anything, in which to believe; thus, Wanga's popularity, not merely as a path of blood magic but as a world view, has begun to grow among the Kindred.

Among the kine, the term "Wanga" refers to charms, amulets and spells, usually of a harmful variety. The Kindred who practice this form of blood sorcery use the term to refer instead to the system of magic itself. Since the Afro-Caribbean religions use different names for their practitioners, we use *wangateur* as a neutral term unless referring to a follower of a specific religion such as Haitian *voudoun* or *candomblé*. The Kindred use the term in the same way: Many *wangateurs* think of themselves as *santeros*, *houngans* or whatnot.

WANGA THROUGH THE AGES

The development of Wanga — and indeed, the religions on which it is based — can be broken into two distinct periods. It is neither fully of Africa nor of the New World, but equal parts of both.

AFRICA

The religious system that would spawn Wanga and the Afro-Caribbean religions developed among the Ewe, Fon, and primarily the Yoruba peoples in what are tonight Nigeria and Benin. The Yoruba — master smiths of brass and iron, weavers and crafts-makers, artists and sculptors — have lived in cities for over a millennium and put the lie to most Western ideas of Africa's "savagery." Some Kindred from that region take credit for influencing the Yoruba to their cultural peak. Precisely how reliable these claims are is open to interpretation, and even the most vocal proponents of this viewpoint tend not to shout all

TRUE BELIEVERS

Wanga is a religious practice, not merely another form of Thaumaturgy tacked on for the sake of cultural inclusiveness. While some vampires adhere to the precepts of a specific Afro-Caribbean faith, most Kindred *wangateurs* practice a mishmash that combines aspects of any or all of these religions. Be they strict adherents or more lax in their interpretations, *wangateurs* must have real faith (though not necessarily True Faith) in the God and spirits revered by these religions. Kindred who don't worship some combination of these faiths have a great deal of difficulty mastering Wanga.

Most *wangateurs* do not teach their secrets to anyone who does not share their beliefs. Even if a faithless *wangateur* wannabe can find an instructor, she can never call upon Wanga's full potential; the *loa*, *orishas*, Saints or whatever you wish to call them do not smile upon those who invoke them spuriously. The player of a Kindred who is not one of the faithful raises the difficulties of all his Wanga-related rolls by 1. Furthermore, the player is always considered to have one automatic inclination toward failure to overcome in her rolls; treat it as an extra "phantom die" in her pool that always rolls a 1. Note that this makes normal failures botches! Wanga is not for the faint of heart to begin with. Attempting it without the proper faith to back it up is just asking for trouble — one request the spirits are only too happy to oblige.

that loudly, for fear of attracting the attention of something even greater.

Modern records — what few exist — fail utterly to reveal how the Yoruba religion first metamorphosed into a Kindred system of blood magic; as long as Kindred have dwelt among the Yoruba, it seems, they have practiced magics rooted in the local faith. The Yoruba worship a single divine being: Olodumare, the "owner of all destinies." Olodumare created the world, and Olodumare maps out the fate of every living being.

Olodumare is present everywhere, and in everything. He manifests throughout the world as a spiritual energy called *ashé*. *Ashé* is present throughout all of creation, but is most concentrated in the essence of living things. Plants possess *ashé*, as does the blood of living animals — and people. Kindred who subscribe to the Afro-Caribbean religions feel that they feed upon *ashé* when they drink the blood of others.

Despite his great power, prayers and petitions never address Olodumare directly. Instead, the God of the Yoruba uses intermediaries, divine messengers who carry word between him and his worshippers, and who manage the little details of running creation with which Olodumare himself can't (or won't) be bothered.

The *orishas* occupy something of a middle ground between the mortal and the divine. Not quite gods but far more than human, they serve as messengers between Olodumare and His worshippers. Many *orishas* are spirits of nature, aspects of weather, geography or human nature. Many others are local or household "gods," patrons of a specific city or family. Some were created directly by Olodumare; others are spirits of the dead who have become something greater.

These ancestor spirits — called *Ara Orun*, or "people of heaven" — are among the most important figures in Yoruba religion. They are the most frequently evoked, particularly in family ceremonies, and their names and symbols were often carved into the beads of the Yoruba kings' crowns (and, considering that there have been Kindred in Africa since the dawn of man, at least according to many origin stories, the odds are good that some of the ancestors worshipped by the Yoruba weren't 100 percent dead at the time). Every year at the time of the yam harvest, most Yoruba cities celebrate a week-long festival in which the *Ara Orun* are said to return to the mortal world to hear petitions and punish those who use evil magics to threaten the community. These ancestor spirits are portrayed by *egungun*, masked dancers swathed in heavy cloths. While some *Ara Orun* — and the Egungun who portray them — can be quite generous when hearing petitions, others are unnecessarily cruel in their behavior. Approaching the *Ara Orun* is never guaranteed to be a safe practice.

Yoruban Kindred used to pass themselves off as *Ara Orun* or other manifestations of the *orisha*, as their powers were usually more than sufficient to convince the gullible of their "divine" nature. This practice thrived — for a time. A number of African Kindred, however, vanished mysteriously during the heyday of Yoruba culture. As *orisha* impersonators made up the vast majority of those who disappeared, the practice halted rather abruptly.

For a time, the Yoruba dominated West Africa. Yoruba tribes held trade routes that spread over the entirety of West Africa, Yoruba kings demanded and received tribute from other tribes (the city of Oyo was particularly powerful in this regard) and the Yoruba Kindred became as princes of their domains.

The situation couldn't last. The beginning of the slave trade to the New World in the 1600s did not

IS THERE AN AFRICAN TERM FOR "MUNCHKIN"?

Somewhere, someone read the previous paragraph and immediately leapt to a conclusion that goes something like: "Hey! If the spirits of Wanga can do all these powerful things, then calling directly on Olodumare must provide even more power!"

Never mind that this simply isn't the way things are done; some power-hungry goober with no real understanding of Wanga or religion (or common sense or roleplaying…) will eventually attempt it. Storytellers are encouraged to consider any use of Wanga that directly invokes Olodumare an automatic botch, regardless of circumstances.

substantially harm the Yoruba as a culture; rather, the downfall of the Yoruba "empire" can be traced to the last years of the 18th century. The fall of the Yoruba Kindred, however, began much earlier. For centuries the cities of the Yoruba warred constantly, with each other and with outside tribes. The local vampires, unable to maintain stable domains, were crippled in the face of Western Kindred who arrived alongside the slave traders. Most were forced to flee. Some traveled to other regions of the African continent, others to Europe or even the New World, where they dwelt near and fed from the slave populations that were the closest simulations they could find to the home they'd lost.

Outsiders discovered West African blood magic in 1794. Louis Doumer Millerand, a well-traveled French Tremere who'd long been fascinated by the strange mysticism practiced by Haitian slaves, fled Paris during the Reign of Terror and used his period of exile to study the roots of those beliefs in Western Africa. While his precise activities and experiences in Benin remain a closely guarded secret, he discoursed with a number of native blood sorcerers and escaped back to Vienna with his newfound knowledge despite a number of near-fatal attempts to stop him. The Kindred of the Yoruba could now add knowledge-hungry Tremere to the list of Westerners who wanted to exploit them.

Two years later, a coalition of lesser chiefs overthrew the (weak) king of the city of Oyo. Vassal territories broke away; wars between the Yoruba cities continued throughout the following century. Other tribes invaded, sensing opportunity in instability. While this was primarily a war of kine, the local Kindred found their domains even further destabilized by the conflict.

In disarray, no longer even marginally unified as a people, the Yoruba fell victim to slave traders in ever increasing numbers. The Yoruba made up the majority of all slaves shipped from Benin's ports from 1820 to 1840.

Most of the Yoruba slaves were bound for either Cuba or Brazil, though some of them ended up in Haiti and the United States.

The Yoruba still exist today, in Southwest Nigeria. They are, in fact, a more unified people than they have ever been. Their religion flourishes, though it is now just one among many. Some African Nosferatu still practice alongside them, as do some more inscrutable elements of Kindred society. By the modern nights, however, *wangateurs* who follow the Afro-Caribbean religions far outnumber those who still practice the faith in its original form (though many Western *wangateurs* still visit the Yoruba, intent on learning the most ancient histories and secrets of their craft).

THE NEW WORLD

The adaptation of the Yoruba faith into other forms began the instant the first captive tribesman set foot, hungry and frightened, on the shores of his new and unpleasant home. Although aspects of *voudoun*, *Santería* and others can be traced back many centuries, the specific identifiable roots of the modern Afro-Caribbean religions first appeared in the 17th century. Slaves needed something in which to believe, and many of them felt that their old gods had proven insufficient to the tasks required of them, else the Yoruba would not now suffer in chains.

It is important to note that these slaves did not actually betray their faith. In many African belief systems, the core of belief was strength. A conquered tribe would often shift over to the worship of their conquerors' gods or *orishas*. Obviously, if this tribe had proven stronger, their guardian spirits were stronger as well, and the strongest gods and *orishas* were obviously most worthy of worship.

This mindset carried over to include the slave traders. The slaves, who had been taken from their homes by men with weapons the likes of which they had never seen, must have thought the gods of the white man to be quite powerful.

This didn't make the behavior of the white man right, of course, but the morality of a people and the power of its spirits were completely separate issues.

The Kindred were heavily involved in the African slave trade. Such a massive source of vitae, people with no rights, people often kept locked up, people expected to die young — it was a cornucopia that many vampires found themselves unable to resist. Some particularly foolish Tremere and African Nosferatu have attempted to claim credit for the development of the Afro-Caribbean forms of Wanga, maintaining that such practices were taught to the slaves by those Kindred who remembered them from the old country.

Such an idea is laughable.

The newly arrived slaves were often expected to abandon their old religions and adopt this strange, foreign thing called "Christianity." The displaced Africans responded the way they always did — by incorporating these new "spirits" and customs into their own beliefs. *Orishas* became saints, and vice-versa. Olodumare was just another name of the "one God" the white overseers kept insisting they worship. And as for Christ — well, Jesus Christ was an unusual case. Many of the slaves accepted the Christian belief in Christ's divinity, incorporating him as a new aspect of their own religion; others lumped him in with the saints as simply another *orisha*.

The religions that developed, while each unique and distinct from the others, share important aspects. All of them revolve around the worship of a single supreme deity and his spiritual agents. Rituals to invoke those spirits differ, but they all involve common themes, such as the sacrifice of food and drink to the *loa* or *orishas*, the use of ritual symbols and the power of music, herbs, and — in many cases — the blood of animals. None of these religions involve human sacrifice. Some truly obscure underground cults — such as Cuban *Abakua* — are exceptions to this rule. Such cults are viewed with fear and hatred by most practitioners of the Afro-Caribbean faiths, and are no more representative of the norm than any other criminal subculture.

More accurately, none of these religions *as practiced by the kine* involve such sacrifices. Kindred *wangateurs*, on the other hand, have developed rituals far bloodier than those used by their mortal contemporaries.

RELIGIOUS DIFFERENCES

Voudoun. Santería. Candomblé. Shango cults. Palo Mayombe. Obeayisne. All these religions and more developed in the slave populations taken from the Yoruba, Ewe and Fon tribes of Western Africa. Had we 10 times the space available, we could not fit a comprehensive — or even moderately cohesive — history and description of every one of these faiths. Thus, much of this discussion is generalized to apply to all of them together; details that pertain to specific faiths are given only where such distinctions are vital to the understanding of Wanga itself. Anyone interested in learning more about these fascinating systems of belief is strongly encouraged to do further research.

Still, some effort must be made to differentiate between the various faiths under discussion because the various *orishas* and spirits of these religions are invoked during the practice of Wanga. Discussed (very briefly) are *voudoun*, *Santería* and Palo Mayombe — three of the most widespread and heavily practiced of the Afro-Caribbean faiths. Brazilian *candomblé*, though equally as widespread, is very closely related to *Santería*; the differences lie primarily in minor details, spelling and pronunciation. For each we list a small handful of its *loa/orishas/Enkisi/*spirits. These represent merely the tiniest sampling — some of these religions recognize literally thousands of divine messengers — but it should be enough to get you started.

VOUDOUN

Voudoun (alternately spelled, of course, Voodoo) developed on the island of Santo Domingo, known tonight as Haiti. Haitian *voudoun* has most influenced American centers of "voodoo" such as New Orleans, and is the system most often portrayed (wildly inaccurately) by Hollywood. *Voudoun* claims fewer links to the Yoruba people than do the other religions under discussion, instead drawing equally from the Yoruba, the Fon, and several other tribes of

Western Africa. Those who practice *voudoun* are called *serviteurs*. Priests of *voudoun* are called *houngans* if male or *mambos* if female. The culmination of many *voudoun* ceremonies involves the possession of the houngan (or, alternately, another participant), by the *loa* being petitioned; this is called being "ridden" by the *loa*. The *loa* of *voudoun* are divided into families, called *nanchons*. The *rada loa* tend to be more benign (though that doesn't necessarily make them nice). The *petro loa* are darker, more vicious spirits. A third nanchon, the *ghede loa*, are associated with death, and function somewhere between the extremes of Rada and Petro. Many *loa* have multiple incarnations that cross family boundaries.

The *Vouodoun* name for Olodumare, the one God, is *Bondye*.

Some of the more important *loa* of *voudoun* include the following.

Legba

Perhaps the greatest of the *loa*, Legba is one of the oldest cosmic forces. He represents the sun, the bringer of life. Legba stands as the guardian of the crossroads between this world and the next. As such, all prayers to the *loa* must first go through him, for he has the authority to allow — or refuse to allow — a *loa* to respond. Legba appears as a man past his physical prime; many *serviteurs* fear that as his own strength withers and his influence fades, Carrefour (a *petro loa* who represents shadow and darkness) will gain prominence as the new guardian of the crossroads. Extremely, perhaps infinitely, knowledgeable, Legba is somewhat prophetic, though what he sees and what he reveals are not necessarily the same thing. Legba is most frequently associated with St. Peter.

Damballah

Also called Damballah-wedo, Damballah is one of the most ancient *loa*, present, some say, at the creation of the universe itself. Damballah is the snake, the great serpent. He is associated with stability and wisdom, and is seen as a fatherly *loa* by many of his worshippers. He possesses great patience, though his fury, once aroused, is terrible to behold. He is associated with the rainbow, which also falls under the domain of his wife, Aida-wedo. Damballah is most commonly associated with St. Patrick.

Baron Samedi

The Baron is the most powerful aspect of the Ghede family of death. Baron Samedi is the patron of the graveyard, and it is said that no human can die before the Baron has measured out and prepared his grave. Often appearing in a formal outfit, complete with spectacles, top hat and cane, Baron Samedi is known for his vulgar jokes and comments. He favors a strong drink consisting of rum with 21 hot peppers steeped in it. Baron Samedi is wed to Maman Brijitte. Because the lord of death is seen as a healer as well as a taker of life, he is often associated with St. Gérard.

Erzulie

A small shrine dedicated to Erzulie, one of the most popular *loa*, is found in almost every *hounfour*. She is the *loa* of love, human beauty and, to a lesser extent, the patron of the arts. The average *serviteur* calls upon Erzulie more often than any of the other *loa*. Although she has several aspects — some few of which even belong to the Petro family — she is normally considered a single *loa* rather than a collection of related spirits. In her great beauty, however, can be seen an element of sadness, of something precious forever lost. Erzulie is associated with the Virgin Mary.

Santería

Santería was born in the slave population of Cuba, though it has long since traveled far beyond the borders of that island nation. It is widely practiced among the Cuban population of the American South and its popularity has spread to other segments of the Hispanic community. The majority of those who practice *Santería* are also devout Catholics who see no contradiction in espousing both faiths. Those who practice the magic of *Santería* are called *santero* if male, or *santera* if female. Priests of *Santería* are titled *babalawos*. *Santería* is more concerned with divination than is *voudoun*, and is somewhat less focused on possession. Offers to the *orishas* are called *ebbó*, and must represent a true (though not necessarily great) sacrifice on the part of the petitioner.

A few of the *orishas* include the following.

Eleggua

Eleggua is the opener of all doors and the holder of all secrets. He sees the future without the need for oracles or divination, and is the messenger of God and the other *orishas*. Although he is always just, his actions may seem capricious or cruel, for the true extent of his own justice is hidden from the eyes of mankind. He is known for creating trouble amongst humanity, and is considered something of an incorrigible prankster. He is associated with fate as much as with justice. Eleggua is variously considered to represent St. Anthony of Padua or the Holy Infant of Atocha.

Oggún

One of the most commonly invoked *orishas*, Oggún represents nothing less than the sum total of work and human (and, among the undead, Kindred) effort. Oggún represents a dichotomy of creation and destruction, energy and violence, controlled strength and brute force. One of the oldest *orishas*, he is the divine ironworker, and he dwells in the woods that also fall under his expansive sphere of influence. He has an explosive temper, but is also extremely persistent; quick to anger, but slow to admit to failure. He is most commonly associated with St. Peter, but also with St. John the Baptist and St. George.

Changó

Changó is the *orisha* of fire, thunder and lightning. He represents raw, primal power. Thunder is supposedly caused by Changó galloping across the heavens on his great white steed. He also represents passion and virility, and believers call upon this incarnation far more often than his elemental one. Finally, he is associated with physical activities, both dancing and the waging of war. Changó is most often linked with St. Barbara, St. George and St. Patrick.

In parts of South America and the Caribbean, Changó (or Shango, depending on region) is often venerated to the exclusion of other *orishas*, and various faiths and cults are dedicated to his worship.

Oshún

The patron of river waters, Oshún is the embodiment of love and sexuality, and is most frequently called upon in matters of fertility. She represents gaiety, art and the creative impulse, and all forms of human pleasure. She is also the patron of gold and wealth, as well as marriage. Many Kindred *wangateurs*, who underestimate her value and power, refer to her condescendingly as "the Toreador *orisha*." Oshún is most frequently associated with Our Lady of La Caridad del Cobre and with St. Cecilia.

PALO MAYOMBE

Palo Mayombe — which is more closely related to religions of the Kongo peoples than to the Yoruba — has a darker, more sinister reputation than religions like *Santería*, though it is not any more "evil" per se. Many *santeros* fear *mayomberos* (practitioners of Palo Mayombe) as witches and supernatural killers. Found across much of South America and Cuba (though it is vastly overshadowed there by *Santería*), Palo Mayombe involves the worship of spirits called *Enkisi*. As with *Voudoun*, these are divided into two groups: a more benevolent family called Ensambi and a darker, more malevolent faction known as Endoki. Priests of the religion are titled *tata* (father) or *yaya* (mother). Many Palo Mayombe rituals involve the use of a *nganga*, a cauldron filled with sacred earth, sticks and human bones (as well, at times, as human blood, dead animals, iron spikes and other accouterments). It is, perhaps, no wonder that outsiders fear Palo Mayombe. Despite its rather grim trappings, however, this religion involves no more human sacrifice than do the others. The parts of the dead used in its practice are taken from those already deceased. Palo Mayombe does not have as pervasive a connection with Catholicism as do the previous faiths. While a large number of *Enkisi* are clearly taken from the Catholic pantheon, many others do not correlate to a particular saint.

Several of the *Enkisi* venerated by Palo Mayombe include the following.

Zarabanda

The messenger of the underworld and between the *Enkisi*, Zarabanda provides the conduit through which mortals can communicate with the other spirits. Zarabanda serves much the same purpose in Palo Mayombe as do Legba in *voudoun* and Eleggua in *Santería*, though he does not claim the same powers of divination as do his more oracular counterparts. Zarabanda manifests through the *nganga*, and is normally the first *Enkisi* addressed during Palo Mayombe rites.

El Cristo Negro

The "Black Christ" is the king of the underworld and the greatest of all the *Enkisi*. Strongly linked to Catholicism, he is seen as and represented by a black crucified Christ. El Cristo Negro functions in much the same role as Baron Samedi, though he eschews the Baron's crude humor. Although all the Afro-Caribbean faiths place great importance on the spirits of the dead, Palo Mayombe focuses on these to an even greater extent. This grants El Cristo Negro is a position of vast importance in the pantheon. El Cristo Negro clearly correlates with Jesus Christ, though the similarities exist primarily on the surface, and tend to break down once one delves into the behavior and persona of the *Enkisi*.

Santisima Muerte

A spirit of death, the dead and cemeteries, Santisima Muerte often works hand-in-hand with El Cristo Negro; *tatas* and *yayas* are usually initiated into the secrets of both *Enkisi* at the same time. Santisima Muerte is called upon by spiritualists and witches, and is something of a patron of workers of magic. She is an extremely jealous spirit; for this reason, most of her initiates are unmarried. Santisima Muerte is often associated with the Virgin Mary.

San Simon

The keeper of the laws for the *Enkisi* and God, San Simon represents the tenets of divine justice. He is also a source of secrets and knowledge, and is often called upon in divinations, though questions for San Simon are usually more of the "Why is this happening?" than the "What is going to happen?" variety. As the spirit of justice, San Simon is often called upon by those who wish to avoid their just fate, and supposedly possesses the power to render his initiates invisible to lawful (mortal) authority.

PRACTICAL WANGA

Most Tremere maintain that it takes decades, even centuries, to create a workable system of magic. Exactly how the slave population of the Americas managed to adapt a new system from their old beliefs is a mystery even to the most knowledgeable of thaumaturges. All that is known is, after a relatively brief period in which to adjust to this new melting pot of beliefs and spirits, the slaves were once again practicing not only their religion but their ritual magic — and it worked.

It was at this point that the Kindred developed a sudden interest in the practices of the slave religions. After all, another system of belief and another pantheon of gods and spirits hardly interested the average Kindred; but a new system of workable magic was another matter entirely.

The Serpents of the Light would have everyone believe that they were the first Cainites to practice the modern forms of Wanga (adorned primarily, but not exclusively, in the trappings of *voudoun*). They weren't. Nor were the Tremere first amongst *wangateurs*, though they were most active in, and most responsible for, the consolidation of Wanga into a practical branch of Thaumaturgy. Nor was it even the Lasombra Gisele Hemmet, who is credited with the first use of *Voudoun* Necromancy (see **Blood Magic: Secrets of Thaumaturgy**). No, the first confirmed use of Afro-Caribbean Wanga (as opposed to the original African version practiced among the Yoruba) appeared — perhaps not surprisingly — within the rare and rotting bloodline called the Samedi.

It is common knowledge that the Samedi bloodline was named (or named itself) after Baron Samedi, the lord of graveyards. No one knows whether or not any real connection exists between the two beyond nomenclature, appearance, fatalistic world view and macabre sense of humor.

The oldest known Samedi master of Wanga — who first made himself known to other Kindred in 1764 — was a Haitian *houngan* who called himself Papa Zombie. His current whereabouts and activities are unknown, but over the course of the last three centuries he has made a practice of gathering together and educating Kindred of *any* clan who follow the teachings and the tenets of *voudoun*. He maintains, when asked, that he learned the practice of Wanga through observing its mortal practitioners and petitioning the *loa* for enlightenment. The Tremere insist, of course, that Papa Zombie must have had a Cainite instructor; but if he did, he's certainly not feeling obliged to name names.

Although Papa Zombie himself taught Western Wanga to only a select few Kindred, they carried the knowledge elsewhere in their travels, spreading it further and modifying its practices to fit their own specific faiths (or interpretations of faith). Even as the Afro-Caribbean religions themselves moved beyond the bounds of their original territories, Kindred knowledge of this form of blood magic traveled with them. While still rare in the modern nights, Wanga has grown somewhat more common than many other non-Western forms of blood magic, particularly among younger blood sorcerers in the Americas.

As mentioned previously, most Kindred *wangateurs* do not restrict themselves to the trappings of any one Afro-Caribbean religion, instead drawing what they need from all of them. At the same time, a substantial minority do indeed practice a specific Afro-Caribbean religion. Papa Zombie has never been observed to call on any power that was a *loa* of Haitian *voudoun*. Clarice Fontaine, on the other hand, childe of Louis Doumer Millerand and one of the foremost *wangateurs* among the Tremere, is well known for calling on any and every spirit she feels necessary for her magic. She has on multiple occasions invoked the spirits of no fewer than five different religions in a single ritual. Some *wangateurs* even maintain that no real difference exists between the various Afro-Caribbean faiths. If St. Peter is already considered a "mask" of Legba, is it so much of a stretch to believe that Eleggua and Zarabanda also represent the same entity? The fact that Wanga is so remarkably freeform in its use and practice causes no end of consternation to traditionally minded blood magicians. Still, not even the most stubborn Hermetic Tremere can deny that it functions.

Wanga in Practice

Wanga operates very differently than most traditional forms of Thaumaturgy. One of the many reasons the practice is so loathed by conservative and custom-bound Tremere (and other thaumaturges) is that it refuses to follow the rules.

Wanga blurs the lines between rituals and paths. The invocation of its paths often requires the presence of specific materials and the vocalization of names of power — requirements reserved for rituals alone in Hermetic Thaumaturgy. Even the most basic tenet of Thaumaturgy — that it requires the expenditure of blood to invoke — is belied by one of Wanga's paths. Some of Wanga's detractors among the Warlocks wish to declare it an entirely separate form of blood sorcery, unrelated to Thaumaturgy at all. *Wangateurs* laugh at this notion; Wanga was separate, after all, until the Tremere spearheaded the effort to bring the practice into the fold.

Except for the path known as The Flow of *Ashé*, Wanga paths require the expenditure of blood for activation. In addition, any time Wanga is invoked, be it a path or a ritual, the *wangateur* must call upon a spirit appropriate to the intended effect. For instance, a *wangateur* invoking Lure of the Flames might call on Changó. Alternatively, were she attempting to call upon the Path of Weather Control, she might invoke Agarou Tonerre, a *loa* of thunder.

In addition, Wanga possesses its own unique set of tools, components and ritualistic items that must often be present for the magic to work. Not every ritual involves all of these tools, but the vast majority of them require at least a few. Listed below are the more common of Wanga's tools; once again, a bit of research on the players' part will turn up a wealth of additional material.

Asson
Used primarily in *voudoun*, this is a rattle wielded by the *houngan* or *mambo*, and is considered a magical and sacred object. It is normally constructed out of a gourd to which has been affixed a wooden handle, and is often decorated with such esoteric items as snake bones and bits of coral.

Ekwele
From the *Santería* faith, this is a thin chain measuring about 50 inches in length, and broken at regular intervals by one-and-a-half inch disks made of tortoise shell. It is used in the practice of *Ifa*, a form of divination.

Ese
Also from *Santería*, the Ese are poetic verses used in the interpretation of *Ifa*. *Babalawos* often have hundreds of these committed to memory.

Farine
This is flour used to trace the *veves* utilized in *voudoun* rituals.

Gris-gris
A *gris-gris* is a charm, talisman or any other small magic item. Many of the faiths refer to such charms as *wangas*; *gris-gris* is the *voudoun* equivalent.

Hounfour
A temple or structure used for ceremonies to the *loa* of *voudoun*.

Kisengue
A human shinbone wrapped in black rags, this is a common component of Palo Mayombe ceremonies.

Nganga
A large iron cauldron filled with graveyard earth, bones, sticks and other disturbing ingredients. It is one of the most

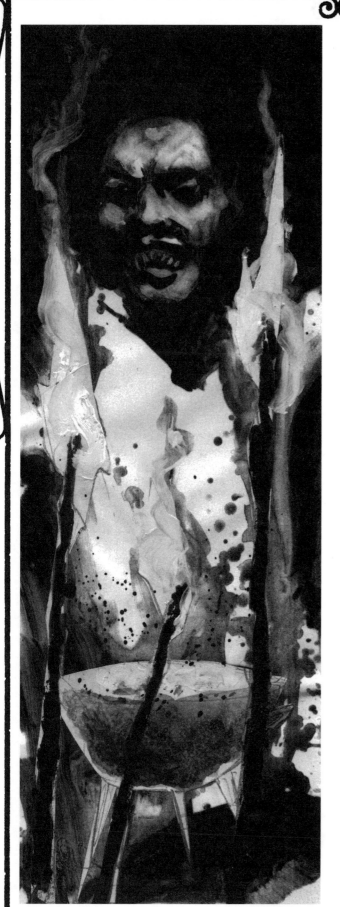

important components of Palo Mayombe. (This term also refers to a priest or shaman of certain African religions, though it is never used in that context in this chapter.)

Peristyle

An open courtyard in which *voudoun* ceremonies are held. There is often, but not always, a *hounfour* located on the property.

Poteau Mitan

The pole that stands at the center of a peristyle or *hounfour*. It is often carved or decorated, and represents the center of the universe and its connection with the spirit world. All dancing during the ceremony revolves around the *poteau mitan*.

Veve

Common to many of the Afro-Caribbean faiths but most prevalent in *voudoun*, this is a symbolic design representing one of the *loa* (or other spirit). *Veves* are used as the focus of rituals, and can serve as a temporary altar when a more permanent construct is unavailable. Although they can be found written or inscribed on all manner of surfaces, they are most commonly constructed by pouring flour on the ground during rituals.

Social Responsibilities

Kindred or kine, you cannot just wake up one morning (or evening) and decide, "Today, I will become a *houngan* (or tata)." As with any position of authority in any other religion, it takes years of learning and initiation to become a priest of *voudoun*, *Santería*, Palo Mayombe or any of the Wanga-practicing faiths. Many are the steps between a simple practitioner and a recognized master of mysteries.

It is relatively uncommon for a Kindred follower of an Afro-Caribbean religion to learn the secrets of Wanga without being initiated as a priest of that religion. Remember, Wanga is as much a religious system as a form of Thaumaturgy, and like any religious secret, it is rarely taught to those who have not gone through the proper steps and initiations.

What does this mean for your Kindred *wangateur*? For starters, it can mean years — often as much as a decade or two — to reach this level of initiation.

Houngans and *mambos*, *santeros* and *santeras*, *babalawos*, *tatas* and *yayas* — they're all religious leaders, which means they have certain social obligations demanded of them by their community and by their own beliefs. In communities where these religions are the norm, the local priest is expected to lead ceremonies on a regular — sometimes weekly if not daily — basis. Many in his community seek his aid, his advice, even his powers of divination. He is expected to use his magics to help those around him, to protect them from evil spirits and the influence of *malice*, or evil spells.

This can cause real problems for those of the vampiric persuasion. Leaving aside the fact that most such events, petitions and request come during the hours of daylight, bear in mind that such a character is constantly standing on the very edge of the Masquerade. Even if you've managed to explain away your nocturnal leanings, what happens if you frenzy in the midst of a ceremony? Many such ceremonies involve the spilling of blood (albeit animal blood). Between the scent of vitae, the pounding drums, the pulsating mass of humanity dancing their ritual dances — the situation is absolutely ripe with disastrous potential.

There are cultures in which the use of magic isn't inherently a Masquerade breach, where magic is almost common — but most Western princes aren't going to see it like that. You can argue all you want that it wasn't really breaking the Masquerade to use Thaumaturgy in front of witnesses because they were expecting you to do magic, but the local sheriff or archon is still likely to stake first and decide later if she should bother asking questions.

At the same time, such a position of authority offers its own advantages. Herd, Allies, Contacts, even a few dots of Fame or Influence, are all easily justifiable — if not mandatory — for such an exalted post. Your position as a religious leader places all sorts of demands on you, but it opens up an equally large host of opportunities. Don't hesitate to make the most of them.

Some few wangateurs do not bear these responsibilities. Perhaps they have left such concerns behind them after years of practice, or perhaps they serve the spirits in some other capacity. The Storyteller should not feel obliged to include these social aspects if they're going to negatively impact the story.

Ritual Practice

Wanga is often a group activity. Although most of its rituals can be performed alone, they prove easier and more effective when cast as part of a ceremony involving numerous participants. Only the primary caster need follow the steps of the ritual itself; all others are involved primarily in the drumming, singing and dancing common to these religious. These other participants need not be wangateurs, or even Kindred, but they must be true believers in an Afro-Caribbean faith, they must be willing participants (no Dominated dancers, though thralls subjected to blood bonds are common among certain less-savory wangateurs), and they must know the true purpose of the ritual. If the number of participants is at least twice the level of the ritual, the difficulty of the Intelligence + Occult roll is reduced by 1.

Note the downside to this: Rituals invoked this way take substantially longer to cast. Although the standard casting time for a ritual is five minutes per level, the casting time for Wanga rituals that are cloaked in these ceremonies is half an hour per level. Of course, nothing forces the wangateur to make use of other participants if she's in a hurry.

The Paths of Wanga

Several standard paths of Thaumaturgy are available to practitioners of Wanga. Particularly popular are the Path of Blood, the Path of Conjuring, the Path of Corruption, Sprit Manipulation and the Path of Curses. In addition, Wanga claims at least three unique paths. Unless stated otherwise, these paths are activated in the standard manner (with the expenditure of one blood point), require the same roll to determine success (Willpower vs. the power level + 3), and carry the same results for botching (loss of a permanent Willpower point). In addition, the wangateur must call aloud (though it need not be at great volume) upon the power of an appropriate spirit (orisha, loa, Enkisi or the like), and many require the presence of specific items or components.

The Flow of Ashé

Kindred who master the Flow of Ashé learn to draw power from sources of ashé other than vitae. The wangateur can perform supernatural feats without the need to spend the blood in his system. He instead draws the power — a "phantom blood point," if you will — from components carried on his person. These materials are consumed in the process. Unlike other Thaumaturgical paths, the Flow of Ashé does not require the expenditure of blood to invoke, as that would largely defeat the purpose. If, however, the player fails or botches the Willpower roll, the character loses two points of blood, in addition to standard penalties.

The player must invoke this path the turn immediately before he wishes to spend the substitute blood point (except for the level five power the Gift of Ashé). If the "blood" is not used in the turn immediately following, it is lost, and the path must be attempted again; the herbs and other components are still consumed. The Flow of Ashé can create only one "phantom blood point" at a time.

Kindred Spirits

Most of Wanga's powers and rituals deal heavily with spirits. Some are primal forces, others the ghosts of long-dead ancestors. Sounds a lot more like the purview of Necromancy than Thaumaturgy, doesn't it?

Many wangateurs would agree, and many of them make as much of an effort to learn Necromancy (particularly Voudoun Necromancy) as they do Thaumaturgy. In fact, in the minds of most wangateurs, Thaumaturgy and Necromancy are two sides of the same system of blood magic — Wanga — rather than two separate forms of sorcery.

Let us stress, however, that this belief has no bearing on Discipline costs or character abilities. A thaumaturge who practices Wanga does not automatically learn Necromancy along with it. A Tremere wangateur is not permitted to buy Necromancy as an in-clan Discipline. Experience point costs, freebie point costs, time required for instruction — none of these are influenced in any way by this belief. All this means is that, in the context of the character, Kindred wangateurs believe Necromancy and Thaumaturgy are both branches of the same form of magic. If your local powergamer tries to use this to explain why his voudoun houngan should be allowed to start with six dots of Thaumaturgy and Necromancy, despite the fact that he's playing a Lasombra, please feel free to push his ass down the stairs.

Powers that require more than one blood point to activate are not affected by this path.

Most requisite powders and herbs are relatively rare and require that the *wangateur* frequent occult and specialty shops in order to obtain them.

• TOUCH OF LIFE

The *wangateur* may perform the most minor feats of blood — causing his skin to flush, causing his heart to beat and the like — without actually spending a blood point.

System: The character must have in her possession two handfuls of herbs and powdered minerals, including *aroeira* (a Brazilian herb used to treat skin ailments) and copper shavings. The character may either cause her heart to beat or her skin to flush or any other single effect, as though she'd spent a blood point. This effect lasts for one scene.

•• STRENGTH OF ROOT AND STONE

The *wangateur* may use the Flow of *Ashé* to power an increase in either Strength, Dexterity or Stamina, as though she'd spent one blood point to raise the given Attribute.

System: The components required include two handfuls of herbs and powdered minerals, including *jurubeba* (an herb often used to cure stomach and liver ailments, and for the treatment of general weakness) and pure iron filings. Otherwise, the effect is identical to that achieved by spending blood to raise an Attribute, and lasts for one scene.

••• BREATH OF LIFE

The *wangateur* calls upon the powers of *Ashé* to heal injuries to himself. Wounds close as though he'd spent a blood point to repair the damage. Note that this power does not allow the Kindred to heal aggravated damage; it has only the effectiveness of a normal blood point spent on a normal bashing- or lethal-damage wound.

System: In order to use this power, the character must smear a paste on the wound. This paste includes crushed *cambara* (a shrub once used for the treatment of cuts and skin injuries), powdered human bone and at least a few drops of blood (this blood may be human or animal, and need not amount to even a single blood point's worth; it cannot, however, come from the *wangateur* himself). The ingredients must be mixed into paste immediately prior to the invocation of the path. If it dries for more than a minute or so after mixing, the power fails to function. Unlike normal healing, a *wangateur* may not use this power to heal while engaged in any other activity; all her attention for the turn must be concentrated on applying the salve and activating its power.

•••• FAVOR OF THE *ORISHAS*

At this level, the *wangateur* may substitute other sources of *Ashé* even when powering Disciplines, including other Thaumaturgy paths (but not rituals). This power may be used only to activate a Discipline; it cannot be used to maintain a power already active.

System: The *wangateur* must possess several leaves of tobacco (this must be pure; a box of cigarettes won't do) and a handful of powdered ivory. In addition, the mixture must include at least a few drops of blood (though not an

THE FAITHFUL FEW

Although any Kindred of any clan can learn the magic of Wanga, the practice rarely appears outside a few select groups.

Wanga is not as widespread among the Tremere as it might be, due to the religious requirements and the mistrust that the practice engenders among more conservative blood magicians. A very small fraction of the Warlocks are *wangateurs* — but because the Tremere make up the largest group of blood magicians to begin with, their *wangateurs* may still outnumber those of the Serpents of the Light or the Samedi. The Tremere tend toward the mix-and-match style of Wanga; very few restrict their castings and procedures to the trappings of any single faith.

Samedi thaumaturges are about as rare as worm's teeth, since the bloodline is so sparse to begin with. Nevertheless, they claim a surprising proportion of *wangateurs* among their numbers; in fact, most Stiffs who do practice Thaumaturgy are *wangateurs*. Samedi blood magicians commonly make an effort to master both Wanga and *Voudoun* Necromancy, often to devastating effect. While some Samedi pull from multiple religions, a substantial number draw solely from Haitian *voudoun*.

Wanga is also seen with relative frequency among the Serpents of the Light, who tend to play up its alien, mysterious aspects in the hopes of causing fear and awe in those (un)fortunate enough to watch them work. A large proportion of the Serpents are *wangateurs*; more, percentage-wise, than any other bloodline. The Serpents rival the Tremere for sheer pragmatism; they draw from any and all of the Afro-Caribbean faiths at will, taking whatever route will most directly lead them to their goals.

Wangateurs can, of course, be found in other clans as well. There has been at least one Nosferatu (of African descent) seen to practice Wanga in the modern nights, though his Thaumaturgy took a form that more closely resembled the original Yoruba beliefs than any of the modern faiths. Also, the Tremere have their eye on a South American pack of Lasombra who have been observed using Wanga; they seem to rely primarily on the trappings of Palo Mayombe.

entire blood point's worth). The *wangateur* may not shed her own blood to invoke this power, though the blood of a foe struck in melee combat is acceptable.

Once Favor of the *orishas* has been used to power another Discipline, all rules and systems of that Discipline — including rolls required, maintenance costs, duration and so forth — apply as normal.

••••• GIFT OF *ASHE*

At this level, the powders or pastes created by levels 1 through 3 of the Flow of *Ashé* may be imbued with enough power that they hold their magic for a time, and need not be used the following turn. Furthermore, the *ashé* in these components may be granted to other Kindred for their use if the *wangateur* chooses to do so.

System: The effects of the power may be delayed for an entire scene. At any point, the character may activate the stored power, either on her own person or on another Kindred. For instance, a *wangateur* who anticipates combat might invoke the Breath of Life and mix the paste, then give the paste to a companion, allowing him to heal a single wound level without spending blood should he be forced to do so. A *wangateur* may have a number of pastes and powders prepared at any time equal to her Intelligence.

Orisha's Fortune

Orisha's Fortune (or *Loa*'s Fortune, or *Enkisi*'s Fortune, depending on the *wangateur*) allows the thaumaturge to manipulate the whim of luck, the vagaries of random chance. By spending his own blood in sacrifice, the *wangateur* beseeches the spirits to bring fortune to himself and his allies, and misfortune to his foes.

Orisha's Fortune follows most standard rules for Thaumaturgical paths. The blood point required cannot merely be spent, however; it must by physically shed by the *wangateur* when the power is activated, and many practitioners carry a small ritual blade on their person for this purpose. The wound required need not be large enough to inflict even a single health level of damage; it is the act of shedding vitae that captures the *orishas*' attention. Many *wangateurs* slice open a palm and symbolically fling the blood at their target, though this is by no means required.

(For those who are concerned about such things, the vitae cannot be retrieved by other thaumaturges for use against a character. The blood point is consumed by the magic seconds after it is spilled.)

The *wangateur* can target anyone in his line of sight.

• Sheltering Hand

At this level, the *wangateur* can use *orisha*'s Favor to prevent catastrophe. The subject is granted just a bit of extra fortune; he may still fail, but he finds disasters occurring far less frequently.

System: The *wangateur* chooses his subject — either himself or an ally. The next action attempted by the subject is less likely to botch; the number of 1's rolled must exceed the caster's successes for a botch to occur. Thus, if the player rolls 3 successes when invoking Sheltering Hand, his next roll must come up with at least four 1's (and no successes) to be considered a botch. Botches avoided in this fashion still carry all the results of a normal failure; this power prevents disaster, but it cannot turn a failure into a success. It applies only to the next action taken by the subject, or for the first turn if the action is extended. If the roll to invoke this power indicates a botch, the subject suffers the opposite effect; every 1 rolled by the player counts as an added botch on the subject's own action.

•• Fortune's Blessing

The *wangateur* requests the *orishas*' aid for herself or an ally. Luck is with her; tasks become simpler and less likely to fail and the recipient may even find herself capable of feats that would normally prove too difficult to perform.

System: The specific task — hacking, driving, shooting or any other mundane action — must be declared when the power is invoked. For the duration of the scene, the recipient finds the difficulty of the specified task lowered by 1 (to a minimum of 4).

Multiple uses of this power are not cumulative, nor can a poor roll be superceded or replaced by a better one. Any attempt to use it on someone already under its influence automatically fails.

••• Fortune's Curse

The reverse of Fortune's Blessing, this power allows the *wangateur* to inflict minor misfortune upon an enemy, making a single task more difficult and likely to fail.

System: The caster must declare a specific sort of action — brawling, sneaking or the like — when the power is invoked. The target of the spell finds his difficulty increased by 1 (maximum 9) when attempting that action; this power lasts for the scene.

This power is not cumulative, and should be considered a failure if used on someone already under its influence.

•••• Fortune's Favor

The *wangateur* calls upon the spirits to perform some truly hefty twisting of the laws of probability. Blows that should land, contests that clearly favor the opposition — all seem to shift inexplicably in favor of the *wangateur*.

System: At the moment of casting, the caster must choose a specific individual against whom this power operates. Once this power is invoked, the *wangateur* is protected by an effect that seems to combine aspects of the previous two powers. All of the target's rolls are at +1 difficulty (maximum 10). All the caster's rolls are at -1 difficulty (minimum 4), but only when in direct opposition to the target (attack rolls, dodges and contested actions). Fortune's Favor lasts for a number of turns equal to the *wangateur*'s successes.

The caster cannot use Fortune's Favor while under the effects of Fortune's Blessing, nor can she use it against anyone already influenced by Fortune's Curse.

••••• Smiting Hand

A truly nasty magic, Smiting Hand sets the power of the *orishas* directly against a foe, transforming almost any attempted task into a catastrophic failure.

System: Every success achieved by the caster becomes a "phantom botch" that the target must overcome on his next roll. Thus, if the caster achieves 3 successes, the target's next roll is considered to have 3 extra dice that all came up 1. Furthermore, any failure while under the influence of this power is considered a botch, rather than a mere failure. For example, if the aforementioned victim rolled 10, 7, 3, 2 and 2, that would normally be a failure — the phantom 1's cancel out the 7 and the 10. Because of the power of Smiting Hand, however, the result is a botch *even though successes were rolled*. The Storyteller is encouraged to have such botches result in truly catastrophic results, even as compared to "normal" botches; those who threaten the favored of the *orishas* deserve whatever happens to them.

VOICE OF THE WILD

A holdover from the ancient Yoruba Kindred, this is possibly the oldest Wanga path practiced in the modern nights. Originally intended to grant influence over the predators of the savannas and jungles, it is often overlooked in a culture of sidewalks and skyscrapers. Enough creative *wangateurs* have found the path sufficiently useful, however, that it has not died out.

In addition to vitae, Voice of the Wild requires the use of materials, much like certain rituals and the Flow of *Ashé*. These components are consumed by the magic during casting.

A *wangateur* may attempt to influence the same animal as another Kindred utilizing Animalism. Assuming successful rolls on both sides, control goes to whomever has the highest level in their respective Discipline. If the Voice of the Wild and Animalism scores are tied, victory goes to the user of Animalism.

• SCENT OF THE BEAST

The magician can produce scents and pheromones appropriate to a particular species of animal. Used in ancient nights to attract game and ward off predators, it finds similar use tonight among more creative *wangateurs*.

System: The caster must have in her possession a sample (tuft of fur, whisker, tooth, drop of blood, etc.) from the animal she wishes to smell like. If successful, the Kindred gives off a scent identical to that of the target animal for the remainder of the scene. Three successes allow the *wangateur* to smell like that animal in a particular emotional state; she could, for instance, duplicate the scent of a scared cat or a dog in heat. With five successes, the power is effective enough to fool an animal ghoul. Five successes will also permit the caster to fool Lupines, Kindred in animal form, or Kindred using Auspex, but these received an opposed Perception + Alertness roll (difficulty 6). If this opposed roll is successful, the Lupine or Kindred notices something subtly off about the caster's scent, and may well investigate further.

Any attempt to attract an animal must achieve at least three successes to inspire the creature to overcome its instinctive aversion to vampires; fewer successes mean that the animal will approach to within a few yards, but no closer. Any attempt to create a scent strong enough to affect a human or a Kindred not using Auspex (duplicating the spray of a skunk, for instance) also requires three successes.

•• HIDE FROM HUNTER'S EYES

The cities of the 21st century may house vicious guard dogs rather than hungry lions, but the effect of this power is much the same as it was in nights past. With this power, the Kindred causes animals to overlook her completely. This applies to scent and hearing as well as sight. Although few animals willingly attack Kindred, this is powerful protection against those that will. Perhaps more importantly, it prevents dogs and other guard animals from rousing the neighbors.

System: The *wangateur* must have a body part (fur, hair or a tooth will suffice) from the kind of animal she wishes to hide from, and a pinch of pepper, drop of perfume or any other strongly scented material. This must be rubbed on the sample as the blood is spent. For the remainder of the scene, animals of the specified variety (dogs being the most common in modern cities) simply don't notice the Kindred's presence unless she specifically does something to attract attention (touching the animal, making any noise louder than low conversation or the like).

This power requires five successes to fool Lupines or Kindred in animal form, but they receive an opposed Perception + Alertness roll to see through it (difficulty 6). It functions on animal ghouls regardless of the number of successes, but they too are allowed an opposed Wits + Alertness roll (difficulty 7 for ghouls).

••• MARKING THE PREY

Working off the premise, "I don't have to run faster than the bear, I just have to run faster than you," this power allows the caster to fix the attention of a given variety of animal on a specific target. The beasts in question will focus only on that individual, unless someone else makes a concerted effort to get their attention. This power does not automatically make an animal hostile.

System: The caster must have a bit of hair or other sample from the variety of animal to be influenced, and a pinch or drop of something that animal might find attractive (catnip for cats, the fur of a small rodent for snakes, etc.). These must be combined at the time the blood is spent to invoke the magic. The target must be visible to the *wangateur*. If the roll succeeds, all animals of the chosen variety in the area will focus exclusively on the target for the duration of the scene, or until the target is able to escape their immediate vicinity (and avoid pursuit) for several minutes. Distracting their attention requires physical contact or an actual attack; shouting at them accomplishes nothing. Friendly animals will frolic and play around the target, whereas hostile animals will attack.

•••• GUIDING SPIRIT

This power allows the *wangateur* to manipulate the emotional state of an animal. This means more than just "angry" or "sad." The caster can achieve a specific degree of control by causing the animal to react one way to some stimuli, and entirely differently to another. Although not as particular as the control granted by Animalism, Guiding Spirit can create some truly impressive results.

System: The caster must have in his possession some body part (again, fur or the like is fine) from the type of animal to be influenced. The caster must make eye contact or direct physical contact with the animal as he spends vitae to invoke this power. The animal may resist with Willpower (difficulty 7) only if the *wangateur* is influencing it to do something totally against its instincts or training (attempting to make a loyal dog attack its owner, for instance). Animal Willpower can be found in the appendix of **Vampire: The Masquerade**. For every success, the caster maintains control over the animal's emotional state for a scene.

The target can be made to calm down, grow enraged enough to attack a specific target, become playful or any other emotional effect on which the player and Storyteller can agree. The animal cannot be made to perform specific tricks for which it has not been trained (like shaking paws or fetching keys), nor can it be made to place itself in the path of certain harm (though it can be made to take risks). The exact limits of this power are deliberately vague, as animals react on a much more emotional and instinctive level than humans. It is ultimately the Storyteller's call as to what is and is not possible with Guiding Spirit.

●●●●● MANTLE OF THE BEAST

The caster may assume a single physical characteristic of an animal. The eyes of a cat allow vision in areas of very low lighting (though not complete darkness). The claws of a bear are sufficient for shredding opponents, and aid climbing to boot. The nose of a bloodhound can tell you exactly where that snooping reporter ran off to. And though Kindred aren't built for flight, a set of wings will at least break your fall, allowing you to glide to (relative) safety.

System: The character must have on her person a sample (as above) of the animal whose feature she wishes to duplicate. This power duplicates a single feature only. Thus, the caster could not take a snake's ability to wriggle through small places, because that is a factor of the snake's body structure and not a specific feature; she could, however, take the compressible ribcage of a mouse and accomplish much the same thing, as that is a single physical feature of the animal.

Claws created with Mantle of the Beast do Strength +1 aggravated damage. They also reduce climbing difficulty by 2. Wings require a roll of Stamina + Athletics against difficulty 7 to use properly. Kindred can glide for a distance of 100 yards per success rolled (further with a strong tailwind), and she can safely fall almost any distance without taking damage. A protective covering like a turtle's shell or an insect's carapace adds 2 to the character's soak pool; these dice can be used to soak aggravated damage. Advantages for taking other features are at Storyteller's discretion.

WANGA RITUALS

Wangateurs have access to several rituals of "traditional" Thaumaturgy. These include many wards and other defensive rituals, divinations, various bone-related rituals and those that are designed to cause injury or consternation from a distance ("curse" rituals). In addition, Wanga has its own rich library of unique magics that call upon the spirits and the *ashé* of the world around them.

To perform a ritual, a *wangateur* must wield an *asson*, an *ekwele*, a *kisengue* or other religious talisman, in addition to listed components. Wanga rituals require a roll of Intelligence + Occult versus difficulty of the ritual's level + 3 (maximum 9). A failure on this roll indicates that the magic has not been properly invoked; any required components are still consumed, and must be replaced if the caster wishes to try again. Botches indicate the *orishas'* displea-

sure and often pervert the intent of the ritual, causing an effect exactly opposed to that which was intended.

Many of the rituals draw upon components and practices taken from a specific religion (*Voudoun*, *candomblé*, etc.). These are usable by any *wangateur*; if, however, a character is willing to draw on only one faith, she might have to make use of a modified variation of the ritual. Players should feel free (in fact, feel encouraged) to do some research in that direction if they're so inclined.

Some rituals, such as Grandfather's Gift, *Ori* Sight and Shackles of Blood, call specifically upon ancestor spirits. The *Ara Orun*, while often generous and helpful, can also be malicious and cruel on whim. Any time such a ritual is attempted and failed, the Storyteller should secretly roll the caster's Charisma. If this roll fails or botches, the failed ritual may be considered a botch, rather than a simple failure — at the Storyteller's discretion; the *Ara Orun* have proven exceptionally hostile this night.

LEVEL ONE RITUAL

SINGING CHARM

A small item is enchanted to send out a constant call that only the caster can hear. This "song" is audible for many miles, and the magician can always determine direction and approximate distance to the charm. On Sunday night, the caster slices off an earlobe, which is then placed in a pot or other metallic receptacle. To this is added one point of the caster's blood and the tongue of a bird. The entire mixture must be burned and the remains mixed with the ashes of a cremated corpse. This ash is then placed in a small leather or hide pouch (perhaps the size of an apricot), which must be sewn shut.

System: The Singing Charm can be heard by the *wangateur* as long as he is within a hundred miles, and the charm sings for a number of nights equal to three times his casting successes. During this time, the caster need merely concentrate to learn the subject's approximate direction and distance (direction is usually accurate to within a few degrees, and distance to within a few yards).

LEVEL TWO RITUALS

CRAFT GARDE

The caster creates gardes (also called *paquets Congo*), talismans designed to protect the bearer against hostile magics. The garde may look like nearly anything — a small leather pouch, a doll or a bit of ornamental jewelry are all common forms. The caster mixes two points of her own blood with various powdered healing herbs (such as *jurubeba*), exactly nine drops of rum and some sample (hair, fingernail, etc.) from the intended recipient of the garde. The garde thus created will function only for that person. This ritual does not allow the caster to create a talisman to protect herself.

System: The garde functions for a number of nights equal to twice the caster's successes on her casting roll. It must be worn at all times to be effective, and it must touch the bearer's skin. For the duration, any attempt to use blood magic rituals (but not paths) against the bearer has its difficulty increased by two (maximum 10).

Craft Gris-Gris

Also called "Craft Wanga," this ritual is referred to by its *voudoun*-specific name to avoid confusion with the practice of Wanga. The *wangateur* creates a *gris-gris* that will bring harm and misfortune to the recipient. The victim feels ill, suffers from ailments such as headaches and muscle pains and is unable to concentrate. The caster must mix two points of his own blood, the finger bone of an infant, nine pinches of graveyard dirt and a sample taken from the intended victim. The *gris-gris* must then be hidden within a few feet of the victim's home or haven.

System: Against Kindred, the *gris-gris* functions for one night for each of the caster's net successes (unless the *gris-gris* is moved first); against mortals, the magic is permanent until the *gris-gris* is located and removed. All actions performed while under the effects of the *gris-gris* suffer a dice-pool penalty of -1. A *wangateur* with a higher level of Wanga than the caster who finds the hidden *gris-gris* can turn its effects back upon the caster with a successful roll.

Grandfather's Gift

The *wangateur* contacts the *Ara Orun* and asks them to grant her their skills and knowledge. The caster must mix one full handful of graveyard earth and an offering to the spirits into a small container. This offering should consist of rum, fruits, cigarettes, pennies and any other gifts she feels appropriate. If successful, the sprits grant her temporary knowledge.

System: Every success on the casting roll must be divided between dots in Abilities and turns of duration. For instance, four successes could be used to raise the caster's Occult by 3 for one turn, by 1 for three turns or by 2 for two turns. The Ability raised must be one that the caster's deceased ancestors — Kindred or kine — could reasonably have possessed (Storyteller's discretion).

Level Three Rituals

Curse Candle

On a Friday night, the magician creates a black candle incorporating the brains and bones of a dead man, nine pinches of cemetery dirt, pepper, the leaves of an itching plant and other herbs. By burning the candle for 20 minutes each night while concentrating on the victim, the magician plagues the victim with poltergeist-like activity such as thrown objects or furniture that moves to trip him. This only happens when no one else is looking. Other people will soon think that the victim is crazy, clumsy or both. Most of the time, the curse is merely a nuisance. If the ghostly force shoves the victim while he walks down a steep flight of stairs, though, or throws something while the victim drives a car, the victim might be seriously injured.

System: The Curse Candle itself does not require any expenditure of vitae to create, but each 20 minutes of use costs the magician one blood point. A single success will

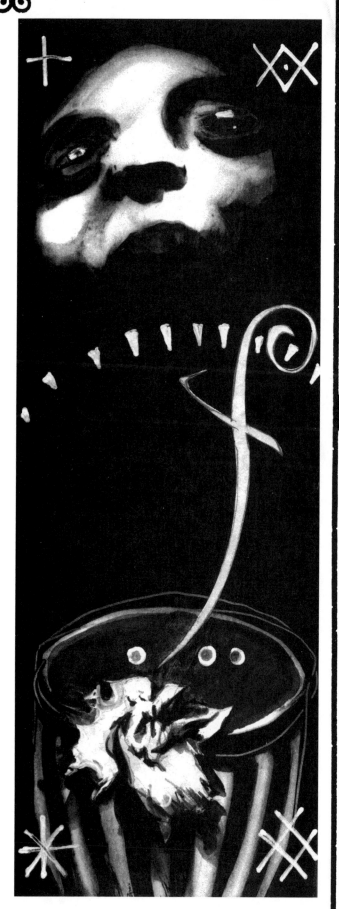

set the poltergeist against the victim for 24 hours. The magician must be within (Willpower x 10) miles of the victim. The poltergeist has a Strength of 2 and a dice pool of 4 for its pranks and attacks. It will try to cause serious harm at least once every night that it harasses the victim, using whatever props it finds on hand. The candle is large enough to burn for a number of 20-minute periods equal to the caster's successes on his casting roll.

ORI SIGHT

In *voudoun*, the *ori* is the soul, of both the individual and her family, that resides in the head. By petitioning the *Ara Orun*, the magician may attempt to use the senses of someone else's *ori*, thus seeing through the subject's eyes and hearing through her ears. The caster must burn one of her own eyes and ears (removing these causes three levels of unsoakable aggravated damage, which can be healed in the normal fashion). The resulting ash must be placed inside a human skull and mixed with a splash of rum, tobacco and an eyelash or drop of blood from the individual in question. The resulting paste must be applied to the caster's empty eye socket and the flesh where her ear used to be. She may then see and hear everything the target experiences.

System: The caster may shift back and forth between her own senses and those of the target at will. If the caster has eyelashes or blood from more than one individual, she may include a number of people in the spell equal to her level of Wanga, and may shift back and forth between her own senses or any of theirs as she chooses. The gauging out of an eye and the slicing off of an ear each require a Willpower roll (difficulty 8). The ritual lasts until the player spends blood to heal the injuries to her eye and ear.

LEVEL FOUR RITUAL

CANDLE OF RAGE

This is constructed much like the Curse Candle, save that the brains and bones must come from a man who died violently, and that nightshade is substituted for pepper. By burning the candle for 20 minutes each night while concentrating on the victim, the caster may influence the victim's emotional state. The most common result is to drive the target into a rage, but other options exist.

System: The Candle of Rage itself does not require any expenditure of vitae to create, but each 20 minutes of use costs the magician one blood point. Every night the candle is burned, the victim may resist with a Willpower roll (difficulty 8) against the *wangateur*'s casting roll when the candle was created; success indicates that the candle has no effect that night, but the magician may try again the

following night. If the ritual functions, the victim finds the difficulty of all Self-Control rolls (or Courage or Conscience, if the caster chooses to go for an emotional state other than rage) raised by 2 for the night. This often results in a great deal of bloodshed as the victim loses his temper or frenzies on a regular basis. The candle may be burned a number of times equal to the caster's successes on the casting roll.

The Candle of Rage will effect mortals and other creatures that do not normally frenzy. These enter into a near-mindless, berserk rage, though they gain none of the benefits normally associated with a Kindred frenzy. Targets that do not have a Self-Control Trait (such as animals) should instead roll a dice pool equal to half their Willpower (round up).

LEVEL FIVE RITUAL

SHACKLES OF BLOOD

The *wangateur* must spill three points of her own blood, numerous herbs (with both healing and hallucinogenic effects), various peppers, tobacco and the heart of a recently deceased person (male if the intended victim of the ritual is female, female if the victim is male) into a *nganga*. The mixture is then stirred with an iron rod as many of the *orishas*, including the *Ara Orun*, are invoked. This takes three full hours of stirring. The result must then be strained through unbleached cotton. The liquid produced, when drunk by the subject, creates an instant — though temporary — emotional attachment that is equivalent to a blood bond. This occurs even if the victim has never fed from the magician. The bond thus created has all the characteristics of the regent-thrall relationship.

System: The false bond lasts a number of nights equal to the caster's net successes. The caster may attempt to create a true blood bond with the victim during this time, if the ritual lasts long enough. If the ritual expires before a true bond is formed, however, any partial bonds are instantly nullified, as if the victim had never fed from the magician. The Storyteller may wish to make the casting roll for the character in secret, so the *wangateur* does not know how many nights remain before the ritual lapses.

Obviously, few Kindred will willingly imbibe this mixture if they have any notion of its true effects, so *wangateurs* have learned to be creative. Kindred who feed from a mortal who has consumed this mixture within the past 24 hours are themselves effected as though they themselves had drunk it directly; practitioners of Wanga have developed all sorts of techniques for taking advantage of this unusual property of the elixir.

Appendix: Mysterious Ways

"There are more things in heaven and earth...Than are dreamt of in your philosophy."
— Hamlet, Act I, scene v.

The Tremere maintain that, as a clan, they have by far the greatest understanding of blood magic. This, for the most part, is true. Some among the Warlocks, however, maintain that they possess a *complete* understanding of blood magic.

They are fools. Or dangerously deluded.

Many mysteries transcend, or at least evade, the understanding of the Tremere. Clan propensity accounts for some. The Necromancy rituals below, for instance, fall under the purview of the Giovanni or the Samedi rather than Clan Tremere's "preeminent" magicians. Beyond these lie forms of blood sorcery most Tremere have never heard of, let alone comprehend.

Beyond even these lurk... *other* things. Things that violate even the most basic laws of magic as the magi understand them. Magic without will. Power without purpose. These "spontaneous talismans" are no more comprehensible to the Tremere than the workings of a nuclear reactor are to a child.

The Tremere seldom admit ignorance, even among themselves, but they'd better do so before many more nights drift past. Without a better understanding of the mysteries that still lurk in the shadows, the Warlocks remain utterly unprepared to deal with the threats they face — and as these forgotten blood magics emerge from the depths of history in ever increasing numbers with the coming of the Final Nights, it may not be the Tremere alone who suffer the consequences of their ignorance.

Other Forms of Blood Magic

Necromancy

These rituals are particularly well suited to *Voudoun* Necromancy (see **Blood Magic: Secrets of Thaumaturgy**). Nevertheless, there is no inherent reason why workers of "standard" (read: Giovanni) Necromancy can't also use them.

Part the Veil (Level Two Ritual)

Called the 6th Sense ritual by young Kindred who enjoy pop-culture references, this allows the necromancer to grant someone else the ability to see wraiths and the Shadowlands as though they'd invoked Shroud Sight. The necromancer spends several moments chanting over an object representing the subject (hair, fingernail or a prized possession, for example) and a fresh human eye. If the subject is Kindred, he may resist with a Willpower roll, difficulty 6; successes on this roll are subtracted from the caster's total successes. If the power is successful, the victim sees the spirits and abodes of the dead overlaid with the living world for a number of scenes (if Kindred) or nights (if mortal) equal to the caster's successes. This can drive mortals mad — or at least to make their friends think they are.

Eyes of the Dead (Level Three Ritual)

The caster may see through the eyes (and hear through the ears) of a corpse. The body can have been dead any length of time if the caster wishes to see through its eyes (or sockets), but it must retain at least the inner mechanisms of its ears if the magician also wishes to hear. While chanting, the caster sheds a point of her own blood (for sight *or* hearing, two points to use both) over either a piece of anatomy taken from the corpse or a possession of great importance to the individual in life, such as a wedding ring or family heirloom. The magician must be able to see the corpse while casting, though it need not be close enough to touch. The ritual lasts for a number of nights equal to the necromancer's successes on her Intelligence + Occult roll, and she may switch back and forth from her own senses to those of the corpse at will. This ritual functions on corpses made animate through other uses of Necromancy (or other Disciplines), but the duration decreases to one *scene* per success. Eyes of the Dead does not require a complete corpse — only a relatively intact head is needed — but the difficulty of the ritual increases by 1 if a partial corpse is used.

Garb of Hades (Level Five Ritual)

Similar in some ways to Daemonic Possession, Garb of Hades allows the necromancer to inhabit a recently dead body, leaving her own form in a torpor-like state. The body may have been dead for no longer than 30 minutes before the ritual begins. The caster dresses herself in the clothes the subject wore at the time of death (the ritual must be performed nude if the subject died that way). The caster spends two blood points and symbolically "breathes" into the corpse's mouth. At that point, the caster inhabits the corpse and reanimates it. While in the corpse, the caster has access to the subject's memories, though only those from the past several days and nights are clear. The caster may even access the subject's Abilities, though only one dot of each, regardless of the subject's original level of mastery. The magician does *not* gain access to the subject's supernatural abilities, if any (such as Disciplines, shapeshifting or other powers). The ritual lasts a number of scenes equal to the caster's successes when casting; after this time, the body rapidly decays and the caster returns to her own body.

Koldunic Sorcery

For more on *Koldunic* Sorcery, see **Blood Magic: Secrets of Thaumaturgy**.

Reflections (Level One Ritual)

The *koldun* draws upon the elements present in a location to learn more information about that area. The caster need simply take any object from the room, area or location. The object must consist primarily of natural materials, rather than synthetic; thus, a pencil suffices, but a notebook computer does not. Within the next 24 hours, the *koldun* may cast this ritual over the item. For a number of turns equal to her successes plus her Willpower, her mind travels to the area from which the object was taken, and she may proceed to examine it in detail, even going so far as to look behind furniture or inside drawers that she did not search before. She observes the area *exactly* as it was when she took the object. This ritual is particularly useful for searching the haven or offices of an enemy at leisure. Any given object may be used only once, after which it becomes useless for purposes of this ritual.

Earth's Embrace (Level Four Ritual)

Of use only to Tzimisce, this ritual allows the *koldun* to call upon the spirits of the earth to empower the soil around him. The Tzimisce may temporarily substitute this soil for the "native" earth he must normally sleep with. The *koldun* sheds two blood points into the soil in question no more than an hour before dawn, and spends a temporary Willpower point. The soil is then capable of sustaining him for *one* day, as though it came from his homeland. This ritual may be performed no more than once per week. It is suggested that the Storyteller make the roll, rather than the player, as the *koldun* has no way of knowing if the magic was successful until he attempts to have a good day's sleep. If the roll indicates a botch, all dice pools for the next day suffer an *additional* loss of one die, on top of the standard penalty for sleeping away from one's favored soil.

Gaze of the Gorgon (Level Five Ritual)

The *koldun* is able to transform a single victim into unliving stone. The subject must be present for the entire hour-long ritual, in which the caster chants constantly, spends two blood points and sheds a third. This last blood point must be consumed by (or force-fed to) the subject. If the subject is Kindred, she may resist with a Willpower roll, difficulty 8; her successes are subtracted from the *koldun's* own. The transformation lasts for one year per success with Kindred; the effect on mortals is permanent. While stone, victims cannot sense their environment in any way. Although they do not expend any blood while petrified, Kindred often come out of the ritual in frenzy when it finally wears off (Self-Control difficulty 9 to avoid). Some Tzimisce *koldun* are fond of sculpting their subjects into more "pleasing" forms with Vicissitude before transforming them into more durable material.

NAHUALLOTL

As strange and alien as *Koldunic*, Setite and Assamite sorcery may seem to Hermetic-minded Tremere, at least the Warlocks know what they do not understand. However mysterious the ways of the Assassins or the Serpents seem, some Tremere recognize that these foreign methods of magic exist, and take what steps they can to study them.

Most Tremere — in fact, the overwhelming majority of Kindred — remain ignorant of the threat that grows nightly in the tangled jungles and poverty-stricken villages of South America. Like shadows in the night, the Tlacique creep forth from the mists of history, and they bring with them magic the likes of which no outsider has seen in centuries. For now, these ancient powers attack the Tremere's foes, but in the world of the Kindred, the enemy of one's enemy is almost never truly his friend.

Tlacique

An extinct bloodline in all eyes but their own, the Tlacique played only a small part in Kindred history. Although other clans have forgotten them, the children of Tezcatlipoca have never forgotten those who invaded their home — and they've certainly never forgiven.

Kindred who came to Mexico with the Conquistadors found that the cities of the New World — far larger and more prosperous than they'd expected from "barbarous heathens" — hosted an active population of native vampires. Some were Gangrel, some Nosferatu, but the most influential native bloodline was the Tlacique. They claimed descent from Tezcatlipoca, the Jaguar, god of night, mirrors, smoke and black magic. They ruled openly, in a fashion not seen since Carthage, in small family groups called cliques. The *nahualli*, Tlacique blood sorcerers, removed the hearts of sacrifices atop the great pyramids and drank of their blood. The Tlacique proclaimed themselves gods, and their people worshipped them.

The Camarilla could have claimed a great ally, for the natives treated the Spaniards as honored guests, and the Tlacique were happy to negotiate with the foreign Kindred. And negotiate they did — until smallpox devastated their people and the Conquistadors plundered their cities and plunged their worshippers into near-slavery. This was hardly the fault of the European Kindred; mortal greed, not Cainite influence, steered the course of the Spanish explorers. But the Tlacique, who ruled their own people, could not conceive that the Europeans did things differently. If the newcomers oppressed the natives, it must be so because the Camarilla Kindred wished it so.

The Tlacique soon learned that they could not confront the newcomers alone. They had learned, however, of another faction of Kindred, newly arrived from Europe, a sect that counted the Camarilla among its enemies. The Tlacique allied with the struggling Sabbat.

This alliance lasted only as long as it took to drive the Camarilla from Mexico. The Tlacique soon realized that the Sabbat exalted violence. The Tlacique had innumerable bloody traditions and rituals, but the Black Hand was all form with no meaning; their enthusiasm for adopting the Tlacique's rites was rooted in sadism, not faith. Their erstwhile allies were more depraved and more dangerous than the Camarilla Kindred they'd driven from their lands.

The Tlacique battled the Sabbat in turn — and lost miserably. The Sabbat all but eliminated the outnumbered natives and diablerized their elders. The few surviving Tlacique scattered to distant communities. The Black Hand thought them dead and gone; the Camarilla forgot them in the face of Sabbat aggression. The Tlacique became an obscure legend in the lands they once ruled.

After four centuries of hiding, that "legend" is vengeful and hungry.

Perhaps fewer than a few score Tlacique exist tonight, hidden throughout South and Central America and the southwestern United States. Slowly, they reestablish lines of communication. For the first time, they work together as a unified bloodline. They seek the resting places of those slumbering elders the Sabbat missed in their purge. They launch guerrilla assaults on Sabbat enclaves, determined to take back their stolen homelands.

The Sabbat is again at war — they just haven't yet figured out with whom.

Nickname: None. Nobody knows they still exist; who's going to give them a nickname?

Sect: The Tlacique claim no allegiance to either sect, but they have one budding alliance. Their interest in purging the Sabbat from Central America and their links to the Aztecs and Maya provide common ground with the Pisanob branch of the Giovanni. Negotiations remain tentative at this point, but the elders of the Sabbat and Camarilla would shudder to think of what these two groups could accomplish together, if only they knew the Tlacique existed at all.

Appearance: The few surviving Tlacique elders are natives of Central America. Some younger Tlacique come from immigrants now dwelling in the United States, though most are drawn from populations south of the border. Whether they dwell in a Third-World, poverty-stricken village or a bustling metropolis, the Tlacique try to blend in with the surrounding population.

Haven: Tlacique in large cities reside just about anywhere, from apartments to abandoned basements. Those dwelling in less sophisticated or rural areas prefer houses and huts with well-constructed cellars. A few paranoid Tlacique who have mastered Earth Meld keep no haven at all, sinking into the soil with every sunrise. Most Tlacique decorate their havens with native crafts and other reminders of their heritage — and purpose.

Background: The Tlacique consider anyone of South or Central American descent for the Embrace, so long as she proves both sympathetic and useful to the cause.

Character Creation: Because they are so few and scattered throughout enemy territory, the Tlacique look for self-reliance in their progeny, either in terms of Abilities or Demeanor. Primary Attributes vary based on why the individual was chosen for the Embrace. They also seek those who show signs of social responsibility, particularly in the areas of native rights and cultural preservation. Although the bloodline remains conservative and dislikes undisciplined childer, the elders relax this restriction somewhat in the modern nights.

Clan Disciplines: Obfuscate, Presence, Protean (The "default" predatory form for Shape of the Beast is a jaguar, rather than a wolf.)

Weaknesses: The Tlacique suffer exceptionally harsh penalties from sunlight and other illumination. Add two health levels to damage inflicted by sunlight, and subtract one from all dice pools when exposed to bright light (such as powerful spotlights).

Organization: The Tlacique still struggle to establish a new social order, much to the chagrin of elders who yearn for the structure of nights long past. Status is based partially on age, though young members are respected simply because they are so much more capable of coping with the modern world. Ancillae hold the real power, receiving blessing and instruction from the elders and mentoring the activities of the neonates. Status is also influenced by mastery of *Nahuallotl*.

Nahuallotl Systems

Like *Wanga* (see Chapter Four), *Nahuallotl* is as much a religious system as a form of magic. The Tlacique believe that their magic comes from Tezcatlipoca and other ancient gods of Central and South America, gods upon whom the Tlacique still call. They believe these gods demand sacrifices, that the sun requires blood and hearts to keep it alive from day to day. Aztec faith maintained that the Earth has already died four times and that the end of this, the fifth age, will be the end of all that is. The Tlacique believe this still, and their religious rites — and their magic — reflect the need to offer constant sacrifice to the powers that be.

No recorded occurrence of a Tlacique willingly teaching *Nahuallotl* to an outsider exists, but even if one did, a "heathen" *nahualli* suffers the same penalties to her rolls as do faithless *wangateurs* (again, see Chapter Four).

The skillful practice of *Nahuallotl* garners substantial respect within the bloodline. A Tlacique can never have more than one dot of bloodline Status unless she possesses some knowledge of the blood magic. Although *Nahuallotl* is not a clan Discipline, the practice is widespread, and any Tlacique character who wishes to purchase *Nahuallotl* with freebie points may do so (unless it violates the specific character concept, of course, or the Storyteller otherwise wishes to restrict it).

Although the practice is growing — as much as it can within so small a bloodline — the elders of the Tlacique weep bloody tears for their lost grandeur. The Sabbat purge destroyed a huge amount of the knowledge and practice of *Nahuallotl*. While many neonates receive basic instruction, fewer than a dozen *nahualli* of any real power have survived to the modern nights, and only a handful of rituals remain.

Nahuallotl employs the same mechanics as Thaumaturgy, but it remains a distinct and incompatible Discipline due to its forms and procedures. Activation of paths still requires a Willpower roll, and rituals still require Intelligence + Occult, with the difficulty based upon the level of the power.

Nahuallotl Paths

Although they were created independently, most of *Nahuallotl*'s paths emulate those invoked in more familiar forms of blood magic; only names and procedures vary. When a *nahualli* invokes a path power, he must physically spill the blood points spent. The Aztecs believed that blood from the earlobe, tongue and genitals was of particular potency, and many *nahualli* carry a large cactus spine used to draw the required blood. In addition, the caster prays aloud to the gods. The most common paths of *Nahuallotl* and their Thaumaturgical equivalents follow. In addition, *Nahuallotl* claims one unique path.

Nahuallotl Path	Thaumaturgical Path
Flower of the Divine Liquor	Path of Blood
Secret Ways of Tezcatlipoca	Path of Corruption
Huehueteotl's Glory	Lure of Flames
Rites of Tezcatlipoca	Spirit Manipulation
Breath of Quetzalcoatl	Weather Control

Lash of Xipe Totec

Xipe Totec, "Our Lord of the Flayed One," is the god of suffering, and many of his rites involve the flaying of the skin from the victim with an obsidian blade. This path allows the *nahualli* to control pain itself.

• Another's Burden

The *nahualli* can lessen the pain of another by taking some or all of his suffering onto herself.

System: The caster touches the subject after shedding a blood point and praying to Xipe Totec. Her successes on her Willpower roll indicate how many dice-pool penalties she can transfer (though she need not absorb the full amount). Thus, if a companion is at the Wounded health level (-2 penalty) and the caster achieves two or more successes, she may take a penalty of 1 die (leaving her companion with only a 1 die penalty) or 2 dice (leaving her companion unhindered). This does not transfer actual damage or health levels; merely related penalties. The power lasts for the scene, or until the *nahualli* chooses to deactivate it. If the subject wishes to resist this power for whatever reason, he may do so with a Willpower roll, difficulty 5; his successes subtract from the caster's own.

•• Obsidian Shattered

The *nahualli* may temporarily ignore wound penalties. This does not actually heal any damage; it simply dulls pain. This power may be used on the caster only.

System: The *nahualli* sheds a blood point and prays to Xipe Totec. The caster may ignore a number of dice penalties equal to his successes. The power lasts for a scene.

••• Burden Another

The caster may reduce his own pain by inflicting it upon another.

System: The caster must touch the subject while shedding a blood point and praying to Xipe Totec. The power may be resisted with a Willpower roll, difficulty 8; successes on this roll subtract from the caster's successes. Her net successes on her casting roll indicate how many dice-pool penalties she can inflict (though she need not inflict the full amount). Thus, if the caster is at the Wounded health level (-2 penalty) and achieves two or more successes, she may inflict a penalty of 1 die on her subject (leaving her with only a 1 die penalty) or 2 dice (leaving her completely unhindered). A *nahualli* may not transfer more pain — or penalties — than she currently suffers. This does not transfer actual damage or health levels; merely penalties and pain. The power lasts for the scene, unless the *nahualli* chooses to end it early.

•••• OBSIDIAN'S EDGE

The *nahualli* may now cause actual damage at a distance. Wounds appear on the target's skin as though an invisible blade is being applied.

System: Obsidian's Edge requires the standard prayers and shedding of blood. The victim may not resist with Willpower, but he may soak the lethal damage. The damage pool equals the caster's Intelligence + her successes on her Willpower roll. This power may target anyone within line of sight.

••••• FLAY

A further enhancement to the power of Obsidian's Edge, Flay may be used to cause severe pain and injury to multiple foes at once.

System: Flay requires the caster to pray, shed blood, and make the standard casting roll. The power can target a number of targets in a single turn equal to the caster's Intelligence; it otherwise employs the same mechanics as Obsidian's Edge.

NAHUALLOTL RITUALS

When invoking paths, the *nahualli's* own vitae serves as sufficient sacrifice. Where rituals are concerned, however, the gods demand more. Rituals require an offering of life, not just vitae. Some less potent rituals function with animal sacrifice, but the most powerful require human life. The *nahualli* normally sacrifice a human by opening the chest and rib cage and removing the heart. When they feel they can get away with it, the Tlacique perform such sacrifices regularly, even when not casting *Nahuallotl* rituals. They see this as doing their part to keep the sun rising day to day.

Most of the Tlacique's sacrifices come from three potential groups. Occasionally, they find members of their community desperate enough to go under the knife willingly, in exchange for promises of wealth and protection for their families. Other sacrifices come from those criminals who dare prey upon a Tlacique's community. Finally, many Tlacique hate the Sabbat so much that anyone connected with that sect becomes an enemy, and a potential sacrifice. The Tlacique treasure those few people who volunteer for the procedure; a willing sacrifice lowers the difficulty of the ritual by 2.

Very few rituals of *Nahuallotl* survive to the modern nights. Still, what follows is not a complete list, but merely a foundation on which Storytellers may expand.

MIRROR OF THE GODS (LEVEL ONE RITUAL)

The *nahualli* utters a prayer to Tezcatlipoca and smears a mixture of his own blood (one point) and the blood of a sacrificial animal (anything the size of a cat suffices) across the surface of a mirror. The blood fades as it is smeared. For a number of hours equal to the caster's successes on his casting roll, the reflection of any person or item currently under the effects of a path or ritual (from any variety of blood magic, be it Thaumaturgy, Necromancy or others) glows softly when viewed in the mirror. If the mirror is made of obsidian, the ritual lasts an additional hour.

SHROUD OF DAY (LEVEL TWO RITUAL)

Developed so the besieged Tlacique might move or otherwise make use of captured foes without their knowledge, Shroud of Day is cast upon a sharp wooden implement of sufficient size to stake a vampire. The ritual requires the sacrifice of two small animals, one nocturnal, one diurnal. Their blood is mixed with a single point of the caster's own vitae, and the stake is soaked in this mixture for two hours. The next vampire staked with that particular weapon is put to sleep (as though the sun was up) in addition to being paralyzed. This prevents the victim from seeing or hearing what is happening around him; he is not aware that time has elapsed at all. This ritual does not grant any other special powers or qualities to the weapon.

BROTHER'S EYES (LEVEL THREE RITUAL)

This ritual is identical, in most respects, to *Ori Sight* (see Chapter Four), in that it allows the *nahualli* to see and hear through the eyes and ears of another. To invoke this ritual, the caster spends a blood point while uttering a prayer to Tezcatlipoca. If she wishes to see through the eyes of a mortal, she must have in her possession the heart of a close blood relative of that person. If the subject of the ritual is Kindred, she must have in her possession the heart (obtained via the Severance ritual, or some other method that does not result in Final Death) of the Kindred whose eyes and ears she wishes to use. The ritual does *not*, however, require the caster to remove her own eye and ear, as does *Ori Sight*.

STRENGTH OF THE VANQUISHED (LEVEL FOUR RITUAL)

The *nahualli* absorbs the strength of her foes by consuming specific portions of their bodies. The ritual requires an hour of prayer to both Tezcatlipoca and Xipe Totec, followed by the sacrifice of the subject with an obsidian-bladed knife. The subject must be alive — or undead — when the ritual begins. The *nahualli's* player must spend one Willpower point to make the character consume the organs, along with one blood point for *each* organ consumed. The consumption is symbolic, as the organs are quickly vomited up in one pulpy mass. The *nahualli* gains a temporary increase to one or more of her Attributes (determined by the parts consumed). If the Attribute of the "donor" is higher than that of the caster, the caster's Attribute is raised to the donor's level. If the victim's Attribute is equal or lower, the *nahualli's* Attribute is raised by 1. Thus, if the *nahualli* has an Intelligence of 2 and consumes the brain of someone with an Intelligence of 5, her own Intelligence becomes 5; if, however, the victim's Intelligence was 2, the caster's Intelligence becomes 3. Attributes can be raised to 1 higher than generational maximum. The increase lasts for one scene per success on the casting roll. This power does not function if the victim is a vampire of sufficient age to decay immediately upon Final Death.

Organ	Attribute
Heart	Strength
Soles of feet	Dexterity
Lungs	Stamina
Lips	Charisma
Tongue	Manipulation
Face	Appearance
Eyes	Perception
Brain	Intelligence
Spine (a portion only)	Wits

SEVERANCE (LEVEL FIVE RITUAL)

This ritual is one of the most important to the Tlacique blood sorcerers, as it connects to fundamental aspects of their religion. It is also their greatest secret. The ritual greatly resembles the Serpentis power Heart of Darkness, but it works on other body parts as well as the heart. Using this ritual, a *nahualli* can remove any part of a vampire's body without killing the vampire — heart, head, whatever — and keep the body part undead and potentially animate. Most often, however, the *nahualli* will remove his or another vampire's heart.

A vampire with a removed heart becomes immune to staking and more easily resists frenzy. On the other hand, the vampire loses some human emotion, becoming more cold and ruthless. What is more, the heart itself becomes a terrible vulnerability. Any attack upon it "echoes" to the body from whence it came. A stake through a severed heart forces a vampire into torpor, or kills a mortal. Holding a vampire's heart in a flame causes the vampire to burn to ash in seconds.

Nahualli who know this ritual routinely extract the hearts of captured enemies, preferring to force service from them instead of simply killing them. A *nahualli* who holds a vampire's heart may use Disciplines on that vampire as if he were actually present, no matter how far away the other vampire might be. More cruel *nahualli* use the ritual to sever an enemy's head and send it, still animate and speaking, to the victim's allies as a warning while keeping the vampire's body.

The magician can cast this ritual only at the dark of the moon, when Tezcatlipoca is most powerful. The ritual itself demands an obsidian-bladed knife, a previously consecrated urn, a variety of amulets, and a human sacrifice to appease Mictlantecuhtli, god of the dead, for cheating him of a death. The magician must inflict one health level of aggravated damage while cutting out the body part, even if she uses this ritual on herself. The severed part must immediately be placed in the consecrated clay urn with a blood point of the magician's own vitae. Cutting out one's own heart or severing one's own head or hand (unlikely, but it could happen) demands the expenditure of two Willpower points.

SPONTANEOUS TALISMANS

My dearest Master,

I set quill to paper (you will remember how I despise computers) filled with chagrin that years have passed since my last report. I hope you will stay your anger long enough that I may explain. I have been privileged to serve you since the beginning. You gave me the honor of choosing my own way, rather than forcing the Traitor's elixir upon me as it was forced upon so many others. I have never forgotten that single act of kindness, and I have striven these many centuries to repay you for it.

I think I may finally do so. Unencumbered as I am by the burdens of guiding our House and Clan in the nights since our Father's descent into torpor, I have seen things in the past millennium that even you, with your weightier tasks, have missed. For centuries, I have studied and compiled rumor and whisper, seeking an explanation to a phenomenon that seems to bear none: items of power that follow no rules of sorcery I can discern, either Thaumaturgical or mortal wizardry.

You know that I am well versed in the mysteries of blood magic, yet these "spontaneous talismans" are as alien to me as our rituals of Thaumaturgy would be to any random mortal off the streets. I can find no pattern to their appearances, no rhyme or reason to their function. They simply — are.

I have observed some commonalities. Every spontaneous talisman of which I've heard is a physical item. Most — all of which I am aware, except one — fall within a common range of size, from items as minuscule as a ball-point pen to a full-length, wood-framed mirror. Many of them seem to manifest in areas that are subject to powerful faiths or magics over a prolonged period of time — such as churches or, though I hesitate to say it, our own chantries — but many do not. Others appear to be the focus of intense emotional resonance, as is the case with the baby rattle discussed below; but then again, I have come across others that were of no importance to anyone until their unusual properties manifested.

I have learned one fact, and one fact only, that appears to apply across the board to these unexplained phenomenon. No matter how beneficial such a talisman might seem — and a few of them do, indeed, appear more than moderately useful to begin with — I have never heard of any of their possessors coming to a good end.

Various fiction and legends amongst the mortals bear more than a passing similarity to the items of which I speak: The King in Yellow. The Monkey's Paw. The Picture of Dorian Grey. While I do not doubt that these specific examples are entirely fictitious, I cannot but wonder if some true knowledge of these bizarre magics has somehow made its way into the popular culture of mankind.

I've included various reports I have come across in my investigations that seem to relate, directly or indirectly, to these spontaneous talismans. They noticed that Brother Philippe was not wearing his customary cross, the cross he had worn every day since we'd both taken our vows, but instead had draped about his neck and partly hidden in the folds of his robe a crucifix, carved of finest wood. The image of our Lord Jesus was portrayed with such fine crafts-manship and skill that even the most minute of details was laid before my eyes, and I felt certain the image itself would at any moment grow animate and spring to life. A marvelous piece of work in honour of our Savior, but perhaps, I felt, inappropriate for one of our humble order, and I told Philippe as much.

I did relent in my disapproval, however, when he told me that this was the cruci-fix owned by his dear mother, not two months dead of leprosy, and that it was her dying wish that he should have it and wear it always to remember her by. The poor lady was mad at the end, as I am given to understand that she swore to her deathbed that her flesh was not in fact rotting off, but was being slowly chewed and consumed by tiny mouths that came in the night. Still, the last wishes of the departing ought to be honored where possible, and as Philippe had already received permission from the abbot for his unorthodox ornament, I let it lie.

Imagine, then, my grief and consternation some weeks later, when Brother Philippe himself contracted the dread illness. Confined to a single room at the rear of the monastery, we could only watch as the wasting consumed him quickly. And I still feel the hair on my neck stand upright when I remember the look in his eyes as he swore to me that he, too, could feel the nibbling, nibbling of tiny mouths in the night. He died far too rapidly, even for one who has contracted leprosy, and he asked, with his dying breath, if I would take his crucifix from him and wear it always, to remember him by.

I will not. I will bury it deep in the earth, as far from the walls as I can go and still stand atop consecrated soil. For I swear by God that the thing on Philippe's crucifix was far less emaciated after he died than it was when it was given him. That rather than the expression of peace that is supposed to adorn the face of our Lord, the figure's lips were upturned in a hideous grin of wanton glee. And that all I heard, echoing again and again in the vaults of my mind, were the words "He that eateth my flesh and drinketh my blood, dwelleth in me, and I in him...

remain in their original form, altered only where I felt it necessary to add my own notes on the subject at hand; I have placed them in chronological order, from oldest (circa 1217 AD) to most recent. I have discovered more such talismans than I have described below. I could, had I the inclination, tell you of three others just off the top of my head, the most interesting of which is actually an old automobile — a Model-T Ford, I believe. Professionalism, however, requires that I be able to confirm such accounts through sources more reliable than word of mouth, so I include in this report only the information pertaining to items for which I have documentation.

For the Storyteller: Katrina's Cross

Brother Philippe's poor mother was not the first to die of slow consumption under the influence of this twisted icon. The first was the man who raped and murdered a young woman named Katrina in a grimy alleyway in a small village in Hungary around the turn of the first millennium. He took every item of even the slightest value —including her crucifix, a gift from her grandmother. The murderer who stole it was the first to suffer for the violence that had imbued the crucifix with an unholy bloodlust, but he was far from the last.

Katrina's Cross grants its possessor several benefits. The owner is calmed by the "holy" aura of the icon, even if such godly emanations are normally anathema. The difficulty of all Virtue rolls is reduced by 2. In addition, the cross improves the owner's health, granting an additional die to all Stamina rolls. These advantages last only until the cross begins feeding on its owner.

Anyone who keeps the crucifix in his possession for more than a few nights will begin to find his flesh slowly consumed, as though by some rotting disease. Starting on the third Sunday since the victim took possession of the cross (whether or not it's been on his person), he suffers one health level of lethal damage every third night. This damage *does not heal* for as long as the victim maintains ownership of the cross. The victim may feel tiny mouths chewing upon him in his sleep, though this is never sufficient to awaken him to full consciousness. The instant the victim suffers the first health level of damage, he develops an emotional attachment to the crucifix, refusing to be parted from it. If the victim can be kept isolated from the cross for an entire month, his "ownership" of the icon is null and he is safe — unless he reclaims the crucifix.

If the owner of Katrina's Cross is Kindred, he may soak this damage normally — but any damage he suffers due to a failed soak *cannot be healed*, by spending blood or any other method, while he owns the cross. Kindred experience the feeling of being gnawed upon during their daylight sleep, not at night. All victims of the cross experience the affects of the Nightmares

June 18, 1864

Dear diary,

I've only just moved into my quarters in Lord Waltham's estates, and I've already been given some truly curious instructions. Apparently, though I'm to thoroughly dust and clean everything else in his upstairs study, I am not to uncover the mirror hanging along the wall. Odd; it isn't as though he's given any such instructions regarding the downstairs mirror, and it's certainly valuable enough. Still, he is the master here, and I suppose anyone sufficiently wealthy to hire a housekeeper is entitled to his quirks and petty mannerisms. Particularly when I am earning my wages as the housekeeper in question.

June 25, 1864

The most astonishing thing happened this evening. I was in the studio atop the stairs, carefully polishing the old sword that Lord Waltham keeps above the mantle, when I swear I heard a voice calling to me, begging for help. I turned about, but there was nothing out of the ordinary in the room — save that I had, in my cleaning, disturbed the purple cloth draped over the mirror. I thought only to straighten it, but it fell from the mirror even as my fingers brushed across it and I saw...

Well, all melodrama aside, I saw nothing abnormal at all. Simply my reflection, staring back at me from a tall mirror. I can't begin to imagine why Lord Waltham is so concerned about it, as it is hardly the equal of the one downstairs. I covered it back up, and I shall continue to ignore it, as instructed.

June 26, 1864

I think Lord Waltham may have noticed something amiss, for he asked me today, "Clara, did you disturb anything in my study?" He seemed to believe me when I told him no, but I'm grateful I decided to ignore the mirror from this point. I'd hate to lose my employment over something so trivial.

July 8, 1864

I hear the voice calling for help in my sleep now. Her name is Rachel; I do not know how I know this, but I do. Strange. Now that I think on it, I believe the name of the girl I am replacing here was named Rachel. How very odd.

I shouldn't go. I've been spending far too much time staring into that mirror. But it's such a flattering image. I can't begin to imagine why, but I look so much prettier in this mirror than in the one downstairs. Perhaps just for a moment or two.

July 14, 1864

I see everything I've ever wanted in the mirror. The lines on my face have faded and gone, and I am as beautiful as I could ever dream. I see, not the dull skirts of a housekeeper, but the lace-edged gowns of a true lady of quality, the handsome Lord Waltham escorting me by the arm. Servants trail behind, cleaning up after me and bringing me all I could ask for. The house grows filthy, and I know Lord Waltham is displeased with me. I'll return to work tomorrow, I swear. I just need one more look in the mirror. Just one.

Flaw (see **Vampire: The Masquerade**, page 299) for the duration (if they already possess this flaw, the difficulty of their Willpower roll is raised by 2).

Once the victim dies, the figure of Christ on the cross appears sated and less gaunt. This appearance lasts for three days, at which point the figure returns to its normal appearance, one more resembling a normal crucifix. Truly observant individuals may notice this abnormal (and rather grotesque) expression and attempt to deal with the cross (though it will not break or burn under normal conditions). It has been buried or locked away multiple times, but always turns up elsewhere.

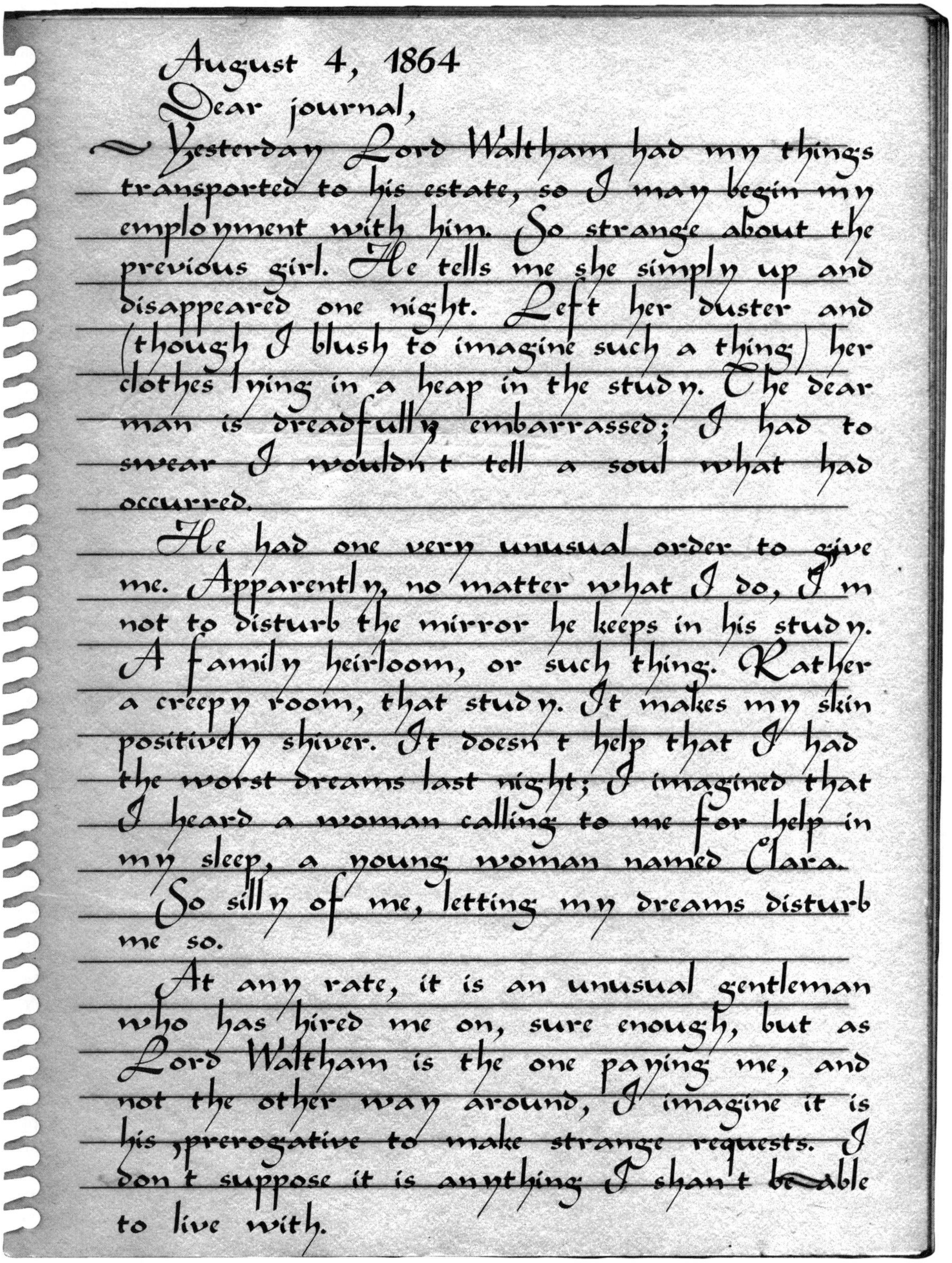

August 4, 1864

Dear journal,

Yesterday Lord Waltham had my things transported to his estate, so I may begin my employment with him. So strange about the previous girl. He tells me she simply up and disappeared one night. Left her duster and (though I blush to imagine such a thing) her clothes lying in a heap in the study. The dear man is dreadfully embarrassed; I had to swear I wouldn't tell a soul what had occurred.

He had one very unusual order to give me. Apparently, no matter what I do, I'm not to disturb the mirror he keeps in his study. A family heirloom, or such thing. Rather a creepy room, that study. It makes my skin positively shiver. It doesn't help that I had the worst dreams last night; I imagined that I heard a woman calling to me for help in my sleep, a young woman named Clara.

So silly of me, letting my dreams disturb me so.

At any rate, it is an unusual gentleman who has hired me on, sure enough, but as Lord Waltham is the one paying me, and not the other way around, I imagine it is his prerogative to make strange requests. I don't suppose it is anything I shan't be able to live with.

FOR THE STORYTELLER: THE MIRROR OF DREAMS

The Mirror of Dreams has existed since the Renaissance, though none know exactly when it was crafted, or by whom. Anyone except the owner who looks into the reflection must make a Willpower roll, difficulty 7. If the roll is successful, nothing abnormal occurs, though the individual can still be affected upon subsequent viewings. Should the roll fail, the victim sees her reflection, not as she is, but as she wishes in her heart she could be. She also loses a point of *permanent* Willpower. If the Willpower roll is botched, two points are lost.

Every subsequent morning (or evening, if the victim is Kindred), the victim must make a Willpower roll (difficulty 7) to avoid looking in the mirror again at her first opportunity. Each time she looks in the mirror, the reflection becomes more enticing, and the victim loses another point of permanent Willpower. When the last Willpower point is lost, the mirror absorbs the soul of the victim (a process that destroys the body), trapping it and slowly consuming it over the course of weeks. Sensitive individuals who spend time near the mirror may hear the cries of victims not yet consumed, though they rarely associate this phenomenon with the mirror itself.

Should a victim succeed in avoiding the mirror (either through successful Willpower rolls or forced separation) for a number of days equal to twice the number of Willpower points already lost, she has escaped the mirror's hold. All lost Willpower points return and the victim no longer feels the compulsion to return to the mirror.

The mirror's owner may, once per week, gaze at his own reflection and gain a temporary point of Willpower, even if this takes him over his permanent Willpower. This point lasts until spent, or for one week. If, however, a victim succeeds in escaping the mirror's influence and regaining her Willpower, the mirror's owner immediately loses as many points of permanent Willpower as the victim regained. If this takes him to zero, he is drawn into the mirror as the victim would have been, and consumed.

What follows, Master, is a partial transcript of a conversation I tape-recorded with a woman in the suburbs of Tulsa, Oklahoma in 1982.

Interviewer: And then what did you do, Mrs. Collins?

Subject: I— well, I didn't want to believe it. I mean, doctors can be wrong too, right? It's not [the subject stopped to blow her nose on a tissue], not as if they're infallible.

Interviewer: Indeed.

Subject: I went into the baby's— that is, the room that Dan and I had intended to be the baby's room. I just remember falling to my knees and praying to God. We wanted a child so much.

Interviewer: You mentioned a baby rattle earlier, Mrs. Collins.

Subject: Oh, yes. I'm, umm, not actually sure when I picked it up, but I realized I had it clutched in my hands while I was praying. It was such a silly little thing. We bought it for about a buck-twenty-five. Just a little pink and blue plastic thing with a ball bearing inside. But I— this is going to sound silly.

Interviewer: Nothing you say is being judged, Mrs. Collins. Please continue.

Subject: Well, I somehow got it in my mind that if I prayed over the rattle hard enough, we'd finally be able to get pregnant.

Interviewer: And?

Subject: And it worked! I was pregnant not three months later!

Interviewer: When did you find out about your neighbor's child?

Subject: Oh. [Subject began to cry again at this point.] About two months before I realized I was pregnant. We saw the ambulance. It's so terrible, when a baby dies.

Interviewer: But you didn't see any connections at the time, did you?

Subject: [Speaking very softly] No. No, it wasn't until three years later, Dan and I decided that Sarah needed a brother or sister and— and we couldn't get pregnant again.

Interviewer: So you tried praying over the rattle again?

[The subject nodded]

Interviewer: And what happened this time? Just before you got pregnant the second time, I mean.

Subject: Janine Summers — that's a woman at my office — miscarried. In her third trimester.

Interviewer: I see. Mrs. Collins, have you gotten rid of the rattle?

Subject: God, no!

Interviewer: And why not?

Subject: Because... [Here Mrs. Collins looked up, and I must admit that I was taken aback. The subject had brown eyes, but when she looked at me at that moment, they were blue — the same light blue as the baby rattle.] Because — what if I want another baby?

[End transcription]

FOR THE STORYTELLER: HEART'S DESIRE

This one's weird, even for a spontaneous talisman. The baby rattle isn't actually the talisman — it was simply *inhabited* by the magic. Heart's Desire is a mobile effect, not a single item. The powers of Heart's Desire can manifest in any object that becomes the focus of impassioned longing. The rattle is one example; it could also manifest in, say, the engagement ring of a man whose proposal was rejected. The item, when prayed over, grants the owner his fondest desire (assuming it's mundanely possible; getting pregnant is feasible, sprouting wings and flying is not). The wishes are granted by stripping the desired object or emotion from somewhere else (as in the lives that were traded for Mrs. Collins' baby, or perhaps the infatuated young man earns the love of the girl by stripping the ability to love *at all* from the rest of his family). Heart's Desire never functions more than a handful of times for any one individual, and it invariably fails when the owner is desperate. The final time Heart's Desire functions, the price demanded (be it a death, a loss of emotion or whatever else) *always* comes from someone the owner truly cares about (or himself, if he cares for no one else in the world).

Long Island, NY — Daniel Locke, controversial horror novelist and author of *Visions in Black* and *They Rise*, was found this morning by authorities in his Long Island home. Although physically unharmed, according to preliminary reports, Locke was said to be in a state of mental collapse. One paramedic at the scene, who has asked not to be identified by name, claimed that Locke "…was like a [expletive] empty slate. Just gibbering, like baby-talk. Nobody home, you know?" Doctors do not yet know the cause of Locke's mental collapse.

The author was found hunched over his computer, the final chapter of what appeared to be his latest novel still on the screen. Locke's novels have developed a moderate cult following, and is most widely recognized by his fans for the astoundingly realistic characters that populate his most recent works. Hundreds of his readers nationwide have taken up candlelight vigils in the hopes that he will recover.

A clipping from a paper two years ago that I thought might interest you, Master. The story itself is fairly unremarkable, except for the details that it fails to mention. When Locke was found, he had apparently covered his entire writing desk, as well as the wall beside it, in various childish scrawls, written with crayon. There was, however, a single relatively coherent thought, repeated multiple times throughout the scrawl. I have included a photo of the wall for your edification.

According to the receipts I backtracked, Locke purchased his computer mere months before he wrote his first bestseller, Surrender the Day (a vampire novel, if I may be allowed a brief ironic chuckle). He bought it cheap, as the small store from which it was purchased was going out of business — due to the mental collapse and institutionalization of its owner. The computer itself,

I am shamed to admit, has disappeared after being claimed by Locke's family, and I have been unable to locate it.

FOR THE STORYTELLER: LOCKE'S COMPUTER

A relatively recent talisman, and proof that the advancements of the 21st century are no protection from the whims of magic, Locke's Computer epitomizes modern fears that technology is stripping away what it means to be human. In fact, stripping away what it means to be human is exactly what Locke's Computer does.

It appears, at first, to be helpful. Any task attempted on the computer proves surprisingly easy. Writers find their characters taking on astoundingly realistic lives of their own. Programmers find themselves cranking out code at astonishing rates. Hackers find no system they cannot access, no security they cannot breach. The computer adds a random number of dice (1 to 5; see below) to any actions attempted on it.

The owner remains unaware that his new proficiency comes from ideas and emotions stolen from previous users. As the user comes to rely on the computer, he loses his ability to function without it — and loses himself along with it.

For Daniel Locke, an author, his self-image and self-identity centered on his creativity and writing skill, and the computer ripped those features from him over months of writing. (Incidentally, Locke is still fully sane and aware — he just can't *communicate* that fact to anyone.) Another user might see herself as a "people person" (and thus lose Charisma or Manipulation to the computer) or quick-witted (loss of Wits); even Willpower or Humanity can be stolen, if these are the basis for the owner's sense of self. The precise Attribute or Virtue lost is determined by the Storyteller's interpretation of the character's self-image.

Because the computer adds a random number of dice to each action, it can take quite some time before the character becomes aware that he is losing parts of himself — and even then, the cause may not be obvious. Furthermore, the Trait loss is not apparent when the victim uses Locke's computer; that is, a character whose Intelligence drops from four to two will still have an Intelligence dice pool of four when using the computer. This effect lasts until the Attribute drops to zero.

Mere proximity to the computer isn't sufficient to render a victim an inhuman or emotional wreck (Microsoft notwithstanding). The effect occurs gradually, as the victim works at the computer. Each time the owner's player attempts a roll using Locke's Computer, the Storyteller makes a second secret roll, with a dice pool equal to the Trait being drained (difficulty 6). If this roll fails, the character loses one point from that Trait; if botched, the character loses two. These points can be purchased back with experience points as long as the victim has at least one dot remaining. Should any of these Traits be reduced to zero or below, the victim suffers permanent mental damage and requires years of treatment before a cure can be attempted.

Some months back, as I compiled the information you have just read, a sudden thought struck me. If such talismans most commonly manifest in areas with a great concentration of magic or emotional resonance, how much more likely would it be to find them in a place of both magic and emotion? And I knew, I realized with a sudden dread, of one such place, a nexus of great power, great deeds and great suffering.

Our old home, long abandoned. The chantry Ceoris.

I'll not include the details of my journey or my exploration here, Master. Bizarre — and, I must admit, terrifying — as some of my experiences have been, they are not germane to the issue at hand. I have chronicled my travels in my journal, which I will happily forward to you at a later date should you express an interest.

After several truly horrific nights, I made my way into the lowest levels of our ancient sanctuary. There, in rooms of cracked and faded stone, in a chamber that appears to have lain undisturbed by so much as a spider or a rat for centuries on end, I found exactly what I sought.

Chains, Master, chains and manacles. The very same, I believe, that held those cursed Tzimisce, the Kindred from whom the traitor first learned the secrets of vampirism — and who gave their unlives in the creation of his elixir. I can still, as I examine them in the glare of the electric lantern, see the old stains of dried blood amongst the patches of rust that adorn the ancient links.

I have not yet performed any rituals to determine the precise nature or extent of the magic in these instruments of imprisonment. I have not needed to; I can feel their power from where I stand, hear ancient voices calling to me across the centuries. As I pen this, I am actually sitting in the chamber across from the iron shackles, for I felt it imperative that I set down everything that has occurred to date before I investigate further.

In but a moment, Master, I shall lay down this document and begin my experimentations with these ancient, blood-soaked chains. Considering the sheer force of history that resides within these iron links, I believe that this could well prove to be the most significant find our clan has made since the development of Thaumaturgy itself!

When next I set pen to paper, Master, it will be to describe, for your eyes alone, the power that will soon belong to the House and Clan Tremere.

The alert Storyteller has noticed that we've given no rules for the creation of spontaneous talismans. Guess what? We're not going to.

Gideon Nils' writings contain enough hints to get your devious minds working. Use them if you like, ignore them if you don't. There are *no* hard-and-fast rules regarding how, when or why spontaneous talismans develop. That's what makes them spontaneous.

Don't feel constrained by rules when deciding what they can do, either. Use the examples above or create your own. Such talismans are capable of nearly anything — within reason. Their power should be low-key, or at least relatively subtle. They should not be used as "magic weapons" or arcane tactical nukes. The idea is atmosphere and creepiness, not more kewl powerz.

Don't overuse them. Mystery loses its impact with familiarity. Such items should appear no more than once in a long chronicle (unless the chronicle focuses on such things specifically), and never just for the heck of it. These aren't random treasures to be found after killing the boojums; these are plot devices — and even entire stories — in their own right.

Only three firm guidelines apply to spontaneous talismans. The characters — and the players — should come away from any such experience with a definite sense of unease. They should come away from their experience with an incomplete understanding (at best) of what really happened. Finally, they should come away from their experience worse off — or at least no better off — than they started.

E,

As per your request, I have investigated the disappearance of your historian and researcher Gideon Nils. I tracked his movements to a tiny hovel of a motel in Romania. The room he'd acquired was unoccupied — and had been for some time — but it did contain a large amount of paperwork scattered atop the table. The above documentation was neatly stacked and tied together, topped with a note addressed to you. The remainder of Nils' writings have been sent to you via a more traditional courier, but I thought you'd want to receive these particular documents as rapidly as possible.

I took the liberty of reading through Nils' report before sending it along. My apologies if I overstepped my bounds, but I felt it prudent to ensure that his findings posed no immediate threat to you, myself, the clan or the Camarilla. I found no journal chronicling his excursion to Ceoris, no report of what might have occurred during his examination of the chains he mentions, and no indication of where he went after returning the journal to this room (assuming it was he who did so).

I think it likely that your chronicler is dead. I also firmly believe that our wisest course of action is to follow up on his investigations *immediately*. You know even better than I the danger Nils might have drawn upon us all by traveling to Ceoris. I anxiously await your decisions on this matter.

di Zagreb